Post-National Arguments
The Politics of the
Anglophone-Canadian Novel since 1967

The search for the Canadian identity has often attempted to unify cultural characteristics into a homogeneous whole, and to idealize national notions of art and thought. In this examination of sixteen post-centennial Canadian novels, Frank Davey argues that there is no monological Canadian nationalism, and that studies that have attempted to define Canadian literature as a unitary cultural category have overlooked the conflict and heterogeneity active in Canadian texts, and also mistaken the process of nationhood.

Using post-Saussurean linguistics and contemporary discourse theory as terms for his debate, Davey presents the argument that it is the presence of internal conflict and debate, national arguments in fact, that signal a separate society in Canada. The high proportion of conflicts, he argues, indicates national health and confidence. A national concept such as Canada receives its definition within an evolving differential system of linguistic signs, specific to individuals, yet overlapping into other constituencies. Different positions are indicated through metaphor, genre, allusion, quotation, specific vocabularies, sentence structure, and textual organization. These reflect concurrent and competing effects of ethnicity, region, gender, class, ideological inheritance, and self-identification with race.

Davey begins with an investigation of the declared positions of writers in the recent free trade debate. There is, he says, a semiotic relationship between these positions and well-known aesthetic and cultural arguments in Canadian criticism, both of which attempt to idealize themselves, one by positing an ideal and homogeneous Canadian nation and the other with idealized notions of art and thought. These idealizations conceal the political natures of the writers' interventions.

FRANK DAVEY is first Carl F. Klinck Professor of Canadian Literature, University of Western Ontario.

Theory/Culture
General editors:
Linda Hutcheon and Paul Perron

Post-National Arguments

The Politics of the
Anglophone-Canadian Novel
since 1967

FRANK DAVEY

UNIVERSITY OF TORONTO PRESS
Toronto Buffalo London

© University of Toronto Press Incorporated 1993
Toronto Buffalo London
Printed in Canada

ISBN 0-8020-2785-7 (cloth)
ISBN 0-8020-6834-0 (paper)

Printed on acid-free paper

Canadian Cataloguing in Publication Data
Davey, Frank, 1940–
Post-national arguments : the politics of the
Anglophone-Canadian novel since 1967

(Theory/Culture)
Includes bibliographical references and index.
ISBN 0-8020-2785-7 (bound) ISBN 0-8020-6834-0 (pbk.)

1. Canadian fiction (English) – History and
criticism.* I. Title. II. Series.

PS8199.D3 1993   C813'.5409   C93-093081-9
PR9192.5.D3 1993

This book has been published with the help of a grant from the Canadian
Federation for the Humanities, using funds provided by the Social Sciences
and Humanities Research Council of Canada.

for Robin Mathews

Contents

viii Contents

Acknowledgments

Many people in various ways contributed to my writing this volume. I would especially like to thank the Université Canadienne en France, where I began writing the book in September 1988, Linda Hutcheon, the series editor for University of Toronto Press, the Canadian Federation for the Humanities and its extremely helpful readers, Harold Heft and Anne Bailey, who assisted with the last revisions of the manuscript, and Linda Davey, who contributed numerous editorial suggestions.

POST-NATIONAL ARGUMENTS

Introduction

That literary texts may have overt political meaning is something few readers, if any, would dispute; writers who wish their texts to have political impact usually require little help from the critic or reviewer to bring this to public note. Several of the novels investigated in this study – like Joy Kogawa's *Obasan*, Gail Scott's *Heroine*, or Rudy Wiebe's *The Temptations of Big Bear* – foreground their political engagements in re-staging recent or historical political arguments, constructing the viewpoints of specific actors or positions, and favouring one or more of these viewpoints by representing them in intimate discourses that operate to 'humanize' and 'naturalize' their postulates. Many of these novels have been framed by their publishers to give emphasis to their political significance. The cover of Kogawa's *Obasan* announces it as 'the moving story of Japanese Canadians during the Second World War'; that of Jeannette Armstrong's *Slash* names it 'a story of colonialism in Canada.'

What this study addresses is not any overt politics these sixteen novels may contain, but the assumptions they take for granted and which become identifiable as political in the context of differing assumptions brought to the text by a reader. In the particular discourses in which a novel narrates its stories, in its array of characters, places, and issues, its narrative viewpoints and structures, its selections of imagery, symbol, and metaphor, the syntax it awards to narrators and characters, and the relative space it may give to any of these, it signals specific understandings not only about human relations, social structure, and political conflict but also about such trans-human questions as the nature of value and being. Such understandings enter a novel because texts are produced not merely by individual wills and perceptions; they are produced also – like the individuals who write them

– by the linguistic conventions and social practices from which their own particular selections and combinations have been taken. Attentive readings of widely read fiction can help in understanding not only what issues are consciously under debate in a culture but also what unspoken assumptions, wishes, or fantasies underlie that conscious debate, influence the terms in which it is conducted, and add psychodramatic significance to what may appear to be pragmatic alternatives.

I began this study in 1988 during the anglophone-Canadian debate about the establishment of 'free trade' between Canada and the United States – a debate in which many Canadian writers, particularly in Ontario, attempted to play public roles. I was intrigued by a number of aspects of their interventions. Although their writing engaged many different kinds of people, in terms of experience, region, and class, the writers had only two positions to take: for or against free trade. Were there relationships between which position they took and the kinds of writing they sought to publish or the kinds of experience they sought to represent? Would the establishment of 'free trade' be likely to impede or assist the circulation of the kinds of text they wrote, or the fortunes of the particular Canadians their texts might be said to 'represent'? I was intrigued also by regional, gender, and ethnic distributions evident among the names of the free trade intervenors. Why did I, both officially and historically a 'Canadian,' feel alien to both positions? Were the political interests of some writers, and perhaps of some segments of Canadian society, not at stake in the debate? Did many Canadian writers not envision their society in either national or continental terms, or perhaps give priority to affiliations that were paradigmatically incongruent with either a 'free trade' or 'status quo' option?

Within a year of the 1988 'free trade' election Canada entered its 'Meech Lake' crisis over the constitutional position of Quebec within the Canadian federation. The implicit cultural politics of the earlier debate was soon subsumed within a many-sided quarrel among numerous well-identified anglophone-Canadian interests: aboriginal peoples who desired that their own constitutional claims not yield precedence to those of Quebec; multiculturalism advocates who wished the Québécois to be merely one ethnicity among many; free trade opponents who blamed Quebec sovereigntists for the Conservative party's 1988 federal election victory and the passage of the trade agreement; Quebec anglophones and allophones who resisted equating the province of Quebec with French ethnicity; provincial rights advocates who wished all provinces to have equal and perhaps enhanced confederal standing; women's groups who feared that a 'special status' for Quebec would end the federal guarantee of women's rights within that province; and English-Canadian linguistic nationalists who sought a unary country freed of the expense of official bilingualism. Particularly after introduction in the spring of 1991 by the Quebec government of referendum legislation inviting anglophone Canada to make it a constitutional 'offer,' a major question in the Canadian media became whether or not there could be a single anglophone-Canadian constitutional position.[1] Was there even a name possible for the area of Canada outside Quebec – English Canada, the Rest of Canada, 'ROC'? Curiously, despite their active participation in the free trade debates, anglophone-Canadian arts groups have been relatively quiet in the constitutional ones. Their strongest interventions have been to oppose the so-called devolution of arts funding – a hypothetical constitutional revision that would allow responsibility for culture and thus for arts funding to 'devolve' into exclusive provincial jurisdiction.[2]

As the constitutional discussions have intensified, my questions about what constructions of 'Canada' and 'Canadians' lay behind anglophone-Canadian writers' positions or non-positions on the free trade issue have grown. The trade debate had demonstrated how deeply fractured the conscious cultural views of anglophone-Canadian writers could be; but how various were the views offered by their writings? What implications did this diversity hold for the constitutional questions into which the free trade issue appeared to have evolved? Were there hints in anglophone-Canadian fiction written in the decades immediately before this constitutional impasse of how deeply fractured the English-Canadian polity was, or of how it viewed the Canadian federation? How had anglophone-Canadian writing in these decades constructed Quebec and francophone Quebecers? What places entered into this writing's imagination of the country, what images, arguments, or symbols? How did it map the world around

1 See, for example, 'Survival Strategies: The Regions Seek Their Own Solutions,' *Macleans*, 12 Nov. 1990, 22, and 'Canada Must Prove to Quebec It Can Reform,' *Financial Times*, 17 Dec. 1990, 30.

2 In April 1991 approximately thirty arts organizations, including the Writers Union and the League of Canadian Poets, founded the Common Agenda Alliance for the Arts, primarily to address the devolution issue. See H.J. Kirschoff and Val Ross, 'Anxiety Spreads over Devolution,' *Globe and Mail*, 17 Aug. 1991, C1 and C10; and Marian Botsford Fraser, 'Devolution of Cultural Policy Symbolizes Demolition of the Country,' *Globe and Mail*, 26 Aug. 1991, C1.

its characters? With what discursively encoded ideologies did it affiliate them? From where did the forces that affected these characters come, where did they travel, what significant lacunae marked their consciousnesses? What relationships with other members of humanity did this writing imagine for its characters? Was 'nation' a significant sign within this imagination?

For during these decades, within the teaching of 'Canadian literature,' a direct link had been assumed between anglophone-Canadian writing and nationalism. Anglophone-Canadian literature in this view was a national literature; it evolved from the colonial to the modern (Woodcock), from the Victorian to the postmodern (Kroetsch), from the romantic to the high modern (Keith), from the colonial to a place among the postcolonial (New). It had developed national mythologies like 'two solitudes' or 'survival,' national images like Atwood's 'ice maidens,' beleagured farmhouses, gothic mothers, Moss's signs of isolation, Sutherland's Presbyterians and Jansenists, and more recently, in Linda Hutcheon's work, national modes of irony and historical metafiction. Throughout the period there had been dissenters from the notion of a national canon, complaints that the canons deployed were too Frygian (Mandel), were an instrument of Ontario imperialism, were unresponsive to anything but realism (Lecker), or insensitive to regional priorities, but the national construction had endured both in historically configured textbooks and historically taught college surveys. Had a gap opened up between the models employed in the teaching of Canadian literature and the cultural assumptions embodied in its latest writing?

My choice of 1967 as the beginning date of this study is a symbolic one, intended to highlight the contrast between that centennial year and the uncertainties of 1992. This is an openly post-centennial study, one that sets the centennial and its nationalist sentiments aside, as it were, at the same time as it accepts the writing that has followed as to some extent caused or enabled by that event. What concerns me here is not those nationalistic sentiments themselves but the constructions of nation that have ensued from them, from 1967 through to the difficult present. Although all the texts engaged here are to some extent products of the centennial period – of its expansion of literary production and its development of the Canadian book market into a potentially primary one for Canadian writers, of the emphasis it placed on the role of artistic construction within cultural construction, and of the stimulus it gave to the institutional development of

Canadian literature as both a teaching subject and a political field[3] – they are also signs of how that national celebration has subsequently been translated in various parts of the country. My choice to study fiction alone is, I hope, a pragmatic one. Among other possible genres, Canadian poetry is poorly and mostly regionally circulated, and read mainly by university-educated readers. Plays tend currently not only to be regionally disseminated but also to be performed only in a handful of major cities. Fiction, however, continues to be written for general Canadian audiences, to be widely read, and to be circulated both nationally and regionally.

I have chosen the specific texts of the study, not with the aim of representing any 'best' books, or even best-selling books, but of representing instead books that have been important to particular Canadian audiences and have offered some portrayal of Canada as a semiotic field.[4] I have looked for novels that have been widely acclaimed, circulated, and studied, giving special attention to texts that have had impact within at least one anglophone-Canadian constituency. I have thus looked, in particular, for novels whose modes of articulating experience elicited powerful and continuing response from at least some group of readers. I have not attempted to consider all such novels of the period, but instead have selected texts from a large number of anglophone-Canadian regions and constituencies. The ones selected constitute a list that, like any list, can be quarrelled with. Its construction involved the epistemologically dubious procedure of my hypothesizing positions other than my own, and doing so on the basis of textual evidence that may not circulate well between variously positioned Canadian constituencies; other readers almost certainly have their own positions *and* lists. But because the focus of my study is on the signs, discourses, and narrative strategies at work in the novels, and because such textual elements tend to operate in a culture

3 Among the post-centennial political organizations in Canadian literature are the League of Canadian Poets, the Writers Union of Canada, the Association of Canadian Publishers (with its sub-group, the Literary Press Group), the Saskatchewan Writers Guild, the Canadian Magazine Publishers Association, and the Association for Canadian and Quebec Literatures.

4 This criterion excludes from direct examination some recent novels of Canadian ethnic communities which are of considerable importance, such as Nino Ricci's *Lives of the Saints*, Moyez Vassanji's *The Gunny Sack*, and Rohinton Mistry's *Such a Long Journey*, novels which contain few if any significations of Canada or of Canadian polity. Their lack of such significations, however, itself has political implications which contribute to the general suggestions of this study.

independently of individual speakers, writers, or texts, I doubt that my readings would have been greatly altered by my having chosen, say, a different 'arctic' novel from that of Van Herk, or an earlier Atwood novel, or by my having included novels from one or two additional constituencies; particular instances of signification would have been different, but the overall array of signs, characters, discourses, and narrative structures and strategies would have very likely been much the same.

The sequence in which the novels are considered is similarly based on the concept of an array of inter-referring discourses and positions rather than on a concept of contrasted authors or texts. Whatever readers may infer from the sequence (and I am sure they will *infer*), it has not been intended to signify evaluation, change, or hierarchy – best to worst, least to most – nor to replicate any 'actual' narrative of my inquiry. Nor has it been designed to match or 'pair' dichotomous positions – there are too many interwoven and nuanced issues and positions at work in these texts for a critic to adopt such simple schemas. Instead I have attempted to arrange the chapters in a sequence that foregrounds the various ways in which the issues and concerns of the novels overlap and contest, and that allows all possible play to the complex dialogue implicit among the novels in their disputation and qualification of various kinds of discourse and position. I have hoped thereby to discourage any preconceptions readers may bring to this study that these particular novels represent polarizations, singularities, or exclusivities of focus, and to encourage appreciation of the complex field of reference and disputation they all occupy.

I am aware that this book is also very much a product of my own *interests* in both senses of the word – that my past situates me in various and mixed relationships with the regional, ethnic, cultural, gender, and class conflicts of Canada, that I am myself conflicted in particular ways that have the potential to alienate me in some way not only from two 'free trade' viewpoints but from elements in nearly every Canadian text which I encounter. I believe, however, that other readers, while not likely similarly positioned, may well be similarly conflicted, and thus find at least some of their interests and desires similarly jeopardized by the possible social dominance of the constructions these novels offer. As someone with contrary interests and desires, in a nation of contrary desires, I find myself in this book seeking, not the elimination of conflict or the establishment of some liberal ideal of social harmony, but continued debate and irresolution.

When the politics of meaning are constrained, the range of all of our hopes and desires becomes diminished with them.

Because of my interest in the implicit rather than explicit politics of the novels, my focus falls on the texts themselves rather than on their authors or on the critical reception the authors or novels have received. Authors themselves may change their conscious assumptions and emphases as their own material interests change, or may have their less-conscious assumptions shift as the discourses they live within clash and change. Readers may adopt particular interpretations of novels to meet their own immediate interests – Atwood's *Surfacing*, for example, was widely read as a nationalist novel when published in Canada in 1973, but as a feminist novel when published in the United States after the growth of feminist thought in Canada; her *The Handmaid's Tale*, first read as a feminist text, has the potential to someday be widely read as a Canadian critique of U.S. political history. As for my own readings, they too are almost inevitably conditioned by the general Canadian political conditions within which I write – those conditions are, after all, their occasion. A text also has meanings, however, that it makes available to readers through the much more slowly changing discourses, structures, images, and signs it deploys – meanings to which a reader may be resistant or blind. It is these I have searched for, and attempted to illustrate by quotation from both the novels and the surrounding field of Canadian social discourse, even when I may not have liked, or liked too much, what I found. As for the ones I am myself blind to, I will trust my readers to find those within the signs that follow.

Beyond Disputation:
Anglophone-Canadian Artists
and the Free Trade Debate

On the eve of the 1988 federal election two statements signed by various members of the Canadian arts community appeared as advertisements in the national edition of the *Globe and Mail*.[1] Both addressed the recently concluded tariff and trade-management agreement between Canada and the United States, popularly known as the 'Free Trade Agreement,' the implementation of which rested on the outcome of the election. One statement urged the reader 'to vote for the party in your riding that will help to defeat this FREE TRADE DEAL,' and was followed by thirty-nine names, among them 'Adrienne Clarkson,' 'Robertson Davies,' 'Don Harron,' 'Gordon Lightfoot,' and 'Sylvia Tyson.' Nothing in the statement offered any identification of these names – the text implied they carried meanings well known to the reader. The second statement announced itself 'in favour of the Canada–United States Free Trade Agreement' and was signed by sixty-two names, each identified by profession. Carrying in addition the heading 'Artists and Writers for Free Trade,' this advertisement suggested that the significance of its signatures – among them 'Ken Danby, painter,' 'Mordecai Richler, writer,' 'Robert Fulford, journalist,' and 'Mira Godard, art dealer' – could be unknown to *Globe* readers.

The rather short statement of the thirty-nine argued 'the Mulroney-Reagan Trade Deal is a hastily-concluded agreement that was made for political reasons, and not for the welfare of our country. It will irrevocably damage the Canada we care about.' Its choice of 'Mulroney-Reagan' rather than 'Canada–United States' for the name of the agreement was a common rhetorical move during the election campaign to suggest that the agreement was an eccentric personal

---

1 *Globe and Mail*, 19 Nov. 1988, 14 and 16

action of two unreliable men rather than one between two elected national governments; the use of 'deal' rather than 'agreement' was also a common move to imply 'sleazy' and 'corrupt' dimensions to the negotiations. This choice of language tended to affiliate the statement with other 'popular' opposition to the agreement rather than to mark it as one from a specially authorized or interested constituency. Somewhat less commonplace was the statement's use of the word 'political' in its claim that the agreement 'was made for political reasons.' This usage implies that 'political' signifies 'self-serving' and that 'the political' is the realm only of corrupt party politics. It implies conversely that honest people are not 'political,' that the statement we are reading is not 'political,' and that the people who have signed it have not thereby performed a 'political' action. Ultimately, it implies that 'the' Canadian identity is undebatable, that it is an idealism outside of politics.

Although the statement offers no arguments against the trade agreement, it covertly signals two major objections. One of these concerns Canadians' construction of their country as a more caring society than the United States ('the Canada we care about') and as having more far-ranging social programs ('the welfare of our country'). The second, hidden in that seemingly innocent phrase 'the Canada,' is that Canada is a discrete, single, uniform entity, fully distinguishable from the United States, that stands in risk of adulteration by too much commerce with it neighbour – there is only one 'Canada we care about.' This monolithic notion of Canada is also reflected in the names of the signators. While the thirty-nine names include at least three from the West, and several of Maritime origin, almost all are associable with Ontario, and specifically with the Toronto region. The silences in the advertisement are large – a silence from Quebec, a silence (apart from Rudy Wiebe) from the Prairies, a silence (apart from Phyllis Webb) from British Columbia, a silence about its own political nature, a silence about which 'the Canada' it defends.

The text offered by the sixty-two supporters of the trade agreement is quite a different piece of language. While the advertisement of the thirty-nine awarded the subject-position of its opening statement to the agreement ('The Mulroney-Reagan Trade Deal is a hastily-concluded agreement ...'), this advertisement gives it to its own signators. 'We are not fragile' (implying that opponents of the agreement are both 'fragile' and fearful of competition), the advertisement begins, even though its heading – 'Artists and Writers for Free Trade' – has already indicated that the signators fear that their reputations may be indeed 'fragile,' perhaps non-existent, within their own country. 'We, the undersigned artists and writers,' it continues – here not only foregrounding its own signators in the subject-position and again reminding its readers of who this 'we' is, but also adopting the authoritative rhetoric of public declamation. 'We, the undersigned artists and writers, want the people of Canada to know we are in favour of the Canada–United States Free Trade Agreement.' Rather than using the intimate 'we-you' discourse of the thirty-nine opponents of the agreement, the sixty-two address Canadians in the more formal third person, 'the people of Canada.' Particularly revealing here, in terms of the explicit claims of both groups to endorse a participatory politics, is the fact that the artists who support the agreement choose not to address Canadians directly, while those who who resist it do.

The statement continues:

> There is no threat to our national identity anywhere in the Agreement. Nor is there a threat to any form of Canadian cultural expression.
>
> As artists and writers, we reject the suggestion that our ability to create depends upon the denial of economic opportunities to our fellow citizens.
>
> What we make is to be seen and read by the whole world. The spirit of protectionism is the enemy of art and thought.

The first of these short paragraphs makes an assumption of the singleness of Canadian identity – 'our national identity' – similar to that made by the statement of the thirty-nine, although it undercuts this with the ambiguity of 'any form of Canadian cultural expression.' The next tells the reader for the third time that the undersigned are 'artists and writers' (they will later also be individually identified as 'writer,' 'painter,' 'author,' etc., after their signatures) and in the repetition of this insistence signals increasing anxiety about the stability of this identification. Reinstating the signators in the privileged subject-position, this paragraph has them 'reject the suggestion' that their 'ability to create' depends 'upon the denial of economic opportunities to ... fellow citizens.' This is a curious statement that on the one hand limits the activity of the artist to 'creation' (excluding such things as dissemination and social intervention) while also implying a separation between 'creation' and 'economic opportunities.' While appearing to affirm a romantic construction of the mystery and integrity of creativity, the statement is also, and rather more significantly, rejecting a materialist analysis of artistic activity. There is no relation, it implies, between art and economics. An artist's perceptions and choice of genres, as well as the time available to work, are unaffected by his or her economic experiences. An artist creates some materially disengaged and inevitable 'creations' and leaves the business of publishing and distribution to those who have dedicated themselves to 'economic opportunities.' A reader may well wonder here whether this assumption of economic disengagement is perhaps behind the signators' uncertainty about how widely they are known by 'the people of Canada.'

The concluding paragraph suggests another explanation, however, for this uncertainty – the 'creations' of the sixty-two were not specifically intended for the 'the people of Canada' but 'to be seen and read by the whole world.' Like the romantic notion of economically unbesmirched creativity, this is also a recognizable element in the Canadian text – the desire to be world-class, found elsewhere in Canadians' fascination with Lester Pearson and Ben Johnson, in John Metcalf's suspicion of the Canada Council, and in Morley Callaghan's pride that he boxed with Hemingway. As Robert Kroetsch mischievously quotes from a 1920s Mackenzie seed catalogue, 'There is no place in the world where better cauliflowers can be grown than right here in the West.' But what if other parts of the world value different properties in a cauliflower? The 'world-class' concept implicit in this advertisement is, like 'the Canada' in the other, a monolithic and idealized construct. There is only one each of 'art and thought,' and these are to be found internationally, in texts written not for any one place but for 'the whole world.'

Such a notion of world-context is also that of multinational business: the world as a homogeneous market-place with uniform rules, practices, and economic forces. Since it is to help realize such a notion that the free trade agreement was conceived – to create for business the 'level playing field' – it is not surprising that the sixty-two should support it. They too are arguing for a level playing field, the 'whole world'; among the sixty-two signators are several – most prominently Metcalf – who have lamented Canadian arts grants and subsidies as distortions of the playing field. 'We are not fragile,' their advertisement began. Here too is evident the open competition theory which multinational capitalism and the sixty-two signators of the statement appear to share. 'We are not fragile, we can survive international competition, we work to world standards and do not need protective legislation' is the subtext here – a subtext which not too subtly places artistic production on the same ground as that of any production which can thrive in an unregulated multinational economy. This message in the advertisement, that the signators represent a tough, internationally competitive Canadian art, an art which can compete economically like any other well-made product, appears, however, to contradict their other message that they represent a pure kind of creativity, unsullied by the market-place. But not quite: for the text also implies that these two are one and the same: the pure disinterested (and thus universal) artwork is also the tough internationally competitive (and thus universal) artwork. An illusion that the gap between these has been bridged is created in the advertisement by its silence on all issues of art distribution, and by the ambiguity it allows to hover around the word 'fragile' – 'fragile' artistically, perhaps like Ogden Nash or Mazo de la Roche, or 'fragile' materially like Isabella Valancy Crawford?

This silence is joined by a silence within the names of its sixty-two signators similar to the silence within the names of the thirty-nine. Here again there are no Québécois (unless one so defines Irving Layton or Nick Auf Der Maur) and few identifiable Westerners. There are more names from the Maritimes, although none of these is a writer. There are thirteen women (there were also thirteen women among the thirty-nine opponents of free trade), with only three of these identified as 'writers.' This low representation of writers somewhat qualifies the advertisement's thrice-stated claim to be a statement by 'artists and writers.'

These two advertisements raise difficult questions about the relationship between politics and art, and between society and the artist. Both constitute attempts by artists to intervene in a nation's political debate either overtly or covertly on their authority as artists. The thirty-nine encode this authority in their assumption that their names possess public meaning; the sixty-two invoke it through their announcing three times in fifteen lines that they are 'artists and writers.' Yet both are uneasy about the political quality of the act they engage in; the thirty-nine speak disapprovingly of the 'political,' while the sixty-two take pains to insist that their 'creativity' has not only nothing to do with national issues but also nothing to do with the 'economic.' The latter insistence is so strong that it leaves their statement without apparent motive except perhaps that of good citizenship. Both statements suggest that the activities of their supporters are in some way beyond politics. The thirty-nine do this through their attaching themselves to an idealized 'Canada we care about,' the sixty-two by attaching themselves to similarly idealized concepts of 'creativity,' 'art,' 'thought,' and 'world.' These strategies are, of course, and ironically so, *political* strategies. The idealization of one's own position – to offer it as archetypal, universal, or natural – is a pragmatic move to foreclose debate by attempting to raise one's position out of, 'above,' the ongoing contingent and continuingly contestable play of social interactions.

In the literary practices of Canada, as in those of most Western countries, readers, critics, and often writers have been diverted from awareness of the political dimensions of literature by the two ideologies apparent in the advertisements above: the aesthetic/humanist and the national. In the former the aesthetic is held to be a celebration of humanity, to be 'above' politics in its enacting of a *homo* both *sapiens* and *fabrilis*. Northrop Frye writes in his 'Conclusion' to *The Literary History of Canada* of an 'autonomous world of literature' (334), and in the *Anatomy of Criticism* of an 'emancipated and humane community of culture' (347) and 'a complete and classless civilization.' He urges 'the ability to look at contemporary social values with the detachment of one who is able to compare them in some degree with the infinite vision of possibilities presented by culture' (348). Presumably this detachment would apply also to the seeking of 'economic opportunities' by one's 'fellow citizens.' A.J.M. Smith similarly writes that the poet must be 'true to the reality of nature and of human nature,' as if such 'reality' again were trans-cultural if not transcendent. Poetry 'draws mankind together'; the poet returns 'through language, rhythm and the sound of verse – to humanity' (188–9). George Woodcock (engaged in 1988 by the ostensibly nationalist publisher ECW Press to write what its 1988 catalogue described as a series of 'succinct monographs that offer fresh, lively readings of central Canadian works of fiction') writes of 'the underlying universality of the personal and national experience' (1970, 23) and of 'the transcending symphony of art' (75).

Nationalist ideology usually presents itself as contending against the aesthetic and humanist in arguing the particularity of human social forms within specific national boundaries. I say 'usually presents itself as contending' because one often finds peculiar links between the two. One is the tendency, as in the two advertisements, to be similarly homogenizing. For the nationalist all literary production can be either recuperated as articulating some facet of the national archetype, whether this be the American Adam, the English garden, or the French struggle for the 'fraternal' state, or dismissed as nationally irrelevant. A nation has, as D.G. Jones suggests in the preface to *Butterfly on Rock*, an 'imaginative life,' and criticism can, 'by isolating certain themes and images ... [attempt] to define more clearly some of the features that recur' in this 'imaginative life' and reveal 'something of the Canadian temper' (3–4). Canadian fiction, for John Moss, reflects a 'geophysical imagination,' 'the progress of the Canadian imagination towards a positive identity' (7). As in the humanist 'art' and 'mind,' the terms 'temper,' 'identity,' and 'imagination' are offered as unitary constructs. The second link is an overt move in many nationalist readings to locate the unitary national text within the similarly unitary humanist one. The peculiarly 'Canadian' imagination is thus validated by its participation in 'themes common to western literature' (Jones, 6), by its sharing 'objectives of art' that are 'universal' (Moss, 8). Canadian writers are not only Canadian, but this Canadianness is of 'world-rank': a Canadian construction such as 'the hostile wilderness becomes, not just a Canadian universe but the whole natural universe' (Jones, 6). This move can allow a nationalist to deflect possible criticism from humanist ideological positions without having to develop a critique of humanism itself, and very likely accounts for the fact that it is possible to adopt both humanist and nationalist positions in Canada – to develop a national identity can also be, paradoxically, to acquire a place in universal culture.

My main concern in *Survival* was to distinguish Canlit from Britlit or Amlit. But to see the theme [victimization] as 'universal' is to view it as a *constant* in human society – like saying 'the poor you have always with you' – and therefore *as an unalterable* fact, like birth and death and the weather. It is to ignore the political and economic context of 'victims.' In fact you have victims only where you have 'hierarchies.'

Margaret Atwood, *Second Words*, 132–3

It is significant that among nationalist theorists Margaret Atwood is one of the few to explicitly refuse humanist valorizations of the national. Although her critique here is fragmentary, it offers two key elements: humanism mistakenly idealizes the 'universal' as a 'constant' in society, and correspondingly neglects 'the political.' All nationalist readings of Canadian literature are in a general sense 'political.' All attempt to construct links between the literary text and the cultural one, to show the literary as contributing in some way to the formation of the cultural. What has prevented nationalist literary theory in Canada from dealing more fully with the political than Atwood does above has been its tendency to construct the national text as unitary and thus as devoid of political contestation and debate. In Atwood's *Survival* politics enters her theory as conflict between the Canadian and the non-Canadian, between 'Canlit' and 'Britlit or Amlit,' between those who view their victimization as changeable (her 'position' Three) and those possessed of what Marxists term a 'false consciousness' in which they experience their own oppression from the point of view of the oppressor as either non-existent or 'natural' (her 'positions' One and Two). Her text suggests little if any contestation within the 'Canadian' position itself and tends overall to totalize this position through the 'victim' metaphor. In a similar way Gaile McGregor's *The Wacousta Syndrome* subsumes the Canadian within one metaphor and portrays the political as a contestation between 'American' and 'Canadian' national ideologies. The analyses of Moss and Jones not only construct the Canadian cultural text as unproblematically first-person plural and conflict-free – as in Jones's 'our own cultural house' (3) and Moss's 'our emergence into national being' – but also, by aligning Canadian nationalism with Western humanism, suggest little conflict between Canadian and non-Canadian interests. For Moss, Canadian fiction 'is continuous with world literature' (7); for Jones literature is a means by which 'man [can] discover his identity and community with the rest of nature' (8). All the nationalist critics, like the advertisement of the thirty-nine, are nervous about the term 'political'; they tend to take shelter behind words like 'culture' and 'identity' and aestheticize literature by concealing its participation in the social and conflictual processes that produce culture.

The two 'free trade' advertisements hint at a different story. The two construct very different groups of writers, each aligning itself with quite different arrays of fellow artists. They have conflicting interests, yet apparently each is Canadian and participating in a Canadian political debate. One group is confident it is known to *Globe* readers, while the other is nervous that it is not; one writes in the discourse of popular Canadian politics, the other in a more formal discourse of educated authority; one foregrounds the issues it addresses, the other foregrounds itself and its own significance; one addresses Canadians in the second person, the other indirectly in the third person; one is assured that it belongs to the community it addresses, the other uncertain; one idealizes the Canada it believes this community to be named by, the other idealizes 'creativity,' 'art,' and 'knowledge.' Beyond the overt conflicts between the two groups suggested by the advertisements are further ones indicated by contradictions and silences. Why does one group of writers find allies in painters and art dealers, and the other in musicians? Why is the proportion of women higher in one than in the other? Why, among sixty-two supporters of free trade, are there only three women marked as writers, but fourteen men? Why, in the advertisement of the thirty-nine, is there no mention of a relationship between art and commerce? What are the positions on free trade of writers in other regions than Ontario?

Although a theory of the literary text which could take into account its roles within various political texts is probably not going to answer such specific questions, it might very well permit such interventions as the two advertisements to be made with less awkwardness and nervousness and possibly with more candour and effect. The misconceptions assumed or suggested by the refusal of the advertisement of the thirty-nine to construct itself as 'political,' and by that of the sixty-two to include 'creativity' within the 'economic,' are fundamental misconceptions about textuality. Moreover, they are very similar to failures which appear to have prevented anglophone-Canadian literary works from participating as fully as they might in national argument, and have delayed the writing of a textually based and political accounting of this literature. Among these have been the failure to observe that gender, class, region, ethnicity, and economic structures can mark texts as decisively as can nation or 'world culture,' that the codes of literature are shared, and produced in concert, with the other written and unwritten texts of a society, that a writer's choice of codes, or positions in relation to these codes, can again be influenced by matters of gender, class, region, ethnicity, and economic practices, and that the usual relationship between codes, as between regions, classes, genders, ethnic affiliations, and economic practices, is one of contestation and/or dominance. This contestation is frequently more intense *within* a society than it is between it and other societies – in fact, such an intensity of internal conflict is probably the distinguishing feature of a separate society. A reluctance to acknowledge this contestation, or to recognize that people located at different positions within the complex of situations and codes that constitute any country have different and conflicting interests on most issues, can result not only in inarticulate debating of such critical issues as 'free trade' but in misleadingly harmonious constructions of

Canadian literature, politics, and culture. These, in turn, blur the edges of political conflict and suppress the positions of those who cannot be assimilated by metaphors of unity – whether 'victim,' 'ellipse,' 'bush garden,' 'mainstream,' 'Wacousta,' 'Laurentian shield,' or 'butterfly' – or who do not, unlike the sixty-two and thirty-nine, enjoy access to the Toronto media.

Basic to such a theorizing of the political role of the literary text in a society such as Canada's is Saussure's observation that the relationship between a signified and its signifier is arbitrary and rests on differentiations between phonemes rather than on fixed connections between signifier and signified – that is to say, language signifies by referring to itself. At an elementary level this observation allows a theorist to account for the signifying by single terms like 'art' or 'Canada' of different meanings to different speakers: terms receive their definitions within the differential system of linguistic signs specific to particular language communities. More important, however, Saussure's observation implies – as later writings by Sledd in grammar, Barthes in semiotics, Foucault in sociology, Hayden White in history, Lacan in pyschoanalysis, Derrida in metaphysics, and Jane Gallop in feminism have explored – that all 'experience' is linguistically mediated. We perceive not raw 'things' but 'things' placed within specific linguistic patterns of meaning.

The concept of the textuality of all experience is perhaps the most enabling one for any attempt to theorize the political functioning of literature, for it partly dissolves the difficult question for criticism of whether to remain 'inside' the text and 'faithful' to it, or to go 'outside' a text into possibly spurious material. If all experience is social and textual, literary texts are produced as parts of this social text, from a great variety of positions within it, and constitute, in company with other sites of textual production, contributing parts of the overall social production of meaning. In terms of Canadian literature such a theory can propose literary texts as one of many producers of meaning through which a term such as 'free trade' obtains significance. Literary texts can be seen as a sinuous and ultimately inextricable part of the general social text, both leaving their marks 'outside' themselves and containing marks which refer 'beyond' themselves. So invasive are their interweavings into the social text that they have, strictly speaking, neither an 'outside' nor an 'inside.' Attempts to discuss how one might read a text thus struggle with and through metaphor. Although it is possible for a reader to bring gratuitously to a literary text materials and meanings neither signalled nor invited by it, it also becomes possible to theorize readings discouraged by formalist criticism. For example, whereas a formalism such as New Criticism was obliged to attempt to expel authorial biography from influencing its readings, a textual reading can read the author-name as one of the marks a literary text may carry, and can inquire into that name's ability to signify. The significance can vary with time and region. In 1965, on a new book entitled *But We Are Exiles*, the author-name 'Robert Kroetsch' carried little signification beyond its not-female, not-Bob, not-ethnically British differentiations. In 1983 the same author-name on a new novel entitled *Alibi* carries numerous significations in Canada, upon which the paperback cover can rely in announcing the book to be 'Kroetsch comedy ... in high gear.' The range and number of these significations will be different, however, in countries other than Canada, and within Canada differ somewhat according to variously marked positions – by gender, region, class, etc. – of the perceiver.

The author-name, in the case of a well-known author, ceases to be merely a signifier and becomes itself a system of meaning, a system which for most readers the literary text will incorporate. Such a reference is 'intertextual,' in the sense that Roland Barthes and Julia Kristeva elaborated in the early 1970s.[2] While a text announcing itself as a 'novel' incorporates the socially circulating conventions of that genre, one announcing itself by an author known to a particular community incorporates not only that community's knowledge of her but its readings of her previous texts. Margaret Atwood's *The Handmaid's Tale*, for example, is marked by a reader's knowledge of her public life and her other books, as well as by the codes of the novel and the dystopia; at its opening it adds to these the semiotic systems of the high school gymnasium, the concentration camp, and Protestant fundamentalism and returns to the latter two throughout. A reading which includes reflection on all these various elements is a textual

---

2 The theory of intertextuality holds that just as individual phonemes acquire their ability to signify by differing from each other, and by occupying differential positions within a linguistic system, so too various *systems of textual organization* – literary genres, professional discourses, oral forms like gossip, cursing, whispering, a disk-jockey's 'patter,' social genres like wedding invitations, eulogies, birthday cards – and *particular patterns of meaning* (also known as 'semiotic systems') – the English garden, the urban expressway, the nuclear family, the sailing ship – acquire meaning by occupying differential positions within the social text. Further, as parts of the social text, that is as parts of the general system of code available for the communication of meaning in one's society, these are reader-activated rather than strictly writer-deployed.

reading – all of these are, in some reading contexts, available 'parts' of the text.

Similarly useful for a nationalist criticism is the observation by numerous linguistic theorists (Foucault, Todorov, Marin) that speakers situated *within* such semiotic systems will often assemble sentences and strings of sentences in characteristic ways or 'discourses.'[3] The various elements of the discourses evident within a text can be seen to carry signification – of point of view, of specific patterns of meaning, of specific ways of constituting knowledge and value. In Margaret Laurence's *The Diviners*, when Morag learns to say 'simply, *Please*, instead of *Oh yes thanks I'd just love some*, or, worse, *Okay that'd be fine*' (197), she is choosing between two discourses, each marked by class and, through class, by politics. The patterns of meaning which discourse signifies have been termed by many linguists (Macherey, Althusser [1969], Pécheux, Eagleton, Kristeva, Hirst) as *ideology*. Although this term has unfortunate connotations of the dogmatic in North American political discourse, in linguistic and critical discourse it is used to designate 'a system of representations (images, myths, ideas, or concepts) endowed with specific historical context and functioning within a given society.' '[I]t is usually taken for granted, considered as "natural," hence neither repressed ... nor intentionally propounded ...' (Roudiez, 15).

Although much recent Marxist debate about ideology has focused on whether or not it is 'material' and/or 'autonomous,' this question would appear to have arisen mostly from confusion over the persistence of ideological formations. Such patterns of meaning arise from specific material contexts, and reflect the circumstances and interests of the social group which generates them. The Prairie pattern of meaning in which Toronto signifies exploitive business practices has a material origin in the dependent economic relationship the

3 Differing systems of textual organization have in recent linguistic theory become widely known as *discourses* or *discursive practices*. *Discourse* acquires its meaning in contemporary criticism from the French *discours*, speech, a much more widely used word than its English cognate, and which more readily signifies a general and characteristic pattern of organizing language. Determinants of discourse include not only characteristic items of vocabulary, recurrent syntactic structures, recurrent fields of image and metaphor, and recurrent rhetorical figures, but also particular ways of linking sentences together, or of structuring a text. Discourse can be described by genre (as in Todorov's *Genres de discours*), by class (as in Foucault's *Les Mots et les choses*), by semiotics (Barthes's *Mythologies*, McLuhan's *The Mechanical Bride*, Marin's *La Critique du discours*), or through diction and sentence structure (Reiss, *The Discourse of Modernism*).

agricultural economy of the Prairies has had with the financial and industrial sectors of Ontario. It is also, however, a pattern of meaning which is likely to persist and to influence meaning production long after this relationship has altered. Similarly, the Prairie pattern of meaning which perceives rural life as more rich and energetic than the urban (see my 'A Young Boy's Eden: Some Notes on Prairie Poetry,' in *Reading Canadian Reading*) flourishes despite the increasing urbanization and industrialization of Prairie society. The aesthetic is another area of ideology which shows extreme persistence. Notions of beauty or aesthetic value arise from the needs of particular sectors of society to valorize certain texts, textual practices, and positions. When these needs change, or the power of that sector to enforce its interests wanes, the particular aesthetic judgment may nevertheless persist, as if it were itself 'material,' and continue to influence new judgments. In the 1960s the 'value' of F.P. Grove's novels rested largely on the needs of students and scholars of Canadian culture to have sufficient texts for a national literature; this value persisted through the 1970s, although that period's rapid production of new texts made the need less urgent. Only in the 1980s does the value of the Grove texts become problematical, and a new and partly mythological ground for this value begins to be articulated on the basis of the Felix Paul Greve story.

A re-situation of a culture's literary texts within its socio-political text, then, needs in no sense to be an impressionistic, evaluative, or (in the Canadian sense) 'thematic' criticism. The various post-Saussurean theories of signification, discourse, and ideology offer a means of reading a text for political signification that, far from generalizing on plot patterns and overt declarations of theme, requires close attention to semiotic and discursive elements. These theories also allow the theorizing of a particular literature, characterized by such specific positions within its discourses as gender, region, class, or even nation, without arguing either its radical distinctness from other literatures or its subsumption within some 'underlying universality' (Woodcock, 1970, 23). Discourses are not compartments which contain or allude to one another, but systems which interact, overlap, and on occasion invoke each other's codes. Practitioners of specific discourses, whether writers or readers, do not occupy a single 'emancipated and humane' position (Frye, 1957, 347), but each a specific and irreproducible position within the global contention and interaction of discourses. A 'Canadian' literature is theorizable as a literature produced at a large number of such positions within discourse. It is neither distinct and isolated from the contentions of global discourse nor identical with them; its marks are those of the specific contentions and nexuses of the sites of its production.

The two election-eve advertisements which began this chapter are, despite their conflicting political aims, both idealizing attempts to deny the heterogeneity of the Canadian discursive field. This is attempted by the thirty-nine through excluding the 'political' from 'the welfare of our country' – an exclusion which might prompt one to reply that it is by recognizing and participating in the political that one ensures that one *has* a country. The sixty-two place against heterogeneity 'art,' 'thought,' and writing and painting 'to be seen and read by the whole world.' In different ways both manoeuvres are counter-productive to a vigorous and 'distinct' Canadian society. The latter, with its implicit 'we are not fragile' aligning of its art with the non-fragile industrial production that seeks the homogenizing of economic rules which the free trade agreement moves towards, endorses one of the most homogenizing forces in the world today, multinational capitalism.[4] The former, by placing Canada beyond political

4 Sociologist Andrée Michel has described the values of multinational capitalism as 'competition, concurrence, culte de la croissance illimitée du profit, asservissement de l'humain à la consommation, à la technique et à l'économisme, gigantisme des projets, valorisations du militarisme, de l'égoisme de la nation et de l'idéologie nataliste.' She continues, '... les multinationales important dans tous les pays grâce à la mondialisation du marché, un marché dans lequel le noyau central tout-puissant exploite et entretient la faiblesse de la péripherie' (*Le Féminisme*, 121). The all-powerful exploit and maintain the weakness of the periphery: no wonder the sixty-two self-indentified 'artists and writers' are determined not to be 'fragile.' Although I would dispute the centre-periphery model Michel uses, I would also argue that her characterizations of 'les multinationales' accord with many of the criteria most frequently invoked by free trade negotiators and supporters – a widening of the market-place, encouragement of competition, rationalization of competitors, greater economic growth, larger and more powerful corporations. A homogenizing self-valorizing social formation, whether it be one that idealizes 'art and thought' or one that seeks unlimited expansion of economic power, is by its own epistemology unfriendly to difference. Difference is a departure from the ideal; it is lesser, if not parochial. Or difference is inefficient; its acknowledgment makes difficult the economic practices on which profit often rests – the co-opting of the unpaid labour of women, the production of uniform products, the making of minimal contributions to pension and health programs, the perceiving of commercial products, even entertainment and informational products, as extra-political. Had there already been in Canada a recognition of the politics of difference, and of the ongoing working of that politics within and between its literary productions, as marking most of its best-received literary productions, the argument that the free trade agreement offered an exchange of difference for efficiency might have been made with force and precision.

disputation, risks depriving Canadians of the only means they have of defending themselves against multinational capitalism: participating in the arguments of a nation that is being continuously discursively produced and re-produced from political contestation.

Representations of Silence
The Diviners

If you are seeking the True meanings of the many aspects of Life then Go
into Nature. Go where You can enjoy evenings studying the Stars from
the porch of your own home, on your own Land. Go where you can see
the trees that provide the lumber for your house. Go where You can see
the crops that provide the food for your table. Go where You can follow
the stream that provides your water. Go where You can wander for hours
and think freely. Go where You can enjoy directly the fruits of your labor.
Go and become what YOU think You are.

Adolf Hungry Wolf, in *The Canadian Whole Earth Almanac*, Winter 1970,
116

Margaret Laurence's *The Diviners* (1974) is presented as a 'life-story-
recollected-in-crisis,' much like her earlier novel *The Stone Angel*. The
novel purports to come into being because the focalizing character,
Morag Gunn, has been spurred to remember her life by the sudden
decision of her teenage daughter, Pique, to journey alone to the Métis
lands of her father's people in Western Canada. This narrative device
gives the novel two concurrent plots, one in which Morag awaits
Pique and reflects upon her memories, and another in which Morag
grows from a young child to forty-seven-year-old single mother. Interestingly, both the plots unfold chronologically – although there
would appear to be no generic or psychological necessity for a character to remember her life in such a specifically orderly way, stage
by stage, neither recalling later events until the preceding have been
remembered, nor being lured back for a second look at things already
remembered. Morag's narrative search, it would seem, is a search for
coherence, for 'something which would explain everything' (4). The

opening image of the book, the river that, like memory, flows two ways, also implies a search for wholeness.

> The river flowed both ways. The current moved from north to south, but the wind usually came from the south, rippling the bronze-green water in the opposite direction. This apparently impossible contradiction, made apparent and possible, still fascinated Morag, even after the years of river-watching. (3)

This implication is reinforced by the title of the book, with its suggestion that there is some validating 'source' beneath the disparate surface of events – a source that can give intimations of personal identity – and that the artist or rememberer can obtain access to such a source.

Yet within the novel itself the discourse of 'divining' participates more in conflict than in harmony, being one of several discourses – dream, song, poetry – that are presented by the text as subversive and in conflict with authorized discourses such as History, Literature, and Law. These subversive discourses are associated with people and classes marginalized from power in their society – with women, the poor, the coloured, the less-educated – and would appear difficult to subsume under some unifying image such as 'a meaningful life' or a river that runs 'both ways.' Does the novel present these conflicts as part of an unfortunate but structurally unchangeable 'pattern of life,' or as arguments that offer opportunities for choice and change?

> That night Brooke has the same (same? who can tell?) nightmare, the one that recurs every six months or so, and speaks the same name.
> *Minoo.*
> She cannot bear the weird monotone of his voice. She shakes his shoulder.

> *The Diviners,* 186

Brooke's dreams of Minoo occur near the middle of the text of *The Diviners,* shortly before Morag, at this point his wife, determines that she must leave him. The two syllables he speaks in this 'weird monotone' constitute the only evidence of the existence of the young Hindu woman who was Brooke's *ayah* many years before during the British raj. In a text in which all the female characters are in some way marked as 'foreign,' Minoo is the most heavily marked and among the most emphatically marginalized. Even Brooke, through whose voice her name asserts itself in the text, is reluctant to talk of her and, when forced to, can remember but a few details which he insists are not 'important.' 'Well, I may as well tell you,' he says to Morag when she insists that Minoo be identified, 'not that it's all that important. She was a Hindu woman – really, at this point, I have no memory of whether she was young or old. She seemed old but she may only have been a girl. I was about five or six. She was my *ayah*' (186). In the young Brooke's life the *ayah* stands in for his mother, who is also marked very much as sidelined in the text – 'My mother spent nearly all her time lying in a hammock, suffering from migraine' (186). But Minoo's care for him, particularly her practice of holding him in her arms and stroking him 'all over' until he had 'an orgasm or whatever is the equivalent in a child' (186) and then went to sleep, is itself far past the boundaries of British practice and, when discovered by his father, leads immediately to the father's beating Brooke and tying him to a steamer trunk outside the front gate of the compound and placing on his chest 'a placard which read *I Am Bad*' (177). Here Brooke himself is placed outside the margins of British culture – outside the compound – and labelled with a sign of being outside its standard of 'goodness.' As for Minoo's fate, the text offers no information; Brooke volunteers nothing more about her, and Morag neglects to ask.

———————————

In a sense it is ironic that Minoo should break out of her repression by speaking her name through the nightmares of Brooke Skelton. Brooke is presented in the text as someone who is particularly interested in the silence of women, in reducing the number of the words they utter and the interference of these words with his life. He enters the novel as Morag's professor of seventeenth-century English literature. His first classroom words concern John Donne's 'The Ecstasy' and assert to Morag the male writer's authority over his text: 'What would you say that Donne meant by this metaphysical image? Miss Gunn?' (154). Two not necessarily congruent things are being asked in this question: 'what ... you say' and 'what ... Donne meant' (the difficult coexistence of these is marked by the awkward double functioning of 'what' in the syntax of the question as both the 'what' that Donne meant and the 'what' that 'Miss Gunn' must 'say'). In attempting to respond, Morag finds herself protesting the presence of 'cruel lines' within Donne's poems generally: 'Well, like "For God's sake hold your tongue and let me love." That's a very cruel line. Supposing the lady had been able to write poetry – I mean, you wonder what she might have said of *him*' (155). Her protest – which mistakes the addressee of Donne's poem as a female lover rather than male companion (a mistake the text appears to make itself by its failure to foreground it) – can be read as one not only against the Donne text but against Morag's own situation of having to 'hold' her own tongue if she is to present herself as saying what 'Donne meant.'

Brooke Skelton's successful attempts to contain Morag's protest move from his initial invocation of author-authority to an appeal both to historical perspective and to polite, authoritative forms of language. 'You would not take it kindly, Miss Gunn, to be asked to hold your tongue?' he asks Morag. The circumlocutional verb phrase 'take it kindly' signals that any request from him to someone to hold their tongue would be made in an indirect and genteel manner. 'No. No, I would not,' replies Morag. The dialogue continues:

> 'Well, quite right, too,' Dr. Skelton says, seriously, frowning a little at the class's general levity. 'But Donne, surely, must be seen as a man of his historical time.' (155)

This is a peculiar response, which offers an affirmative to unrestrained speech but in a formulaic British-English phrase, 'quite right, too,' and which accompanies the affirmation with a restraining frown against the class's utterance of 'general levity.' Semantically the modifier of his utterance, 'seriously,' acts against the lightness and non-seriousness of the class's 'levity.' Syntactically the entire affirmation is then withdrawn by the qualifying 'but' with which Skelton's second sentence begins. It is appropriate to insist on one's right to speak provided 'historical time' has not already foreclosed the issue about which one wishes to speak. The stock academic phrase 'a man of his historical time,' together with the redundancy of 'historical,' emphasize the 'already-saidness' of the things Morag may wish to argue. In all of the figures the novel deploys in this scene, even its apparent misreading of the Donne text, it works to associate the male poet or critic with oppression, history, hierarchy, power, privilege, and the silencing of woman; and the woman, with silence, colonization, and hopeful impropriety.

———————●———————

The three women above, Minoo, Morag, and the lady who had not 'been able to write poetry,' are gathered by the novel under the sign of the silenced woman, the woman who if she 'speaks' at all speaks through the words or by permission of the words of a male authority. They are not alone but have the company of at very least Brooke's mother, lying in her hammock with a migraine, Prin Logan, Morag's adoptive mother, Bridie McRaith, the wife of her Scottish lover, Eva Winkler, her childhood neighbour, and her Métis lover's sister, Piquette Tonnerre, beaten by her white husband and later burned to death in the Tonnerre cabin.

Prin's silence is constructed by the novel as having grown from deep feelings of inferiority. Early in life she has apparently been identified by the school system as mentally handicapped (205); she has married the town garbage collector – the only man she believes would have her; she has lost her only child in childbirth (36); increasingly discouraged, she has lapsed into a passive life in which she sits in a rocking-chair eating jelly doughnuts (36), growing fatter, and speaking less and less (108). The last fifteen years of her life she spends either in that chair or in bed, 'obese and silent and almost motionless' (140). Piquette Tonnerre's silence is presented as of another kind – she is the Métis child who rarely attends school and who is seldom heard when there. Her failure to attend appears sometimes to be because of a lack of clothing and sometimes because of the tuberculosis that infects one leg. Cured, she immediately leaves town and marries a man in Winnipeg, returning later, deserted, with two children, having 'grown flabbily fat' and walking 'with the lurch of the habitual drunk.' 'She has been arrested several times, like her father before her, for outrageously shrieking her pain aloud in public places, usually in the form of obscene insults to whoever happens to be handiest' (128). Even more effective than arrest in quietening her is the fire that destroys the Tonnerre cabin, killing her and her children – a fire blamed on a 'wreck of a stove' and on Piquette's drinking.

Eva Winkler's silence is presented as also partly a product, like the silences of Prin and Piquette, of poverty and brutalization by structures of authority. Her father beats her because 'he just likes beating his kids,' or 'because she's gutless' (50). She is silent about needing a bathroom on the first day of school and is known afterwards to her classmates as 'Eva Weakguts' (28); later one of her teachers remembers her as 'poor little Eva Whatsername' (51). Bridie McRaith's silence is presented by the novel as only slightly different, as stemming from her marriage to Dan McRaith when she was only seventeen and from a kind of intellectual aggression on his part as he has grown and changed and she has not:

> These famous silences of hers, Morag now thinks, are caused because he
> hands her lines to which she cannot respond either angrily or wittily. Her
> response is silence, possibly because she has not ever figured out any
> other response. She was seventeen. He has moved on, into other areas.
> Bridie has not, and knows it well. (318)

When she first hears of Bridie, Morag reflects on the 'connotations'
of her name – 'connotations of perpetual bridehood, something child-
ish and affected' (305). 'It's a form of Bridget,' McRaith replies. But
although McRaith may defend the nickname as an innocent and culturally endorsed diminutive of 'Bridget,' it is anything but innocent
within the text of the novel itself. The text links the silence of many
of its women characters to the concept of immaturity. Minoo 'seemed
old but she may only have been a girl' (186); the French suffix 'ette'
in 'Piquette' can mark either a feminine (*Jean/Jeannette*) or a diminutive (*couche/couchette*); Prin Logan's lapsing into silence is paralleled
by the reduction of her name from Princess to Prin. The text implies
a need among many of the male characters to keep women not only
quiet but, as Morag intuits, perpetually young and unthreatening.
McRaith reports that, of his older sons, 'one's a teacher, and the other
is at university in Edinburgh,' but his daughter, 'just eighteen,' is
'taking business courses in Inverness' (316); the sons participate in
the making of texts, but the daughter is in training to reproduce the
texts of others. In Morag's marriage to Brooke his almost reflexive
insistence on her immaturity becomes a major point of conflict. 'Hush,
child,' he says to her when she has displeased him, thus insisting on
both her silence and her youth (183); 'idiot child,' he says to her when
amused by her mistrusting him (162); 'little one,' he says to her when
instructing her (177, 185), and 'hush, love,' when she doubts his
instruction (177); 'Have you been a good girl, love?' he asks her each
time they are about to make love (200).

In fact, the namings, both informal and formal, of *The Diviners*
appear to participate overtly in meaning-systems that denote or dis-
tribute power. The women are associated not only with diminutives
but frequently with courtly meaning-systems in which the woman
enjoys a high if not idealized position but only at the expense of
power. Prin's full name, 'Princess,' is the name of the child who
cannot inherit the crown or who can inherit it only in the absence of
male rivals; McRaith's second nickname for Bridget – one which he
appears to use when he is most unhappy with her – is 'my queen ';
the queen, like the princess, is one who normally has rank but not

power. Women themselves in the novel can aspire to the role of princess, including the young Morag, who on first meeting Brooke 'secretly thinks he is a prince among men.' The courtly meaning-system is in turn linked to the European: Brooke 'is English (from England that is)' and has 'a fine-boned handsomeness that gives him an aristocratic look' (153). His first name, 'Brooke,' evokes a European naming of watercourses and contrasts throughout the novel with 'river' – with the river beside which the mature Morag lives in Southern Ontario and with the Wachakwa River, beside which the Tonnerre family lives. His last name, 'Skelton,' connects him with British literary history but also marks both that history and himself with death, or with what remains after a death. It links him also with Morag's Scottish lover, McRaith – who, as his name suggests, may be similarly 'deathly' to women.

───────────●───────────

'Brooke – couldn't we make love and not mind if we had a child? I mean, just let it happen if it will?

...

'Aren't you happy as we are, Morag?'

The Diviners, 179

The signs in the novel that link the names of men and women with systems of meaning that inhibit woman's speech are linked through the seme of silence with practices which control her ability to reproduce. All of the women above in some way have their reproductive functioning influenced by the meanings that have limited their opportunities to articulate. Even Bridget McRaith, with her five children, appears (if one can trust her husband's perception of her) to have had these as substitutes for speech or other creativity: 'Bridie believes in large families, and as having children turned out to be her chief interest in life, it did not seem fair to object to it. She has not objected to my painting, although she sometimes had cause' (305). He speaks of her childbearing as something she does, rather than he and she do together, and equates it with his own painting. His statement also implies that she bears children by his permission and tolerance ('it did not seem fair to object to it'); he apparently would have objected if he could have found a 'fair' way to do so.

The increasingly silent and obese Prin's only child is born 'strangled on the cord' (36). Piquette's two children die with her in the

Tonnerre fire. The oft-beaten Eva Winkler 'aborts herself ... with a partly straightened-out wire clotheshanger' (123) rather than face her chronically angry father, and is consequently unable to bear more children. Brooke Skelton fears both Morag's becoming a successful writer and her bearing children. He subtly discourages and patronizes her about the former and repeatedly defers the latter. Morag's rebellion against him by claiming her right to speak takes the double form of writing and publishing a novel he has not approved and becoming pregnant by Jules Tonnerre. The text thus marks women's speech as both reproductive and linguistic. The strangling of Prin's son presages the slow strangling of her voice; Gus Winkler's silencing of his daughter and Brooke's silencing of his wife are as much silencings of their sexuality as of their other abilities to declare themselves. Christie's burial of Eva's aborted child in the town garbage dump, its 'Nuisance Grounds,' where he has previously buried without comment another foetus he has discovered among a family's garbage, associates these silencings with a further sign, that of the 'reject,' the object dismissed from one's life as if putting it in the garbage bin were 'the end of it' (62).

The aristocratic namings of 'princess' and 'queen' connect with various class signifiers within the text. Morag's home town of Manawaka is hierarchically arranged, from the lowest, the Métis who live in the Wachakwa Valley, to the unemployed and the labourers whose families live, like the Logans, on Hill Street above the valley but *below the town*' (24), to the middle-class homes on the other side of the main street. Among the middle classes are the variously empowered of the town: the doctor, who can decide whether or not to make the special effort needed to cure someone like Piquette of her TB; the teachers, who can decide which children are encouraged or promoted; the lawyer, who can decide whether someone like Jules can also have the opportunity to become a lawyer; and the newspaper editor, who decides whose activities enter into print, in what words, and with what excisions. These people and the institutions they represent enforce class privileges: the grade six teacher chooses the doctor's daughter to sing the Christmas solo even though her voice is inferior to Morag's; lawyer Pearl smiles at Jules's ambition to become a lawyer and offers to help him apprentice as a mechanic; Lachlan McLachlan, as editor of the newspaper, removes the line from Morag's obituary for Piquette that notes that her grandfather fought with Riel in the Northwest Rebellion. On all three occasions the despised sign – the

working-class, the Métis, the rebellious – is excluded from some instance of official discourse.

Contrasts between various marginalized and officially sanctioned discourses are established very early in *The Diviners*, and language practice established as one of the main grounds on which power in the
novel is distributed. The possibility is also created very early that
European-derived discourses of authority may somehow be less 'natural' or even less 'Canadian' than those discourses associated with
the marginal living conditions of women, the poor, and the Métis.
The main site of discursive conflict in the early sections of the novel
is the history of the Selkirk Colony and the subsequent Red River
and Northwest rebellions. This history is told from two different 'Scots
Colonist' perspectives by Christie Logan, from a Manitoba Métis perspective by Jules Tonnerre, and from the view of official history by
Morag and her school books.

Christie's first 'tale' of the Selkirk Colony recounts the consequences for the villagers of Sutherland of the eighteenth-century enclosure of the highlands pastures, their voyage to Hudson Bay, and
overland journey to the Red River. Lord Selkirk is not part of this
recounting, nor are the economic and political forces that led to the
enclosures. The hardships of the crofters are caused by a locally dwell-
ing 'Bitch-Duchess,' who wants all the lands of Sutherland to be
'raising the sheep.' The journey is led from within the Sutherlanders
by a 'Piper Gunn,' whom Christie, the text implies, has invented in
order to delight the young Morag, to whom he tells his tale:

> The Bitch-Duchess was living there then, and it was she who cast a dark-
> ness over the land, and sowed the darkness and reaped gold, for her heart
> was dark as the feathers of a raven and her heart was as cold as the gold
> coins, and she loved no creature alive but only the gold.
>
> ...
>
> And Piper Gunn, he was a great tall man, a man with the voice of
> drums and the heart of a child and the gall of a thousand and the strength
> of conviction. And when he played the pipes on the shore, there, it was
> the pibrochs he played, out of mourning for the people lost and the people
> gone and them with no place for to lay their heads except the rocks of
> the shore. (40–1)

This tale is marked by coordinate and appositive syntactic structures which add to and amplify each sentence. The amplification is emphasized by parallel syntax ('voice of drums and the heart of a child and the gall of a thousand and the strength of conviction') and by redundant doublings ('the people lost and the people gone'). Both this syntax and the diction are literary, rather than colloquial, and resemble biblical or European folktale narrative more than they do Christie's usual speech. The diction is one of extremes and draws on romantic and gothic meaning-systems: the 'Bitch-Duchess' is associated with darkness, gold, ravens, fire, and with her castle; the crofters, with children, homes, rocks, and with emotionally powerful music. This opposition is particularly visible in the characterizing of the two women of the tale: the woman with power is evil, the 'bitch' of 'darkness '; Piper Gunn's wife is the good woman associated with the traditional female marks of beauty, domesticity, and piety – 'the beauty of a deer and the warmth of a home and the faith of saints' (41).

When Christie sometime later continues this tale, however, his language changes abruptly:

> Now that bloody ship, there, who would know what its name was, but with all of them from Sutherland on board, and struck with the sickness and the fever and the devil's plague, well, then, that ship with the children dying of the fever, it crossed the ocean, do you see, and it came to the new land, which was HERE, only very far north. But what happened? What almighty catastrophe struck that ship? Well, the first catastrophe was that ship had a bloody idiot as captain, then. And he landed the christly vessel, if you'll believe it, away up north there, *at the wrong place.* The wrong place. Can you feature it? Them people, see, Piper Gunn and his woman Morag and all them, were supposed to be landed at the one place, up there by Hudson Bay (that's the water, the sea, like, not the store). But the silly bugger landed his ship at another place. Oh yes. The bloody captain didn't give a hoot. (68)

Here, although there are parts of sentences that offer the appositives and parallelism of the earlier passage ('with the sickness and the fever and the devil's plague'), the syntax overall tends to be clausal rather than phrasal. The clauses tend to be short, and to be interrupted by markers that signal an intradiegetic context – 'do you see,' 'if you'll believe it,' 'see.' The grammar tends to be substandard ('that bloody ship, there,' 'them people'). Rather than extending itself through amplification, this passage presses forward through question and answer

– 'But what happened?' 'Can you feature it?' The diction mixes the high and the colloquial ('almighty catastrophe,' 'christly vessel') and signals an irreverent perspective on both an authority that rests on elevated diction and a 'bloody idiot' captain.

Christie's discourse on this second occasion closely resembles that of Jules Tonnerre when he narrates his father's story of the Métis response to the arrival of the Selkirk colonists:

> So a bunch of the Métis, there, they said *Shit on this idea: they're not coming here to take over our land and stop us from hunting.* But they sat on their asses all the same and didn't move. So that Rider Tonnerre, he says *We're gonna hunt these Anglais and Arkanys like we hunt the buffalo, so c'mon there, boys* ... So Rider Tonnerre and the others, they make an ambush, see, and the other guys fall for it and ride straight in. (118)

Again the passage offers substandard grammatical constructions and interrupting elements that indicate an intradiegetic context. The sentence structure, however, is mainly coordinate and balanced, and the diction lacks entirely the 'high' or European literary items that marked both of Christie's narrations. 'Chevalier' Tonnerre, with its signalling of European aristocracy, has become 'Rider' Tonnerre; although in the opening passages of his narration Jules indicated that Rider was also known as 'Prince of the Braves' (117) and his horse as 'Roi du Lac,' these terms fall from the story after the opening. The imagery centres instead on terms from the buffalo-hunting culture of the Métis: 'rider,' 'shit,' 'buffalo,' 'hunt,' 'gun,' and 'ambush.'

Both Jules's and Christie's narratives amplify their heroes and diminish their villains. Rider Tonnerre is 'about seven-feet tall' (118) and Louis Riel 'a very tall guy, even taller than Rider Tonnerre' (119), while Piper Gunn was a 'great tall man' (41) and his adversary, Louis Riel, is a 'halfbreed,' 'a short little man ... with burning eyes.' Each also portrays his hero as being the only man of action in an otherwise passive community: the Métis 'sat on their asses' until Rider Tonnerre led them; Gunn's Sutherlanders, when confronted by Riel's Métis, 'had kind of forgotten how to fight' (106).

Against both men's narrations Morag asserts yet another narrative, one she has learned in school. When Christie claims that the Sutherlanders had retaken Fort Garry from Riel's forces before Canadian troops arrived, she protests, 'They didn't. We took it in History' (106) – a response which has the revealing hidden meaning 'we Canadians recaptured the fort in "History."' When Jules recounts the Métis ambush of the Sutherlanders, she correctly points out 'the battle would be Seven Oaks, where they killed the Governor' (118).

Four different discourses and perspectives are coded here: a factual discourse of 'History' that names events and dates as if these were part of a logical process; a romantic and literary discourse, European, of exaggerated, near supernatural events, a discourse which conceals human conflict by constructing it as literary and beautiful; the angry colloquial discourse of Christie, with numerous adjectival expletives, which, despite its defiantly substandard grammar that openly declares social conflict, still offers echoes of a glorious past that is paradoxically part of a European class system against which the discourse's anger is directed; and the similarly colloquial discourse of Jules, which lacks, however, both the anger (its expletives are nouns rather than adjectives) and the paradoxical romanticism of Christie's. The similarities between the latter two discourses mark the similar class positions of their speakers; the differences mark both Jules as less torn between Europe and North America than Christie and the Métis as less free to be angry than a working-class white.

None of these discourses is entirely suitable for Morag, although she is touched by all. Christie's romantic discourse, with its evocations of a lost European Eden, links in the text with her fascination with Brooke, 'English' and 'princely,' and with her continuing desire to visit the Scottish homeland of the Sutherlanders. The official discourse of History connects with her desire to attend university, and with the rationalism of Brooke Skelton and his success as a university administrator. Christie's mixed and angry discourse gives her a rebellious language with which to resist Brooke and his condescending paternalism, but it is not one she can recognize as her own:

> 'Little one. Brooke, I am twenty-eight years old, and I am five feet eight inches tall, which has always seemed too bloody christly tall to me but there it is, and by judas priest and all the saints in fucking Beulah Land, I am stuck with it and I do not *mind* like I did once, in fact the goddamn reverse if you really want to know, ... and that's the everlasting christly truth of it.'
>
> 'You,' Brooke says, 'are hysterical. Are you due to menstruate?'
>
> Morag stands absolutely silent. *I do not know the sound of my own voice. Not yet, anyhow.* (210)

Jules's impassive and substandard language is also not made by the text to seem hers; although she chooses him to be the father of her child – choosing him, it would seem, as a North American over Brooke's Britishness – she remains so removed from his heritage and perspective that she never manages to stop mispronouncing his name as 'Jewels.'

Morag, upstairs. Writing in her scribbler. This one is nearly full, and what it is full of is a long story about how Piper Gunn's woman, once the child was born, at the Red River, went out into the forest and built a chariot for them all, for Piper Gunn and herself and their girlchild, so they could easily move around in that country there.

The Diviners, 70

From the time she is nine years old Morag attempts to write. A lot of what she writes as a child appears to be addenda to Christie's tales, addenda that amplify the small roles women have within them. After Christie relates his 'First Tale of Piper Gunn,' Morag writes a brief 'Tale of Piper Gunn's Woman' (42); and after his 'Tale of Piper Gunn and the Long March,' the above passage about Gunn's wife as a chariot-builder. Each of these replaces Piper Gunn in the subject-position of the narrative with his wife, although the only name Morag has available for this wife, 'Piper Gunn's woman,' continues to signal her being possessed and subservient. Morag's addition of these to Christie's narratives and her changing of perspective signal both the incompleteness of his stories and their unsuitability to her as both narrative and discourse. Much like Minoo breaking out of silence through Brooke's dreams, we can see here both 'Piper Gunn's woman' and the young Morag attempting to break from their own silences via the stories of Christie Logan.

The story of *The Diviners* is arguably a story about breaking into language – about a character who by becoming a novelist becomes one whose words enter the official and published records of her culture. Throughout, the mature Morag, whose memories and reflections are the focus of the text, is writing yet another novel, which, in the last line's of Laurence's narrative, is about to receive its 'remaining private and fictional words.' But the last lines of Laurence's narrative are not the last words of the novel: it concludes with the section 'Album,' which contains the texts of two songs by Jules Tonnerre and one by Morag and Jules's daughter Pique. The final words are those of Pique, who like Minoo has been doubly marked as silent through being both non-white and female. Curiously, although readers see Pique's text, they do not get to see any part of Morag's novels. The main indications of the narrative discourse Morag has adopted lie in the texts in which she passes on to Pique the stories of Christie and Jules, her 'Tale of Christie Logan' (300) and 'Tale of Lazarus Tonnerre' (301). The discourse of these 'tales' is a meta-discourse, a discourse about tale-telling:

> Well, a long time ago, when I was a kid, Christie used to tell me all sorts of stories.
>
> ...
>
> When he told me the tales about Piper Gunn, at first I used to believe every word. Then later I didn't believe a word of them, and thought he'd made them up out of whole cloth.
>
> (What means *Whole cloth?*)
>
> Out of his head – invented them. But later still, I realized they'd been taken from things that happened, and who's to know what really happened? I started believing in them again, in a different way. (300)

Her tale about Lazarus Tonnerre gets off to a stumbling beginning because of the absence of a woman's story:

> Well, your grandfather, Lazarus Tonnerre, he brought up his children in the Wachakwa Valley, there, just below the town of Manawaka, where I grew up. And there was your dad, and the two girls, Piquette and Valentine, and the two younger boys, Paul and Jacques. And their mother, Lazarus's wife, she – I'm not sure what happened. Maybe she died, or – well, I don't know.
>
> (Why don't you know?)
>
> I just don't. Maybe someday you'll see your dad again and he can tell you. Anyway, Lazarus used to tell stories ... (301)

Morag's stories here are, like *The Diviners* itself, about the impossibility of telling an unambiguous story – an impossibility that rests in there being so many competing discourses and perspectives, each with their 'truths' about what 'happened' and each with their exclusions, quite often an exclusion, as above, of women. The woman's entry into language appears linked ideologically in *The Diviners* to an acknowledgment of this competing multiplicity of discourses, discourses that all constitute possible ways of constructing events from some perspective.

In turn, this acknowledgment of the relativity of 'truth' and power connects with various other overt signs the text of *The Diviners* contains of affiliation with marginalized and relatively silent positions. Offering Morag as the orphaned daughter of struggling farmers and adopted daughter of a town garbage collector who expresses pride in the work he provides, it affiliates itself with the under-educated and poorly paid, and with a rejection of bourgeois values. It also affiliates itself with a conception of the rural that is both 'afraid of cities' (47), as Morag is, and angry at them, as are the young 'refugees' from Toronto the mature Morag finds herself living among at her farm at McConnell's Landing. In its unfavourable characterization of Brooke Skelton, whom it associates with Winnipeg and Toronto, with an upper-middle-class lifestyle, with canonical literature, with British imperialism, and with condescension towards women, it joins together signs of both class and region and adds to these considerations of gender, international politics, and textuality. In its favourable characterization of Jules Tonnerre, it not only reinforces its association with the rural and the disadvantaged, but also affiliates itself with the indigene, the francophone, and with an orality that contrasts sharply with the canonical texts which Brooke prefers. The contrast between Jules and Brooke is itself constructed, through the title of Morag's novel about her relationship with Brooke, 'Prospero's Child,' as one between a Caliban and Ferdinand, a 'primitive' and a 'prince.'[1] The most emphatic affiliation of the text is with the female, not only in its presenting itself through a woman's consciousness but in its making Morag's child a girl, and in its concern throughout for the emergence of woman from both reproductive and linguistic silencing and control.

Near the end of *The Diviners* the narrative act of recollection on which the fictional existence of the text rests, an act which has been implicit rather than explicit since the opening pages, becomes explicit once again. Once again Morag is visibly attempting to achieve an overview of her life which will give it coherence and meaning:

> Morag walked out across the grass and looked at the river. The sun, now low, was catching the waves ... The waters flowed from north to south, and the current was visible, but now a south wind was blowing, ruffling

1 For a detailed discussion of the *The Diviners* intertextual relationship with *The Tempest* see Barbara Godard's '*The Diviners* as Supplement: (M)othering the Text,' *Open Letter* 7, no. 7 (Spring 1990), 26–73.

the water in the opposite direction, so that the river, as so often here, seemed to be flowing both ways.

Look ahead into the past, and back into the future, until the silence. (370)

Although the final words of *The Diviners* are constituted by the songs in which Jules and Pique make an entry into authorized discourse, the final narrative passage is this one, which begins as above, returning to the river image with which Morag's reflections began. This 'return' constructs a frame around Morag's narrative, a frame which appears to enclose the various social conflicts of the novel – between Jules and Brooke, Manawaka and Toronto, River Street and Main Street, between Morag as proud daughter of a garbageman and competent hostess of gatherings of University of Toronto honours students, between Morag as inquisitive young woman and as worried mother – within some mysterious 'natural' process. The passage has the effect of diminishing the meaning of these conflicts, of suggesting that Morag's life 'turned out all right' both despite and because of them, of both poeticizing the conflicts as one resonant, ambiguous image of plenitude, and firmly containing them within Morag's life. Like the images recurrently offered by anglophone-Canadian criticism for Canada and its literature, this 'river of now and then' (2) is a humanistic image, one that operates to unify all the disparate and conflicting elements of *The Diviners* within a single universally accessible sign. Morag's equanimity here in the 'sunset' of her life and at the end of her latest novel is figured by means of the river image as both resting on and rendering 'acceptable' Piquette's tubercular leg and alcoholism, Valentine's death as a drug-addicted prostitute, Eva's crippling abortion, Prin's retreat into obesity and silence, Jules's exclusion from white culture either as a student hoping to study law or as an Indian entertainer who sings songs his audience 'don't wanna know about' (283). These things are just the 'pattern' of life, a continually eddying river, an 'apparently impossible contradiction' that 'still fascinated Morag, even after the years of river-watching' (3). Implicit here is not conflict but complacency, a kind of visionary apotheosis which serves ultimately to confirm the middle-class advantages of 'the Camerons and MacLeods and Duncans and Cateses' (89) and of Brooke Skelton, which Morag feels she has left behind by coming to her cabin at McConnell's Landing.

———————————

So isolate yourself enough and finally you have to accept the conditions of your existence. Clumsy, messy though they may be. Sitting in front of the A frame. Brown rice cooking on the coleman which leaks and stinks up the air.

Judith Copithorne, 'Wild Inlet – a Community,' *Georgia Straight*, 9–16 Sept. 1970, 5

It is strange that a novel which declares so emphatically its dismay at the exclusion of women, Métis and the less-educated from power and influence should end so weakly. While it is able to see these oppressions as socially constructed rather than 'natural,' it can imagine only individual, rather than social, solutions to them and in the end finds itself poetically and humanistically envisioning them as 'natural.' Although it can illuminate group issues, it can focus only on the well-being of a single individual, an individual who by the end of the novel is a university-educated, land-owning, published novelist with little in common with the small-town working class that ostensibly inspires her writing. This class remains as alien to power as when the novel began, despite having been sympathetically 'represented' by Morag. Similarly, Jules and Pique, as individuals and as Métis, remain outside power despite Morag's publishing the texts of their songs. The fact that she has appended the songs to the texts of *her* reminiscences, that they have only entered official discourse through the act of a white novelist, tends if anything to underline their exclusion rather than to negate or mitigate it. The novel that appears to end with their texts ends equally with Morag's appropriation of them, and with them of their signs of connection to the land, aboriginality, inheritance, and 'naturalness' Morag (and much of 1970s Canada) desired: 'My sister's eyes / fire and snow' (379); 'There's a valley holds my name / now I know' (381). Despite *The Diviners*'s emphatically foregrounded affiliations with the oppressed (and a text can never be merely the sum of its declared signs, no matter how successfully declared these may be), despite its attempts to affiliate itself with, and even symbolically incorporate, the silent Minoo, Prin, Jules, Eva, and Piquette, the novel becomes a text through which the Camerons or MacLeods may be comfortably linked to indigenous rhythms and subversive discourses from which they may have feared themselves estranged. It becomes a text through which an older, rural, organic Canada, close to both pioneer simplicity and aboriginal wisdom, can be made newly available – Morag's neighbours *can* raise organic vegetables, her daughter *can* return to her Métis people –

without any fundamental change being made to the industrial society which miseducates Prin and Jules, publishes Morag's novels, or hires Jules to sing. In this text the voices of the oppressed may at times sound out like a voice in a dream or like a mysterious counter-current in a river, but the overall result is finally offered (much as Christie has offered the story of the 'Bitch-Duchess') as mere beauty – 'undulating lines of gold' whose meaning transcends social contradiction and human action:

> How far could anyone see into the river? Not far. Near shore, in the shallows, the water was clear, and there were the clean and broken clamshells of creatures now dead, and the wavering of the underwater weed-forests, and the flicker of small live fishes, and the undulating lines of gold as the sand ripples received the sun. Only slightly further out, the water deepened and kept its life from sight. (370)

Towards the Green Utopia
The Temptations of Big Bear

... at
last we become them

in our desires, our desires,
mirages, mirrors, that are theirs, hard-
riding desires; and they
become our true forbears, moulded
by the same wind or rain,
.and in this land we
are their people, come
back to life again.

John Newlove, 'The Pride,' (1965), *Weekend Magazine*, 28 Dec. 1974,
14

The political engagement of Rudy Wiebe's *The Temptations of Big Bear*
(1973) is explicit in the historical event it considers – the abrupt collision between European industrial culture and North American Indian culture occasioned by the construction (1874–85) of the western
sections of the Canadian Pacific Railway and the opening of the prairie
lands to European immigration. Conflicts between cultures and regions, treaty negotiations, land settlements, and military conflict are
things conventionally recognized as 'political.' Wiebe's novel, however, goes beyond any administrative or procedural sense of 'political.'
Politics here is primarily the clash between various discourses, which
themselves 'produce' the contestants and combatants. *The Temptations of Big Bear* repeatedly foregrounds the discursive aspects of belief, the relativity of the various cultural systems that come into conflict,
and the particular histories and circumstances that have made each

of them seem 'reasonable' and 'natural' to those born within them. The anonymous third-person text attempts to reproduce within itself the social codes of these cultures, their uses of discourse and genre, the ways in which each linguistic practice produces a specific and enclosing view of experience. One important question the text raises thereby is whose political interests these reproductions themselves may serve.

The public events of *The Temptations of Big Bear* − the Canadian government's purchase of the Hudson's Bay Company lands in 1870, the building of the CPR, the Indian treaty negotiations those two events encouraged, the dissatisfaction of many Indians with the resultant treaties, the unhappiness of many Métis at being excluded from the treaties, the Indian killing of whites at Frog Lake in 1885, the Métis declaration of self-government in 1885, and the Canadian government's successful use of its army to reimpose its rule of law − are in their overall shape neither represented by the text nor produced by it. Rather they are assumed by it, gestured to as intertexts. In place of a construction of event, *The Temptations of Big Bear* offers discourse itself, collisions between contending discourses, foregroundings of genre and semiotic code. Again one might ask what ideological preferences are also implied.

The literary code-system in which this text must present itself is that of the mid-twentieth-century anglophone-Canadian novel, with its various implications concerning Canadian nationalism, industrialism, capitalism, and the history of Western European expansion.[1] Perhaps because this code-system inevitably implies some privileging of a European field of discourse, and thus of the discourses that arrayed themselves during 1874−85 on the European-industrial side of Western Canadian conflict, *The Temptations of Big Bear* gives much of its space to the relativizing of European viewpoints and to an attempt to reconstruct and affiliate itself with a Plains Indian meaning-system. Presenting itself as a collage of conflicting discourses, the most extensively represented being that of the River Cree chief, Big

---

1 I refer here specifically to the origins of the English novel in the seventeenth and eighteenth centuries as a genre made possible by emergent capitalist business and production practices, and to its close relationship to those practices as evident in the genesis of Richardson's *Pamela* from instructional manuals and in the celebrations of mercantilism offered by Defoe. In Western Canada, at least since Stead, Ostenso, and Grove, the novel has been conceived as a discourse that articulates a particular 'Prairie' cultural experience.

Bear, it emphasizes the differences among these and the different assumptions about power, value, and knowledge each of them makes.

———————————————

Sweetgrass had signed the treaty. The Honorable Alexander Morris, P.C., Lieutenant-Governor of Manitoba, the North West Territories and Keewatin, looked down his long wide nose again, past his mustache and the clerk's serge shoulder at the heavy x on the paper. Heavy, and broad enough to break the steel pen when it struck, as he had thought then. Break it, old man, hold it like a gutting knife and break it and every one of these Cree will do it in ceremony and we'll have one great splattered original with – twenty-nine pens? Not enough between Pitt and Carlton, more likely Fort Garry, to get it finished.

The Temptations of Big Bear, 9

The opening paragraph of the novel begins an investigation of semiotics and semiotic systems that will become the major accomplishment of the text. Two names, from radically different naming systems, 'Sweetgrass' and 'The Honorable Alexander Morris, P.C., Lieutenant-Governor of Manitoba,' occupy the subject-positions of the first two sentences – one locating identity and value in the organic world, the other in hierarchical social rank. 'Sweetgrass had signed': subject and verb connect through syntax and alliteration but come themselves from contrasting systems, as the violence of the act of signing – 'heavy ... enough to break the steel pen when it struck' – indicates. The text dwells here on significant detail, as it will throughout, to amplify its cultural contrasts: the industrially woven 'serge' cloth of the clerk's shoulder, Morris's 'mustache,' the 'gutting knife' that Morris imagines to be more appropriately wielded by the 'signing' Indian.

The two meaning-systems evident here are within a few pages joined by two other European ones that are, like that of the Indian, declining in power. These are the paternal/colonial system of the Hudson's Bay Company, which has constructed the Indian as the child of the firm, and in times of need has provided free food and weapons because it required able-bodied Indians as fur-gatherers within its system of production; and the missionary one of Christian evangelists, who have needed Indians as souls upon which the Christian practice of conversion, confession, and redemption can be operated. These systems are the European ones with which the Indians are most familiar, and with which many of them confuse the representatives of the Canadian government which has newly 'acquired' the western lands from the Hudson's Bay Company. Sweetgrass, a baptized Christian, mistakes the treaty ceremony as a religious one, telling the Governor,

> The Great Spirit has put it in our hearts that we shake hands once more, before all our brothers. That Spirit is above all, and under His eye every person is the same ... If I am spared until next year I want you, who has come to us from the Great White Queen, to act for our good: to protect the buffalo. I am thankful. When I hold your hand I feel the First One is looking on us both as brothers. (17–18)

The government representatives are shown to encourage such errors, not only engaging both missionaries and ex-company officials to fill government roles, but using the paternal discourses of each to represent government policy. Governor Morris tells Big Bear that he can 'see the Governor and the commissioners of the Queen taking the Indian by the hand, saying, we are brothers, we will lift you up' (28); he speaks of 'The Great White Queen' (34), 'the Queen Mother' (33), and of Indian and European Canadians as 'all the Queen's children.'

Although the company and missionary discourses have both been written ones, and to that extent incomprehensible within the oral culture of the Indian, both have operated without requiring the Indians to surrender their own views of knowledge and value. The Indians have been able to retain their social organization, their hunting economies, and nomadic residencies. Both discourses have thus been able to maintain the fictions of their own benevolence. But the newly arrived legal discourse of the Canadian government promises not merely to touch Indian life but to enclose it within grids of law, regulated economic practice, and land ownership. It is these grids that Big Bear alone among the Indian characters of the text is portrayed as able to see and somewhat understand. Only he is able to think past the phrases of compassion and paternalism with which the Canadian negotiators disguise their project, and identify the radical shifts in ideology and practice the treaties will bring:

> Big Bear: 'The Governor says we will live as we have always lived. I have always lived on the Earth with my people, I have always moved as far as I wished to see. We take what the Earth gives us when we need anything, and we leave the rest for those who follow us. What can it mean, that I and my family will have a "reserve of one square mile"? What is that?'

James McKay: 'Since you are a chief and have a large family, you will receive land in proportion. All your band can receive land in one place.'

Big Bear stared about his circle. 'Who can receive land? From whom would he receive it?' (29)

In addition to being able to identify contradictions in the Canadian arguments, as above, and the alien beliefs on which the arguments rest, Big Bear is also alone among the Indians in being able to understand Canadian legal concepts well enough to see that they are being extended to the Indian only when it suits Canadian purpose. He understands the concept of negotiation which purportedly governs the treaty process:

Big Bear: '... I come from where my people hunt the buffalo and I am told the treaty is such and such. I and my people have not heard what the treaty says and already nothing of it can be changed. It is already done, though we never heard of it. I told you what I wish. That there be no hanging.'

Governor Morris: 'What you say cannot be granted; why do you keep talking about bad men? The law is the same for red and white.'

Big Bear: 'That may be. But itself, it is only white.' (31)

He understands also the concept of representative government, protesting that no Indians yet wear the 'blue coats' of the territorial councillors (31). His ability to understand these concepts and the contradictions attached to them operates deconstructively within the novel, exposing the legalistic discourse of the Canadians to a level of critique its own users can never manage to direct at Indian discourse, no matter how contemptuous they may be of it.

Governor Morris is presented by the text as particularly limited by his inability even to 'name' Indian activities or give words to his feelings about them. Indians who engage in legitimate dissent are 'malcontents' (26). Those who, like Big Bear, question the punishments required by Canadian law are 'cowards' (25). When he is moved by Sweetgrass's oration to see the assembled Indians as a Rousseau-esque 'wild people coming in kindness,' he feels incapable of communicating such a concept to the Ottawa government, incapable of speaking anything but 'such crudities, such make-shift jumble, ... such stench' (18).

The most important sign in the Indian systems of meaning offered by the novel is the buffalo. It provides the main food resource of the

Indian; the necessity of hunting it shapes the Indian lifestyle and economy; the personality attributed to it by the Indian provides a basis for concepts of morality and honour. 'I am fed by the Mother Earth,' says Big Bear early in the novel, in answer to a suggestion he be baptized. 'The only water I will be touched by comes from above, the rain from the Only One who makes the grass grow and the rivers run and the buffalo feed there and drink so that I and my children live' (23). Horses are the most important Indian possession, as both buffalo 'runners' and haulers to carry a band's skin lodges and possessions as it follows a herd. 'We want only the plains and our whole living in buffalo' (97). The buffalo's own nomadic habits offer a model of independence and dignity that Big Bear finds to be a culturally significant contrast to the domestic animal of white culture. 'The buffalo is of the world as The Main One gave it to us,' he tells his son. 'He eats and runs and bellows anywhere, he is angry and can't be talked about like a castrated thing that's tied up as soon as it drops from its mother and won't move unless you beat it with a club' (125). The buffalo has 'gone away,' Big Bear suggests, because Indians have accepted land reserves and become as sedentary as cattle; the buffalo 'would die of shame to be run by hunters whose arms hang slack as pig's fat' (205).

The corresponding sign the novel offers for white Canadian/ European culture is not a single object but merely systematization – measurement and duplication. It is this sign that is offered as the antithesis and nemesis of the buffalo, in the form of the railway that mechanically duplicates itself across the prairies and blocks buffalo migration routes. 'There is no way to go north or south now but to cross those two iron rails they have bolted down into the land, split it open like a thong jerked too tight' (201). It is the sign that makes Big Bear feel 'choked' (201) when offered land marked by 'iron posts driven into the ground' (198) or when told to conform to the proscriptions of criminal law. The promiscuous reproducibility inherent in this sign is indicated by Kingbird's jest that he has shot the railway engine 'in the penis,' in 'the slippery thing near the ground going in and out, just like a man doing it' – doing it, Miserable Man adds, 'to itself' (136). It is indicated also in several perceptions the text offers of the white military:

> Little Pine spoke suddenly, 'Those soldiers ride everywhere, fast, fighting. They never have women or children with them and they never stop it. They're just made to fight.' (60)

'The trouble,' Sitting Bull said, 'is they never do it properly. They never give you any rest to heal up and get your horses bred and hunt meat. They do nothing but fight and fight so even if you kill them and then ride away from one place, you never get it back. If you ever see that land again there are whites on it, scratching and tearing up the grass ... American soldiers have nothing to do but kill.' (95)

The line of police was issuing smartly, in order, from behind the barriers, folding into a double file with banners and gleaming full-dress uniforms ...

The short police column trotted forward steadily until it reached the centre of the plain. There it halted and the shorter column on foot came marching from behind the barriers to join it ... Sixty men outside, all so exactly alike they looked churned from one mould. (188)

These two signs, the unpredictable and honourable buffalo and the system that asexually reproduces itself, are connected in the text with the two radically different political structures: a Cree Indian tribe in which a chief like Big Bear can be both powerful and unable to control his 'Worthy Young Men' when they wish to go to war, and a hierarchically organized Canadian government in which no matter which spokesman one speaks to 'there is always one of them higher who hears nothing' (201). The first structure is misread by the second when the police charge Big Bear with 'insurrection' against the Queen as if he had been able to restrain his young warriors; the second is misread by the first when the Indians assume that negotiations and understandings made with district governors and commissioners will be communicated to and endorsed by the Canadian federal government.

Friday, April 3: Fine weather. Mr. Mann, Farming Instructor, wife and family arrived from Onion Lake at 1 a.m., reports Indians at Frog Lake have massacred all whites. Fatigue all night barricading Pitt. Extra guards posted etc. Henry Quinn arrived from Frog Lake having escaped just before the massacre, confirms reports of Indians risen and all whites shot.

And Big Bear already understands more than anyone will ever think to ask him. Amelia knows this like I know it at one glimpse of his massive head, but Papa does not for he understands only single words of Cree and the sound of Big Bear's voice can't be understood in the exact words he says, which are sometimes silly Amelia insists. He simply says 'Princess of the Yellow Hair' to me, a man barely as tall as I with his almost black bare right arm outside the worn blanket, looking at me.

The Temptations of Big Bear, 268, 277

The Canadian/European meaning-system is in no way constructed by Wiebe's novel as monolithic. Numerous genre shifts suggest different positions are possible within the system depending on a subject's age, gender, education, personal or political interest, and access to power. The genres include letters between civil servants (110–23, 209–10), a treaty text (44), an army officer's serene and self-serving autobiography (86–7), the sardonic memoir of 'a Canadian Volunteer' (315–28), criminal charges (352–3), courtroom testimony (360–81), a crown summary of evidence (357–9), a judge's instruction to a jury (388–92), a policeman's log (268–71), and a young woman's memoir (271–94). In the first of the two passages quoted immediately above, the son of Charles Dickens, 'Francis J. Dickens, Inspector, N.W.M.P.,' records events in a factual discourse, constructing an inventory in which weather records, departures, arrivals, and deaths have equal weight as items to be noted and managed. In contrast, in the second passage, Kitty McLean notes the nuances in Big Bear's speech, her sister Amelia's subjective reading of him, and the puzzling sense of kinship with herself his short height and indirect rhetoric suggest. Her discourse emphasizes not fact and measurement but 'understanding,' not 'single words' but the overall meaning of words, voice, and gestures.

Dickens's name invokes yet another European discourse, the sentimental one of his father, which, like Kitty's, attends to context and relationships among facts but, unlike hers, organizes them hyperbolically to construct a young woman as brave, powerless, and pathetic. Here Kitty openly distinguishes her own experiences – in which her perceptiveness and linguistic abilities as a translator allow her some limited power over events – from such literary ones:

Papa said an Indian captive had to supply himself, though I never noticed that in the books I read. Food usually appeared there without the least worry by the heroine, though she could rarely eat any and was always perfectly clean and disdainful and aloof about the fate worse than death suspended over her head and any instant about to fall if the hero continued not arriving; though in her heart of hearts she was dreadfully afraid in a way that only showed as brilliant courage outwardly. (272)

Inspector Dickens seems to have felt another sort of distance from his father's writing. Kitty recalls that at a 'Fort Pitt Literary Evening' her sister Amelia once recited, 'with great dramatic effect,' from the elder Dickens's death of Little Nell, with some soldiers 'wiping their eyes openly and Corporal Sleigh and Sergeant Martin almost bursting with suppressed laughter while Inspector Dickens stared ahead, small and stiffly purplish among his big men as his famous father's most famous story crawled sweetly on towards its doom' (273). Several contrasting positions in relation to the Dickensian discourse are evident here – the ostensibly mock 'sweetness' of Amelia, the textual empathy of the weeping soldiers, the awareness of irony of Sleigh and Martin, and the embarrassment of the inspector.

The novel depicts Indian discourse as also fragmented, not only through Indians individual adoption of various European ideologies as they become 'missionary,' 'company,' or 'government' Indians, but also by contextual shifts and by differences in the rank and age of speakers. Big Bear tells Kitty that 'a good life should be told in four parts, like everything is four in the life of a Person. The first is to be a child, the second a man proving himself, the third to be known to your band as a good man. And the fourth, if The Only One gives it, is to be known to all the People, everywhere; and honoured' (290). To some extent these 'parts' correspond to the ways of speaking of various Indians, particularly the intemperate, belligerent utterances of warriors like Wandering Spirit, still jealous and eager to prove himself, and the circumlocutionally temporizing speeches of Big Bear, the 'good man' who would soon, had not European history intervened, have become 'known ... everywhere; and honoured.' These 'parts,' however, have almost nothing to do with Indian women, whose position of subservience in the tribe leaves them vulnerable – as the story of Sits Green On The Earth seems to imply – to rape-marriages to Indian men and to molestation and abuse by whites.

Yet despite the rash rhetoric of some of the younger Indians, the unenviable situation of the women, and the apparently unique 'wisdom' of Big Bear, Indian belief overall is constructed in the novel as much more coherent and consistent than that of the Europeans. The discourses of nearly all the Indians assume a natural world entrusted to humanity by a deity, construct human behaviour in terms of honour and dishonour rather than honesty and criminality, construct a man's wealth in terms of the 'number of his friends' (204) rather than his possessions, and construct leadership as responsibility rather than power. Although they may differ about the strategy to use in facing white culture, they are shown to share repeated amazement and disbelief that land can be owned, that warfare can be a capitalistic specialization of soldiers rather than a family or tribal duty, or that social status can be materially rather than spiritually derived.

Then he was going to lie down, and realized that he had no robe or even blanket to spread on the sand. He would arrive naked in the Green Grass World. Well, they would have an immediate opportunity to feel good by showing him their kindness. So he lay down then on the sand, his head to the north. It was very cold. He rolled onto his left side, pulled his knees up against the yellow claws. It was so quiet he could hear sand grains whisper to each other as they approached ...

He felt the granular sand joined by snow running together, against and over him in delicate streams. It sifted over the crevices of his lips and eyes, between the folds of his face and hair and hands, legs; gradually rounded him over until there was a tiny mound on the sand hill almost imperceptible on the level horizon. Slowly, slowly, all changed continually into indistinguishable, as it seemed, and everlasting, unchanging, rock.

The Temptations of Big Bear, 415

Big Bear's death scene, the concluding passage of the novel, depicts the chief's death as both a possible entry into the naturalistically conceived afterlife of Indian belief – a 'Green Grass World' – and a reunion with 'natural' landscape. Lacking the man-made robe or blanket, Big Bear is enveloped by a caring earth, its sand and snow enveloping him in 'delicate streams.' The earth takes him out of temporality and into 'everlasting, unchanging rock.' This passage is the culmination not only of the novel but of the organic imagery through which it has depicted its Indians throughout. The text has gradually built on the animistic beliefs historically associated with the Plains Indians – a belief in a deity who works through weather, landforms, and animals, and a practice of naming themselves through relationships to the physical environment (Big Bear, Sits Green On The Earth, Bear Son, Mountain Child, Little Poplar, Born Upside Down) – to give an interpretation of them as 'children of nature,' as potentially wise primitives whose wisdom arises from and returns to the earth itself.

While indeed this may be legitimate Plains Indian discourse, in a novel in which this discourse becomes part of a major structural motif (a dichotomy in which it opposes a dominant instrumentalism in 'white' culture) and the concluding image, it has – like the passage from Newlove's widely circulated 'The Pride' which began this chapter – unavoidable resonances of European romantic primitivism and Lawrentian vitalism. A structural contrast between an 'original' world of natural innocence and a soulless one of human contrivance has been a part of the language of English literature at least since Wordsworth, and has had strong international impact in texts as diverse as *Michael, Adam Bede, Moby Dick, Women in Love,* and *Brave New World.* In the late 1960s and early 1970s this discursive contrast vigorously asserted itself throughout North America in the commune movement, in new interest in organic farming, and in renewed interest in Indian and, in Canada, Métis inheritance, such as that expressed in the same year as *The Temptations of Big Bear*'s publication by George Woodcock:

> Riel is one of the perennially attractive figures in Canadian history, inside and outside Quebec.
>
> ...
>
> Dumont ... was the natural man *par excellence,* adapted perfectly to the life of the wilderness, and in this alone he was profoundly different from Riel, who was as alienated as any modern Canadian from that existence. (Woodcock, 1973, 19–20)

It is this contrast that *The Temptations of Big Bear* repeatedly invokes not only in its general portrayal of Big Bear's Cree as custodians of the earth but especially in its construction of their sexuality as more 'natural' and spontaneous than that of whites: Sits Green On The Earth unknowingly enables Delaney to release decades of puritan repression; the aging Big Bear virtually seduces Kitty McLean with his sensuous implacability. This structural contrast in *Big Bear* also invokes earlier uses of it in other novels by Wiebe: the contrast between the spirit of Christ's teaching and the machinery of institutional Christianity in *Peace Shall Destroy Many* (1962); and contrasts between Christian faith and materialism that underlie *First and Vital Candle* (1966) and *The Blue Mountains of China* (1970). Intertextually *The Temptations of Big Bear* marks its title character as much as a Wordsworthian or an Anabaptist as it does as a Plains Cree.

With unwitting irony the novel's discursive strategy achieves in language the harmony between races which the nineteenth-century soldiers, civil servants, and colonists scorned. Big Bear's animistic discourse is brought towards that of European organicism and found compatible. As his face is covered with sand, his beliefs are uncovered for the white reader and found congruent with familiar values. Much as Margaret Laurence's doubly running river brings together all the incompatible and barely compatible beliefs of *The Diviners* into a metaphoric and humanistic harmony impossible in the actual social relations of the characters, the movement of the sand hills delivers Big Bear into an ideological harmony with white culture which only he and Kitty, and then only briefly, were able to achieve in his lifetime.

In her essay 'History and/as Intertext' Linda Hutcheon has suggested that in *The Temptations of Big Bear* there is no 'Big Bear of actuality,' only one 'of history texts, newspaper accounts, letters, official and unofficial reports, ... imagination and legend':

> The very fabric of the novel refuses any naïve separation of fictional reference from that of so-called 'scientific' descriptions of the past ... But it also refuses, just as firmly, any formalist attempt to make language into the play of signifiers discontinuous with representation and with the external world ... There *was* a Big Bear – though we can only *know* him today from texts. The novel is both an inscription and an invention of a world.
> (171)

Although Hutcheon is undoubtedly correct that the novel's inclusions of so many and diverse white textual versions of Big Bear demonstrates all to be inadequate representations of him, I have less confidence in her argument that 'the very fabric of the novel' refuses to privilege its own fictions over the 'so-called "scientific" descriptions' it cites and qualifies. Nothing in the novel suggests that its own status as a white discourse producing a new and 'more Indian' Big Bear is equally as unreliable as the Big Bear produced by Governor Dewdney or Crown prosecutor D.L. Scott. In fact, the anonymous third-person narrative that gathers the scenes and documents of the story and imagines Big Bear's animistic consciousness is given overwhelmingly more power than any other discourse in the book. It controls, assembles, and frames these discourses; its own observations begin and end the novel and occupy most of the pages between. The new Big Bear produced by this discourse, a humane, sensuous, generous, god-respecting, and environmentally aware Big Bear, is more than an alternative invention; it eclipses and displaces the ignorant Big Bear of Dewdney and trader McLean, and the villainous one of Scott, and, in its final words, privileges itself as 'everlasting, unchanging.'

Both Wiebe's and Laurence's texts work their elaborations and, in effect, their appropriations of Indian culture within larger cultural missions. Both are concerned to distinguish Canadian experience from a European one that is constructed as more thoroughly instrumental, hierarchical, and self-preferring. Both tend to associate Central Canadian cultural ideologies with the European (and with the written, the legitimized, and the empowered) and to advance a revised construction of 'Canadian' that incorporates 'Prairie' history and its oral memories and aboriginal 'forebears.' Both paradoxically choose inclusivist organicist myths from European history to propose a Canada that can ultimately neutralize a Brooke Skelton or Governor Dewdney, and incorporate the generosity and non-possessiveness of a Jules Tonnerre or Big Bear within its own soul. In the general culture in which the novels are written the Canadian Prairies are also building on historical foundations assertions of their own specificity, assertions which within two decades will be manifested in the 'triple-E' discourse of provincial equality adopted by their governments at federal-provincial constitutional conferences. In Manitoba and Saskatchewan the once criminal Louis Riel is rehabilitated as a regional hero. John Newlove, born in Regina, writes in 'The Pride' that the Plains Indians 'still ride the soil / in us, dry bones a part / of the dust in our eyes.' Margaret Atwood, in her widely read *Survival* (1972), endorses Newlove's call for Euro-Canadian appropriation of Indian culture by approvingly quoting 'The Pride' and suggesting that for Canadians a knowledge of Indian peoples may constitute 'a knowledge of our origins' (105). A Canada that can forgive and identify with the once-imprisoned Big Bear is in these discourses a utopian Canada, humane and non-directive, racially tolerant, rejecting of European hierarchy and General Custer instrumentalism. It is utopian also within the structure of dystopian fiction, rejecting railway, army, and other rationalistic systems of human management, and affirming sexuality, the wide sky, and the 'Green Grass World.'

A Necessary Canada

Slash

Someday western Indians will write novels and their voices will tell us, at last, the authentic version of how their nations contracted culture of the reservation after a millenium of running buffalo and dying of old age. These novels may also tell us that People are reassembling for a retaliatory war, but that is a chapter no white person can write.

Myrna Kostash, 'A White Man's View of Big Bear,' *Saturday Night*, Feb. 1974, 32

As the sound of the drum and voices raised in song rolled out of the National Indian Brotherhood Council room to the lawns of the Parliament Buildings, on National Solidarity Day (Nov. 19, 1981), the future of the First peoples in Canada was guaranteed. Not guaranteed in any absolute sense, but guaranteed in spirit. With the strength and guidance of the Creator, the banner of freedom and survival for the First Nations was raised above the land and the people to be held proudly against any assault.

'Satisfaction Guaranteed,' *Ontario Indian*, 5, no. 1 (1982), 25

Jeannette Armstrong's *Slash* (1985) is signed by an Okanagan Indian, narrated from the viewpoint of a young Okanagan man, published by a publishing house operated by the Okanagan tribe, and yet is paradoxically both more comprehensively 'Canadian' and more 'North American' in the signs it deploys than almost all post-centennial Canadian novels. These signs are not only associated with the novel's construction of the dominant 'white' culture its characters seek to resist, but also with the large geographic field in which they seek to assert their oppositional politics.

Slash presents itself as the retrospective narrative of Tommy (Slash) Kelasket, who recounts his childhood in the South Okanagan, his confusion at the apparent conflict between his parents' traditional Indian values and those of the provincial school system in which they wish him to succeed, and his angry adolescence and young manhood in which his struggle to overcome the racist views of himself and others he has internalized from white culture leads him through prison, intermittent alcoholism, drug abuse, and frustratingly ineffective periods of political activism. The generic signs of this novel are multiple and conflicting. Its first-person narration and focus on Slash's 'growth' from childhood to adulthood identify it as a coming-of-age novel in which the central character both achieves a coherent sense of self and demonstrates this achievement by creating a coherent life-narrative. The strong moral emphasis of the novel, conveyed through the many passages in which characters argue or declaim about matters of personal or political conduct, and the disjunction between the novel's author-sign (female, adult) and focal character (male, adolescent) give it signs of the morally instructional youth novel, like Connor's *The Man from Glengarry* or Richardson's *Pamela*. Slash's preoccupation with learning something he can only dimly conceptualize and his restless journeys to sites of white-Indian conflict in search of some understanding of Indian needs give the novel some of the marks of a quest romance. But in the intermittence of Slash's search, his casual sexual liaisons, and his bouts of self-hatred and alcohol- and drug-abuse *Slash* carries also many of the signs of the picaresque novel: a protagonist disaffected from family and culture, careless of laws or social conventions, more in search of a goal than possessed of one; an episodic plot that enacts the impulsiveness of the protagonist; a series of actions that are satiric in their implicit exposure of the hypocrisy of the established culture. The novel also has many of the signs of an oral tale; it is often narrated not with the precision and framing which indicates the presence of either an achieved subjectivity or a didactic authorial presence, but with excesses, indirections, formulaic representations, and repetitions which characterize narratives that are heard rather than read, and remembered rather than written. Yet it also bears signs of the historical novel, a novel that recovers, organizes, and frames historical events; Slash's search often turns out to be for a North American Indian history that he 'hadn't even heard of' (95); his narrative becomes specifically a history of the North American Indian movement from the early 1960s to the present, from Red Power, AIM, Wounded Knee, the occupation of Alcatraz, and the early landclaims struggles, to Canadian Indians' attempts to block patriation of the BNA Act.

In its generic contradictions *Slash* resists not only general Western discursive practices for framing and constructing experience and knowledge, but also specific Western conventions for framing the aborigine: the savage Indian of eighteenth- and nineteenth-century travel and settler literature; the tragic, incompetent Indian of twentieth-century social and political practice; the romantic, spiritual Indian with shamanistic wisdom and a healing presence that recurs in so much Canadian writing, from that of Duncan Campbell Scott to that of Rudy Wiebe. The Indian characters of *Slash* are at times angry, violent, incompetent, and spiritual; they are also constructed as cosmopolitan, pastoral, pragmatic, motivated, constructive, articulate, and able to move and negotiate among spiritual, legalistic, angry, communal, and other discourses. As Barbara Godard has noted, this double refusal of both general conventions of representation and specific codes for representing Indian subjects has the potential to make the novel difficult for non-Indian readers: 'there has been no progress, no development and almost no action: the narrative is composed mainly of reported speech. In short this has been a "flat" book not likely to make the bestseller list in Canada' ('The Politics of Representation,' 218).

Signs of this difficulty in white reception of the novel appear even in the two endorsements the 1988 edition carries on the cover. '[T]his story is well crafted and worth reading,' the *Vancouver Sun* is quoted as saying, its faint praise qualifying the book simultaneously as oral ('this story'), surprisingly literary ('well crafted'), and morally obligatory for conscientious non-Indians to read ('worth reading'). The quotation from a review by M.T. Kelly is only slightly more complex:

> Intense tale ...
>
>   Through the search of her hero Slash, author Armstrong presents a vivid picture of the difficulties encountered by Native people in their struggle to find liberation and self-determination.

Kelly too invokes the signs of both the oral ('intense tale') and the written ('author Armstrong'), and supplements these with those of the romantic quest ('the search of her hero') and the political ('liberation and self-determination').

The generic contradictions and tensions of *Slash* imagine a discursively violent North America. The book cannot be a coming-of-age novel because it can find no agreed-upon codes for how a young Indian male might come of age. Such codes are among the objects of Slash's quest but, because they are unavailable, the novel can also not succeed as a quest romance. The only achievement it can offer Slash is a knowledge of how to carry on an unending and potentially wearying negotiation between values and discourses. The novel's picaresque aspects are subverted by its moral and political preoccupations. Its determination to recover a usable Indian history both gives coherence to Slash's wanderings and frames them as part of an Indian historical record; his journey from farm to skid row to Indian self-help to political activism and violence, to recovery of Indian history and spiritual practice, becomes a metonymy for changes in North American Indian culture.

———————

The instability of the language of both the novel's narrative and its characters offers an unmistakeable suggestion of the Indian people's colonization. Fragments of bureaucratic and sociological discourses collide here with the highly colloquial oral discourse with which Slash claims to be most comfortable. At times these other discourses appear to overwhelm his attempts to 'personally' articulate his narrative:

> That summer the provincial government announced a fishing ban on the Fraser River because of what they said was salmon stock depletion. From the meetings that I went to, I understood that to the Indian people who lived on the salmon along that river it meant a serious infringement on their right to fish for food. I understood their view was that there were no proper restrictions placed on industrial fisheries and sport fishing and no proper enforcement of laws on industry pollution that destroyed estuaries. It seemed logical that all of that needed to be investigated and acted upon before food was taken from the mouths of people who depended on salmon as their source of protein. It seemed to me that it was a question of corporations having more right to make profits than people to eat food that was provided by the Creator for that purpose. (213)

At the start of this passage Slash uses the phrase 'what they said was' to mark 'salmon stock depletion' as foreign to his own discourse and to signal thereby his awareness that not only are the white culture's fishing regulations intruding into Indian life but its language is intruding itself into his. In the next sentence, however, he marks the phrase 'serious infringement,' also from white bureaucratic discourse, in an opposite manner, as part of both his own and 'Indian' understanding: '... I understood that to the Indian people ... it meant a serious infringement ...' He positions the next observation also within markers of both his and general Indian understanding: 'I understood their view was ...' This observation is also articulated in bureaucratese: '... there were no proper restrictions placed on industrial fisheries ... no proper enforcement of laws ...' Only two sentences later does Slash return to language that constructs experience in non-white abstractions: 'food that was provided by the Creator for that purpose.'

This ambiguity about how Indian understanding is constructed, whether through its own imagery and phrasing or whether through the conceptualizations asserted by the white culture, is evident in the dialogue of other characters as well as in Slash's narration. It is also enacted in Slash's personal life, as when he first tries standard medical means of freeing himself from drug addiction, but later successfully submits to traditional Indian rites of purification, or when he removes his father, who has had a heart attack, from the city hospital and cures him at home through 'ceremonies and sweats' (207). It also constitutes the major issue of the novel: whether Indians like Slash are going to accept having their lives formulated through white discourse – 'second class people stuck on reservations, living in the dark ages' (43) or whether they are going to find their own self-definitions. At the political level this issue becomes whether or not the Indian peoples should attempt to gain recognition through the Canadian constitution, a white discursive framing of experience, or whether they should claim an alternative legitimacy founded on their culture's landed existence prior and external to any white constitutional discourse. Slash himself argues for the second option:

> Think of the song that everybody sings, the so-called Constitution song. It clearly says, 'We don't need your Constitution, B.C. is all Indian land. We don't need your Constitution, hey yeah hey.' How much clearer can it be? We don't need anybody's constitution, what we have is our own already. We hold rights to the land and to nationhood. We just need to have it recognized. We want to keep it. They are trying to make us hand it over by telling us that we have no choice. That's a lot of bull. They want us to believe it and are coercing us into negotiating with them by pretending to write us out of the whole thing, unless we negotiate ... (241)

Nevertheless, at both the thematic and discursive levels, *Slash* – unlike *The Temptations of Big Bear* – refuses to seek some pure traditional Indian culture, rejecting this as an anachronistic and museum-like goal. The Indian culture the novel implies is heterogeneous, both different from white majority culture and heavily marked by it, both retaining what is useful from its past and responding to new social challenges which the dominance of white culture has brought. It is a highly oral culture, discussing its future in a seemingly endless number of conferences, meetings, sit-ins, retreats, and ceremonies. These discussions result in few if any documents, yet often assume the decisive role written records fill in the majority culture. It has many leaders, but no pre-eminent leader. Slash assumes neither a major leadership role among his people nor a dominant role as narrator of his own story. On nearly every page he defers to the voices of others, offering unusually lengthy quotations from people who variously counsel, oppose, endorse, or challenge him on one matter or another. The effect of such repeated and substantial quotation is to intensify the portrayal of Indians as an oral people with a collective and multi-voiced culture. Not only does no one person summarize or represent them, either discursively or politically, but no one position or set of circumstances can characterize them. As Slash argues late in the book, 'we can all support each other on whatever position each of us takes. It doesn't mean each has to take the same position' (235).

The paradoxical assertion of unity and difference, of unity in supporting one another's differences, that is made both thematically and narratologically in *Slash*, pervades its geographic signs as strongly as it does its discursive ones. More than in any other novel of the post-centennial period, the characters of *Slash* take Canada and North America as single fields of action. Characters who must fear assault even on a simple shopping excursion in their home village range with considerable confidence from British Columbia to Ottawa, from Ontario to Washington, D.C., from Washington to Iowa to California to Oklahoma to Alberta. Characters who conceive of political discourse as oral, and politics as primarily local, also construct Canada as a homogeneous field for political action, and North America as everywhere 'Indian territory.'

Despite repeated insistence on Indian differences, on the differing needs of urban, agricultural, and frontier Indians, of Northern, Maritime, Pacific, and Southern Plains Indians, *Slash* also declares an underlying historically constructed commonality. As Slash travels, he feels increasingly that Beothuck, Micmac, Sioux, and other tribal histories are also his history; he comes to feel comradeship and siblinghood with the Indians of many different tribal backgrounds whom he encounters: 'Nobody questioned which Band or which Tribe a person belonged to; everybody was Indian and that was good enough' (181). The Indian who rescues Slash in Seattle from his deepest period of alcoholism is an 'Ojibway from Ontario' (198). The most influential person for Slash at the U.S. camp the Ojibway takes him to is a Plains Indian medicine man. Slash's experience here leads him to similar pan-Indian 'survival camps':

> I found out that there were places like that springing up all across the country. Most of them were not advertised around. A wider and wider circle of people knew about them. At these places there was sameness in the ways things were done. The use of the pipe and sweats were common to all. All kinds of ceremonies and traditional practices were revived. Some of the things were held open to people of all tribes to participate in. Survival gatherings and survival schools, working with those concepts, started up in almost every part of the country. (202)

To some extent, as the ambiguity of 'country' in the last line above suggests, North American white culture is also envisioned as monologic. The detox centres of Seattle are little different from those of Vancouver. The suppression of Indian traditions and construction of the Indian as savage and temperamentally unsuited for white educational and labour practices are similar on both sides of the Canada-U.S. border. The bureaucracy of the 'BIA' (the U.S. Bureau of Indian Affairs) is as self-serving as that of the 'DIA' (Canada's Department of Indian Affairs); the DIA's ostensibly more peaceful approach to Indian protest is constructed by Slash (127–8) as merely more devious and machiavellian than the BIA's openly violent methods. Yet the book also depicts Canada and the United States as separate political fields. Following the Wounded Knee protests, Slash and several Canadian-Indian companions flee, much like Sitting Bull before them, to the Canadian border for safety from U.S. vigilantes and National Guard. Although individual Canadian-Indians seek personal and cultural salvations from tribal wisdom on both sides of the border, Canadian Indian political protest focuses in *Slash* almost entirely on the Canadian federal government and its agencies. Indians occupy various offices of the DIA. They organize cross-country caravans that are to terminate in Ottawa. They send delegations to Britain to try to prevent patriation of the BNA Act, and to the United Nations to attempt to shame the federal government into including them in constitutional discussions. Without the Canadian federation assumed by *Slash* the various political goals of its Indians would have no meaning; there would be no common ground for negotiation, no reliable framework to guarantee an agreement. A federal Canada structures the Indian arguments, and it acts as both a unifying adversary and a necessary context and measure for Indian achievement.

While the seme of difference within commonality marks the novel's sense of North American Indian bands and tribes, it is mostly absent from its view of white Canadian culture. White culture here is not regionally, ethnically, or linguistically differentiated. 'Canada' is a field of signs in which patterns of similar occurrences mark each intersection between Indian and white:

> Things started boiling all over in Canada that summer. We read that in B.C., the Union of Chiefs had made pretty strong statements about owning all of B.C. and that it was not for sale. In Alberta some people made headlines by demanding the return of sacred medicine bundles, held in museums, that belonged to Indian families. In the Northwest Territories, at the request of the North West Indian Brotherhood, the courts put a freeze on all land transactions where a pipeline was being considered for development. At James Bay, the Crees strongly resisted the hydro-electric project that would flood much of their ancestral lands. (123)

There is no evidence in the book even of a French-language presence; the struggles of Quebec Indians such as the James Bay Cree are articulated in English, to an English-speaking federal government, as if francophone culture were an irrelevant minor factor in a cultural field characterized mainly by clashes between a majority anglophone society and a psychologically and territorially alienated native population. The one area of white dissent noted in *Slash* is environmentalism; Indian protesters against the use of 2-4-D to control the spread of weeds in a lake are joined by 'other people who were concerned about the environment' (214) who later call in 'Greenpeace people ... to help with the protest' (216). Slash's comment about these people that 'some of them were beginning to become real North Americans,' that they had begun to feel some of the things Indians felt through their 'ties to the land or the "Mother Earth"' (216), again offers a continental construction of Indians as 'North Americans,' and a provocative construction of continental politics as ultimately grounded on environmental and economic relations rather than on region, race, ethnicity, or nation.

Perhaps the major departure in *Slash* from the codes of the coming-of-age and quest novels is in its highly conflicted deployment of gender signs. The novel has a female signator but sympathetically presents a male focal character. It constructs the Indian struggle as largely that of men but constructs Slash himself as significantly less able than some of the women who become important to him. Most notably the novel constructs admirable women but idealizes none of these within the conventions of literary beauty or sexual desirability common to the coming-of-age novel. The young women of *Slash* for the most part are viewed by the narrator as 'chicks' whose sexual availability offers diversions from boredom and political frustration similar to those offered by alcohol and drugs. This view appears to encode a mild accusation of sexism within Indian culture, a sexism within which the young men expect the women to provide a complete range of support services; this accusation in turn creates tension with other gender elements in the text. However, in the two young women with whom Slash develops lasting relationships the novel offers female characters who speak strongly at public meetings and assume organizational and leadership roles. Again, though, despite their courage and abilities, neither woman is romanticized, and both in fact are rather unsentimentally written out of Slash's story.

These two women, the activist Mardi, whom Slash would like to marry but whom he believes he must 'allow' to travel North America pursuing her political work, and Maeg, a young woman from a South Okanagan band, whom Slash does marry and with whom he has a son, are both from the United States. The phonetic similarity of their names hints that they represent a common sign, as do their deaths while organizing dissent and the hints of an archetypal Mary behind both their names (224–5). Both are linked with semes of difference and of a lost natural paradise. Mardi, Slash exclaims on their first meeting, is 'extra deluxe. Tough with hard eyes and long black hair that hung below her hips. I could tell she knew her way around' (59):

> I had a lot of chicks from the time I was fifteen upwards, but none made me feel so warm inside just by smiling ... She smelled fresh like sage and cedar and her skin was even brown and smooth like those hills in the Okanagan. (62)

On first meeting Maeg, Slash sees her as 'really something to look at although you couldn't say she was pretty':

> Her hair was thick, brown and wavy. It hung past her shoulders and her

skin was smooth and light brown ... She was dressed too plain to have been one of those people who were 'into' Indian medicine ways, in a cult kind of attitude. (224–5)

This refusal to romanticize is paralleled by the relative lack of importance the women have in Slash's life. Although he often thinks of Mardi, and is troubled by the deaths of both women, his preoccupation continues to be his own state of mind and his relationship to Indian culture. Whereas, within the codes of romance, the woman usually stands in symbolically for the hero's gaining of maturity – in that magic fictional moment when he gains either her or the wisdom to accept that he can never gain her – in *Slash* these elements are differently related. Within its plot structure Mardi and Maeg occupy 'helper' roles; one helps him to perceive political action as an alternative to alcoholism and despair; the other enables him to accept himself as a responsible father and citizen within the Indian community – as someone whose social responsibilities transcend his individual pain. Having accomplished these things, the two women are written from the narrative, one through a mysterious disappearance during the Wounded Knee incident and the other through an automobile accident on the way to a political meeting in northern British Columbia.

While the novel's 'killing' of these two women characters can be read as part of a subtle but pervasive male gender bias (such a reading is supported by the tendency of Slash's struggles to become representative in the novel of Indian struggles, and to render them male, and by the novel's making his child and inheritor a son rather than a daughter), the unsentimental characterization of the women also emphasizes once again the political and secular over the romantic and spiritual, and a refusal to offer them as either sexual or spiritual objects. The sweat lodges, purification ceremonies, and archetypal Mary figures are not goods in themselves but must eventually lead to responsible citizenship and social action. The deaths of Mardi and Maeg, whatever their nobility and dedication, are not to be elegized or rendered eternal as was the death of Big Bear, but to be given meaning within an active Indian social order. Maeg's, in particular, is to be given meaning, as the novel's epilogue makes clear, by Slash's telling of his story 'for his son and those like him' (253).

The commitment *Slash* implies to the recognition of social conflict and political process – here both within Indian communities and between them and surrounding culture – and to the situating of this conflict within a stable national context, is extremely rare in recent Canadian fiction. The novel's invention of a political 'Canada' occurs, in part, because it perceives the experiences of Indians as uniformly oppressive no matter what differences may occur within either the Indian or non-Indian population – as so uniformly oppressive, in fact, that they almost prevent signs of difference among non-Indians from entering the text's field of consciousness. The 'white' 'they' of the novel appears nearly homogeneous in its will to exploit and deprive. 'They mean extinguishment and sell-out' (242); 'they stand to gain ... Indian land with all its resources.' Yet it is also a necessary and strategic 'they' – 'our people really want to have our rights recognized,' Slash declares (241) – a required intertext for Indian self-representation and implicit agent of their 'recognition.' While *Slash* at times essentializes white culture nearly as much as *The Temptations of Big Bear* essentializes native culture, the effect is to enable political process within Indian culture rather than, as in the Wiebe novel, to transcend it in both.

There is considerable irony in an Indian novel giving such seriousness to constitutional process and national Canadian political discourse – particularly at a time when the nation itself finds such process and discourse virtually unworkable. But it is an irony that will recur. Within a year of the publication of *Slash* Manitoba Indian legislator Elijah Harper will cast the ballot that blocks the 'Meech Lake' constitutional amendment's recognition of Quebec as a 'distinct society'; within three years Indian representatives will sit at the August 1991 Canadian premiers' conference, and the James Bay Cree will declare their preference to attach their vast ancestral lands to an anglophone Canada rather than have them become part of a sovereign Quebec. The BNA Act's 1867 award of 'Indian Affairs' to federal jurisdiction may have brought, as *Slash* argues, little happiness or justice for Canada's native peoples, but it can apparently create unlikely federalists.

Maritime Powerlessness
Nights below Station Street

Joe got up at five every morning. He would look out the window, wonder what type of day it was going to be, smoke a cigarette, and then go downstairs and put on the kettle. Then he would go about town playing punch-boards and sit in the malls.

Each day Joe would go downtown and see how people were doing. Then he would go to the unemployment office to see if there were any jobs. Then, on those days Rita was out, he would come back and do the housework, make lunch, and then go back downtown again. Sometimes he would stand about the corner listening to men talk, and then he would go up the hill once more, walk along the highway, and back to his house, where he would peel potatoes and wait for Adele.

Nights below Station Street, 84

Most of the narration of David Adams Richards's 1988 novel *Nights below Station Street* is presented in simple sentences or in simple sentences joined by *and, but,* or *then,* often elaborated by appositives or an appositional series of main clauses. Subordinate structures appear infrequently, usually no more than one or two to a paragraph, and often towards the end of the paragraph:

The Russian ship *Gorki* had been stranded here for three weeks. A Petty Officer, Terrisov, became friendly with Myhrra. And she showed him about the river, took him to the curling club, and explained the rules of the game to him, and for a time seemed to forget her problems. (77)

Although arguably appropriate as an indicator of the halting consciousness of the nearly illiterate Joe Walsh, one of the book's six or seven prominent characters, this narrative discourse is employed by the omnisicent narration no matter which characters it focuses upon – even the town doctor and his Oxford-educated niece Vera. Moreover, it is rarely used to indicate what Sherrill Grace has called a character's '"hidden dialogue" within discourse' (125), but almost entirely to indicate the narrator's own 'wise' observations:

> Vera's sickness persisted. Her temperature rose and she vomited.
> At first she thought she could doctor herself, and for a week she drank vegetable soup. Then she took a cold bath followed by a hot bath to change her temperature, and this gave her a case of pneumonia. Her temperature rose to 104, and the doctor was called to the house.
> After seeing his patients that morning he got in his car and drove down to the lane, and leaving the car on the road, walked down to her place. The snow was up to his knees, and he seemed to enjoy the fact that he was out walking through the field, where at every step he had to break the crust and shield his eyes from the glare of the sun. (166–7)

As Walter J. Ong notes in *Orality and Literacy,* the use of 'additive rather than subordinative' syntax and of 'aggregative rather than analytic' (37–8) sentence constructions are major features of oral discourse and particularly common in cultures which have not developed written language. These are features of a discourse which, rather than arranging its materials into greater and lesser, independent and dependent, primary and auxiliary, and attempting to specify the relationships between these, uses its resources to list, accumulate, and remember items of indeterminate and thus roughly equal significance. It is a discourse that has difficulty attributing cause, assigning relative values, or producing empirical descriptions. The deployment of this discourse appears linked to the narrative structure of *Nights below Station Street,* which consists of twenty-seven chapters, in which seven characters to whom the narrative keeps returning – Joe and Rita Walsh, their daughter Adele, their neighbour Myhrra, Adele's boyfriend, Ralphie, his sister Vera, and his uncle Dr Hennessey – and two nearly as prominent characters, the elderly Allain Garret and Myhrra's occasional companion Vye, participate in a series of repetitive separate events and activities, without a great deal of intention or without much awareness of causal relationships among them. The narrative constructs these characters as living without much ability to plan, reflect on their actions, or consult with one another, each acting arbitrarily and impulsively. Joe joins Alcoholics Anonymous and later gets a job as a bouncer without informing Adele or Rita; Adele gets to the ninth month of pregnancy without informing anyone; Ralph gets a job in a coalmine; Vye decides to marry Myhrra: all in moments that not only surprise others but surprise themselves. One of the recurrent frustrations experienced by these characters is a sense that they cannot perceive the shape of their lives well enough to control or, therefore, change them, and that what is happening to them may be 'inevitable' or 'natural.' Joe would like to be free of his tumultuous bouts of alcoholism but fears that 'it was in his nature to drink, and he had to drink – he wouldn't be himself if he didn't' (59). When Ralphie 'finds' himself 'a mile under the earth' working in the mine, he has 'no idea how' this has come about, 'except he believed it was all natural once it happened. And that there was nothing unnatural or not supposed to happen' (220). Adele experiences rage and chronic vomiting because nothing in her home changes: Joe remains year after year without steady work, without a cure for his back pain; Rita continues to do menial work for others; the quarrels among the three of them persist but resolve nothing.

The unspecified narrator of the novel, however, has none of these difficulties with perspective or control. It[1] not only is privy to the concerns of all these characters, but is able to relate them in the past tense, apparently in possession of a sense of history which the characters – who in effect live only in the present tense – lack. This narrator is also able to perform the very acts of grammatical subordination and analysis of motive that the characters apparently cannot:

> ... Ralphie tried to talk as if the strike was important and he, like everyone else, needed the strike. But he didn't want to strike because he'd just started to work – and he didn't seem to realize that a lot of men talk about a strike because they want a holiday, and after a week or so, are not only wanting to go back to work but are angry with their union representative who they believe got them into the strike in the first place. (195)

---

1 I use the pronoun *it* here to refer to the narrator of *Nights below Station Street* in order to distinguish this impersonal narrator both from the novel's signator, David Adams Richards, and from any suggestion of a character-bound narration such as that of a first-person narrator. This usage follows Simone Vauthier's analysis of fictional narrative ('The Dubious Battle of Story-Telling: Narrative Strategies in Timothy Findley's *The Wars*') as potentially bearing evidence of a receding series of 'narrators': a signator, a constructor, an I-narrator, and an impersonal narrator. It assumes that a narrative can have an ungendered and non-personalized 'narrative voice' that is distinct from both 'author' and characters.

The effect of this narration, which for the most part adopts a simple additive syntax, as if this were the 'syntax' of its characters' lives, but can, whenever it wishes, use an analytic subordinating syntax to explain things the characters could never understand, places the narrator and the reader in a different relationship to the events of the novel than the characters. The narrator and reader have 'knowledge' and 'understanding'; they know why characters act and feel as they do, while the characters are fated to find these things forever mysterious. In addition, the narrator's persistent use of what it implies is its characters' oral syntax, even though it is not its own syntax, operates as a kind of parody, which both mocks and patronizes its characters:

> Ralphie had gotten a job at the mines around this time. He worked underground, and he had gained weight. Often, he would come straight from work and arrive at the Walshes' door at five o'clock. That he was now doing the same job Joe had done years before made Adele happy. She was happy when Joe thought she would be angry.
>
> ...
>
> Ralphie, with blasting caps still in his shirt (it was illegal to take them off the mines [sic] property but he had forgotten them) and a big piece of ore in his pocket which he wanted to study under a microscope, and the smell of the soap that was as familiar to Rita and Joe as the smell of life, walked about in absolute contentment.
>
> He was now going to chew tobacco. He was now going to build himself a camp. (194)

One of the most puzzling aspects of *Nights below Station Street* is the source of the discursive power that the narrator holds and its characters lack, and that allows it to incorporate them within its own knowing and patronizing discourse. On the fringes of the events of the novel there are signs of power: there is the 'M.L.A.' (16) whom Joe can never manage to ask for a job; there are the operators of the mine in which Ralphie finds work; there is Vye's steady source of income; the medical schools which have trained the young doctors Savard and McCeachern and the hospital nurses; and the distant college at which Rita once dated young men who are now 'in business in town, and had done something more than swill wine for the last seventeen years' (172). But neither these signs nor the people who appear to have discursive and analytic power are ever focused upon; the people the novel presents up close are ones who are discursively impaired, like Joe, 'who stutters his head off whenever he talks to anybody half important' (16), or who have had some contact with discursive power but been unable to claim it. Myhrra 'had almost gone to university ... she had her father haul her trunk out to the car and drive it to Fredericton' (23); Rita 'went away for a while after graduation – to the teacher's college – but she left without her diploma' (21); Ralphie 'had gone to university for a while, and then to technical school' but 'did not know what to do' (43); Vera had been to university for about three years, had spent a year at Oxford, but had returned, not empowered and knowledgable like the narrator, but merely a captive of 1960s intellectual fashion.

The text also offers a very narrow range of place references outside the town: Fredericton, where Rita almost attended university; Montreal, where Myhrra advises Ralphie's dying father to seek treatment; Calgary, to which Adele imagines escaping; Lethbridge, where Rita's brothers live; Oxford; and the Russian freighter *Gorki*, which docks in the town harbour. Again, this range seems to signify the fragmentary range of knowledge of the characters rather than the range of the narrator's own 'knowing' discourse. When Myhrra accepts the invitation of a Russian seaman to visit the freighter, the narrator invokes this 'knowing' to tell the reader 'It was all so different from how she thought it would be, and all so different than he himself had led himself to believe it would be' and to twice condescendingly describe Myhrra's style of smoking as an 'affectation of sophistication she had learned from childhood' (82).

———————————— • ————————————

Similarly puzzling is the discursive determinism to which the text repeatedly insists the characters it focuses upon are subject. When Ralphie rents his own apartment after his father dies, and young people from the university begin using it as a place to meet, hold parties, and talk about social issues, the narrator comments: 'It was becoming a cultural thing to be dismayed at the right times about the right things' (48). When casually life-threatening events occur at the apartment, the narrator emphasizes their scriptedness: 'Suddenly, the more offhanded one was about everything, the more well informed and the better that person was' (50). When Vye is about to marry Myhrra, the narration tells us he

> ... wanted everything done the way everyone else did it, including the stag party – where they showed four skin flicks – and Vye sat with his friends, as if stag films and all the rest of it were things he was now going

to leave behind. The talk, which he had no interest in, was about hockey and ball. The book, which showed a variety of things that would happen on a honeymoon, he took to be funny because it was supposed to be. (200)

This implication that the opinions and actions of the characters are scripted from without is particularly noticeable in the construction the narration offers of Vera and her husband Nevin. 'Vera was one of those people who is normally infuriating because every new opinion is suddenly hers – and hers alone – and in another year or so she will move on to something else' (132), the narrator remarks – with a startlingly sexist shift of pronouns. Vera is presented as embracing every 'revolutionary' social fashion of the early 1970s. She wears 'granny glasses with golden frames and big long flowery dresses' (91) and 'rubber boots' (184). In college she takes a black lover. Returning from college, she aspires to be 'the head of a corporation.' With her new husband she then buys an old farmhouse and makes it 'exactly like it used to be' (167). She embraces organic foods – 'jars of spice, and wholewheat flour, and packages of granola' (166) – 'the causes of French [-language] equality' (160), and 'books on Margaret Sanger and George Sand, and Greer's *The Female Eunuch*' (168); and she adopts the 'self-important strides' (168), the 'assertive step she believed was very new for women' (131). She learns to use a chainsaw and axe. Her husband is similarly presented in 'flowered shirt, medallion and bell-bottom pants' (91). He applies 'for a grant from the government to build a windmill – something which was suddenly considered by everyone,' the narration reports, 'to be totally innovative and new' (166). Indeed, the narration offers considerable material to suggest that human beings may construct themselves out of an array of scripts which are available to the culture; but what it does not offer is how its own discourse and command of semiosis can stand outside such an array. What is the source of the authoritative discourse that makes such sardonic comments on the derivativeness of Vera and Nevin? – what has constructed it? Or if it stands autonomously outside the discursive determinism it has depicted, how has it achieved such standing?

Everyone wants to change the world; but no one will change themselves.

Leo Tolstoy

There is blood on their lips, you fight back, and it's you they blame.

Alden Nowlan, *Vampires*

After the title and copyright pages, and immediately before the opening chapter, the text offers these two epigraphs. Appearing before the numeral one that announces the first chapter, the epigraphs appear to have been placed here, not by the omniscience that narrates the text, but by the constructor of the *book* that contains it. Tolstoy and Nowlan are not part of the field of reference of the narrated text; their citation seems to imply a consciousness that reflects upon that text, rather than the narrating consciousness that limits its own field of reference to the one it constructs for its characters.

The two epigraphs appear to ask for change and struggle. While the Tolstoy statement is silent on whether 'the world' should be changed, its antithetical structure implies strongly that individuals should not only change but be the conscious agents of this change. The Nowlan epigraph suggests discursive oppression – 'there is blood on their lips' – of a 'you' by a 'they.' The 'you' seeks change by 'fighting back'; the 'they' effectively resists not only by continuing the oppression but by 'blaming' the 'you' for the need the 'they' feels to oppress. Again there is the implication of a conscious will to change, although interestingly the Nowlan text involves the reader in this change, naming the reader as the oppressed 'you,' while the Tolstoy positions the reader as spectator to the intransigence of third parties. Both texts, however, suggest pessimism: in the Tolstoy 'no one' will change; in the Nowlan resistance is deflected as 'blame' back upon the resister.

If we compare the two reader-positions of these texts to that given by the narration in the main text, we find it is the Tolstoy 'I-they' rather than the intradiegetic 'I-you (they)' of the Nowlan that the narrator offers. The narration thereby dissociates itself from the condition of the characters much like it dissociates itself from their language by its *ex cathedra* analyses of motivations obscure to them. That is, it is with the overt pessimism of Tolstoy that the narration discursively affiliates itself ('change is desirable but people are individually incapable of it'), rather than with the resigned indignation ('you, my friend, at least fight back before being blamed for your own oppression') of Nowlan.

Overall, the narrative of *Nights below Station Street* appears to foreclose the possibility of personal growth and significant change even more decisively than does Tolstoy. The characters who attempt to change their lives are mostly depicted as having merely the illusion that they are choosing to change; what is *really* happening to them is that they are being shaped, moulded, and scripted by large social forces beyond their understanding. The apartment Ralphie rents quickly emerges as a generic 'hippie' pad – 'a communal apartment, with everyone having the "same ideas" and everyone friends' (47). Vera's attempts to lead a different and better life than her parents are presented by the narration as embracings of passing fashions for natural foods, rural living, and French-language culture. Other characters' attempts to change are constructed as simple wishes to exchange one class discourse for another. Adele's desire that her family change by moving 'upward' is at one point represented by her wish that Rita play bridge with Myhrra and her current friends:

> One night Adele saw a group of cars in Myhrra's yard.
> 'Go on up, go on up, 'Adele said to Rita, excitedly. 'I'll babysit, I will I will.'
> ...
> 'They're having a bridge party up there,' she said. 'I'm not going to intrude on a bunch of ladies sitting down to play a game of bridge. I have a load of ironing to do as it is.'
> 'Ha, you could beat any of them,' Adele screamed, throwing a sudden tantrum and throwing a dishcloth over Milly's head, and then kicking a chair.
> 'I haven't played bridge in my life,' Rita said.
> And then for some reason Adele got doubly angry at this. (65)

An undisciplined discourse, marked by tantrums, ironing, and a dishcloth, collides with a polite and rule-bound discourse, 'ladies sitting down to play a game of bridge,' which Rita is unable to use or enter. A similar collision occurs when Myhrra visits the Russian freighter and talks to a sailor about his wife, who is 'studying engineering' in Leningrad; Myhrra begins to feel 'ugly' and shabby in her 'dyed hair and blue slacks, which were carefully upturned at the cuffs, and the zipper of her pants, which seemed to protrude as if she had a paunch' (81).

The most determined effort to change is that of Joe, whose attempt to stop drinking is announced on the first page and is a recurrent element in the text. This attempt is also presented as a discursive change, one from regarding compulsive drinking as 'hell' (61) to 'knowing' it to be 'a disease' (75), from seeking help through the discourse of the church to seeking it through that of Alcoholics Anonymous. Although Joe's attempt is not satirized by the narrator to the extent that Myhrra's or Vera's attempts to change discourses are, it is similarly constructed as unsuccessful. At the end of Myhrra and Vye's wedding dance Joe finds what he thinks is a plastic bottle of water on the porch and drinks 'deeply,' only to discover it is vodka.

His chance taking of this drink, and his continuing to drink from the bottle afterwards, contribute to a network of concluding incidents that offers an overdetermined statement of the powerlessness of the characters to, in the smallest way, direct their futures. Myhrra and Vye drive away from the wedding dance down a back road into a rising blizzard; soon 'both of them ... felt that they should turn back, and yet, *strangely*, on they went around a turn' (213, italics added) – and around this turn they become stuck, seven miles from the nearest house and without boots or outdoor clothing. Meanwhile Joe has drunk more of the windfall vodka, has forgotten that he was planning to drive to the hospital to see Adele and his grandchild, and has driven into the forest – 'why he had come here *he had no idea*' (222, italics added). Vye leaves Myhrra in the car and attempts to walk for help. A short time later she leaves the car 'to pee,' quickly gets lost when she panics at the sound of what she thinks is a small animal, and inadvertently stumbles to safety. The narrator takes pains to emphasize the inadvertent and chance nature of her rescue:

... by not finding the road – and by taking a turn to the left because of a windfall that tore her dress, stumbling down a hill and grabbing a branch in the dark – by coming to a brook and being frightened that it was a swamp, and moving back up the hill – and stopping just an instant to realize that she had lost both of her shoes – and by waiting a few seconds to taste the blood on her gashed cheek – she had saved her life.

For if she had done anything else, moments sooner or moments later – or taken another direction in any degree, or stopped for any longer on the windfall when she checked the time, or got out of the car any later to have a pee – she would not have stumbled out in front of Allain Garret's truck lights just as he was backing out of his wood lot. Similarly, if Allain had not left the house when he did, he would not have spotted her. (217)

Meanwhile Joe has driven and snowshoed to his hunting cabin, slept for an hour, woken with the sudden recollection that he had wanted to go to the hospital, begun to snowshoe back to his truck, and '*hap-*

pened ... to cut along a side log road' (224, italics added) that leads him to the helpless Vye. Again the narrator emphasizes the inadvertence of the character's actions: Joe drives down one road on 'an impulse'; he has an intention to be elsewhere but 'at every point on his journey he [is] doing other things' (222); he chooses another road on 'a sudden inspiration' (223); he locates Vye 'not knowing' (225) how he has come to do so.

The actions of these dimly conscious characters, who manage to complete plot sequences without even knowing they have entered them, are paralleled in these concluding pages by the events Adele and Ralphie 'discover' themselves within. Sixteen-year-old Adele, who declared in the first chapter that she was going to differ from her mother by 'starting her own life where there will be no such thing as loads of kids' (16), gives birth, like her mother before her, to an unplanned child. Ralphie finds himself unexpectedly working in the mine, like Joe before him, even though 'he had not intended to.' Again the narrator emphasizes the powerlessness of the character vis à vis that of the invisible teleology that directs him – 'an object falls, it has no idea where it will land, but at every moment of its descent it is exactly where it is supposed to be' (220) – although it is silent on what agency or force governs where an object 'is supposed to be.'

Both characters who perform rescues in the concluding chapter, Joe Walsh and Allain Garret, not only are linked to older rural activities and knowledges – hunting, woodlore, and subsistence farming – but are in positions to rescue because they are practising these. The narration signals that the two endangered characters lack these older knowledges, marking both with signs that identify them with urban culture and its reliance on advanced technology. When Joe drives his truck into an evening blizzard and towards the forest, the text notes that he checks to make sure he has his snowshoes, despite his having no clear understanding of why he is driving to the forest or recollection that he should be driving to the hospital. He parks the truck when the road conditions become difficult and sets out on snowshoes towards his hunting camp. When Vye drives into the same blizzard, the text comments that he has 'no boots, only his leather shoes' (214). When road conditions deteriorate, the text has him '[try] to make it through the drift' (213) but spin off the road. Having 'not liked the woods' since getting lost many years before, he is frightened, lights his cigarette lighter, and 'stumble[s] forward with his lighter lighting the way' (218). The wind blows it out. The text describes Myhrra as similarly entering the woods without adequate clothing, and with fear of the animals and trees. She borrows Vye's watch before he leaves, but after a few minutes in the snow it stops. She is rescued by a seventy-year-old man who is 'at home' in the woods (184) and appears to be making his daily visit to his woodlot despite the weather.

The mistrust of the urban and endorsement of the rural that this ending suggests, are echoed elsewhere in the novel in both the history of Joe Walsh and the eccentricities of Vera's uncle, Dr Hennessey. Despite his abilities as a logger and enjoyment of the woods, Joe became a diver in the navy and was once nearly killed in the Bay of Fundy when he swam 'without knowing' (71) into an underwater turbine. He has been trained as a diver, a boiler mechanic, and a heavy equipment operator but can never find work in these areas. He suffers from a disabling back injury caused by having had a large tractor roll on him. Joe is the kindly logger who comes 'out of the woods' (112) to marry Rita when Adele's biological father, a student from Windsor, leaves without knowing she is pregnant. Dr Hennessey is described by the narrator as an 'old fashioned and anachronistic thinker,' with 'one old-fashioned trait which helped ... he made house-calls' (161). He is outspoken in his contempt for the modern – does not like 'talking about ... aid for poverty-stricken countries, helping people in general, seeing to it that things changed, changing anything in general ... anything that had to do with believing that you could change the system – systems in general' (176). Yet he is also described as not wanting 'to be unkind' (174), as concerned for 'fairness' (179), and his dislike of change is explained as frustration that nothing is really changed. He is portrayed as opposing the volunteer visitor program at the hospital because the volunteers 'could be *selective* about what they volunteered for' (179), and as mocking pacifists because they only 'see the obvious' and give no credit to those 'who have suffered' for peace. His conservatism is constructed as resting on more profound moral concerns than do the liberalisms he opposes.

Together with the powerful implication in the novel that it is useless for individuals to try to give shape to their lives, that what happens to anyone is no more than the chance coincidence of disparate events, these positive portrayals of three characters strongly rooted in the rural past argue a pastoral 'anti-change' view of New Brunswick life. The only moments of even marginal contentment occur when Joe is at his camp, Dr Hennessey is cooking smelts, or Vera and Allain Garret are sitting on a rail fence at his woodlot. Otherwise life is a frenetic round of activities occasioned by urban civilization – attempts to obtain education, to look after others' children, to find work, to rise in social status, to be fashionable and progressive. The language of these characters – even the better-educated Dr Hennessey and his niece Vera – is inadequate either to give them insight into their motivations or effective communication with others.

The narrator and novelist, however, are in a much different position. They have command over a diverse semiotic field that moulds and pushes their unknowing characters. They have access to language which allows not only analysis of motive far beyond the capabilities of the characters but also the shaping of a narrative that can gather these characters together in a final chapter that offers a birth, a wedding, a new career, and two fortuitous rescues. This large superiority in linguistic power the narrator and novelist enjoy over their characters opens a wide political gap in the text. Narrator and novelist are able not only to construct their own version of a story, but also to legitimize this version through commercial publication in a distant province and literary award; the book's characters, however, are construed by this narrator and novelist as better off leading passive, acquiescent, non-constructive, geographically limited lives, rather than ones of ambition and effort. For them, the narration argues, chance events – fortuitous stumbling in snowstorms, drunken forgetfulness of a grandchild's birth – will produce more life-affirmative results than will education, technology, or the desire for literary production or even for self-improvement. The ultimate effect of this gap is the same as that produced by the narration's incessant use of simple and additive sentence structure: condescension.

Such an effect may be difficult to avoid in the writing of texts which endorse pastoral ideologies. To achieve any circulation in our culture, such a text usually must occupy a position outside this ideology, at the very least coming to the reader with 'Cataloguing in Publication Data'; at most, coming in a technologically produced discourse like the novel and through a knowledge of generic and linguistic codes far beyond that of Joe Walsh or Dr Hennessey. The text which suggests that New Brunswick culture would have been better without the arrival of tractors and universities and the impinging of Russian and mainstream North American culture also suggests a New Brunswick which could not have produced *Nights below Station Street*. It also implies that the power to produce such a text had best remain where it is, away from the confused and unknowing of Station Street, and safe with the text's concealed elite – an elite who can mysteriously think and write from outside the determinations of additive syntax and semiotic fashion.

———————•—————

We live in a world whose inhabitants are more and more cut off from nature. Even in little rural settlements like the one in Nova Scotia where I grew up, it is now possible to live in a totally artificial environment, where the temperature depends not upon the weather outside, but on the flick of the switch that turns on the furnace or the air conditioner. Having lived for nineteen years in a house without central heating, without indoor plumbing, without refrigeration, without a telephone, and without electricity, I am not given to romanticising the primitive life. I am merely pointing out how, during my own short lifetime, the city has been swallowing up the country.

...

When everything that is wild and free vanishes from the earth, true civilization will vanish with it ...

Alden Nowlan, 'Sable Island: Symbol of Enduring Life,' *Atlantic Advocate*, 71, no. 10 (June 1981), 86

In the recent discourses of Atlantic Canada there are often profound ambivalences about nature and progress, together with both strong attachments to the past and a clear perception that technology comes, as above, from outside: the 'country' does not achieve 'city' amenities; the country is 'swallowed' by the city. At its most benign this discourse displays itself in usages like the employment of 'Canada' to denote only provinces to the northwest of New Brunswick; at its most problematic it displays itself in figures of helplessness or pyrrhic resistance: the Stellarton miners who, only days after the May 1992 explosion at the Westray coalmine, announce they would likely return to the mine should it reopen; the Newfoundland government that reconstructs and opposes the Meech Lake Accord as something done to Newfoundland rather than negotiated by it.

In *Nights below Station Street* such binary conceptions of power and powerlessness virtually prevent any sense of Canada as an active polity within the text, and alienate the text itself from its subjects. Power is distant, alien, international, and associated (along with the text's own narrative discourse) with figures of education, travel, and fashion that, whether linked to Montreal, Oxford, or Leningrad, have no roots in Atlantic experience. Canada here blurs with the multinational, becomes as alien to the novel's characters as a chess game on a Russian freighter. The Atlantic region itself not only lacks power but possesses authenticity only in renouncing it, like Joe, surprised in the text's concluding sentence that he has inadvertently rescued Vye, 'not knowing the processes of how this had all happened, only understanding that it was now irrevocable because it had' (225).

BC Dreams Quebec
Caprice

... on a 30-mile-long island in the St. Lawrence, sprawls metropolitan Montreal, the world's second largest French-speaking city. European fads and fashions are said to catch on faster here than anywhere else in North America. I always find it a nice place to visit.

Office girls bounce through the busy Place Ville Marie shopping complex, epitomizing up-to-the-minute chic. 'They look a bit like hippies,' says a Virginia lady, 'but such nice hippies.'

'One Canada or Two,' *National Geographic*, April 1977, 461

My interest in Comparative Canadian Literature began on a Saturday night, in a dancehall on the outskirts of a small Quebec town. With the others in the hall I was relaxing after three or four square-dance sets, while an attractive dark-eyed girl entertained us with French-Canadian *chansons*. As I recall, she had a soft, hypnotic voice ...

Ronald Sutherland, *Second Image: Comparative Studies in Quebec/ Canadian Literature* (1971), [vii]

Caprice is the title of George Bowering's 1987 novel and the name of its most prominent character, but her name is not necessarily the title of the novel. 'Caprice' – 'a sudden turn of the mind without apparent motive' – may in this text be as much a name for the writing of texts as it is for a personality formation.

Generically *Caprice* appears to belong both to the western novel and to the story of vengeance. A strong young woman rides canyon and cattle range to seek the killer of her younger brother, shot down unarmed in a cattle-ranch quarrel over a bottle of whisky. As she travels, she ponders the text of Goethe's *Faust* in the context both of her own irresistible desire to avenge her brother's death and of the calamitous end which that death has put to the life she had been building for herself as a poet. But, not only are these sets of signs – North American action, European introspective romanticism – conflicting, they are themselves further qualified and rivalled by other signs and sign-systems – among these a federal, expansionist Canada of railroads, customs officers, and Mounties, a cloistered Quebec of church and family, a knowing yet violent Europe signalled by both French elegance and by Spanish whips, Luger pistols, and the crumbling Austro-Hungarian empire – all of which are themselves qualified by the presence of even more competing signs.

The action of *Caprice* could be said to take place in and near the town of Nicola in south-central British Columbia during 1888–90. It can also be said to take place in a western–North–American semiological field that extends from Tombstone, Arizona, to Kamloops, from Walla Walla, Washington, to Calgary, a field marked by *cowboy, Indian, miner, sod-buster, stagecoach, Winchester, drygulcher, bushwacker, rustler, wrangler, gunfighter, saddle tramp, outlaw, lawman, dancehall girl, saloon, buckboard, buckskin, coyote, tumbleweed, sagebrush, ponderosa,* and *lodgepole pine.* But again we have conflict: the extension of the 'American' wild West into southern British Columbia creates a fissure in the notion of 'wild West.' The miners of Fairview, BC, tip their hats as Caprice rides into town from Arizona – 'the first time she had seen that since [she] had left here in the late spring' (51). That Caprice is a Québécoise from Ste Foy and her brother Pierre is the Québécois cowboy 'Pete Foster' introduces a further fissure, as a convent-educated Caprice, whose mother had wanted her to 'be a nun, so that someone else will have protected her from the things in books' (21), tracks and ultimately faces down the U.S. gunfighter who had killed her brother. The implicit ideological assumptions of 'western' signs – individualism, open spaces, freedom of movement, natural justice – are thus interrupted, qualified, and interrogated by collectivism, closed space, socially defined justice, international boundaries, and the sinfulness of the over-reaching individual.

In addition, the action of *Caprice* takes place within the generic conventions and discourses of the North American 'western' – a matter which is underlined in the text by Caprice's own awareness of it. She is presented as someone aware that when she begins her search for her brother's killer she is entering textual determinations; 'I feel like saying howdy,' she reflects when she rides into what appears to be an archetypal homesteader's farmyard. In the usual practice of the western its conventions include an omniscient narration (the western protagonist is not introspective or reflective), a clear demarcation between good and evil, and either a quest action – search for a 'Lost Something Mine' (245), kidnapped woman, outlaw, or journey to a haven – or a regaining-of-paradise action – the recovery of a ranch lost by fraud, the expelling of evil from a town or territory. The protagonist is usually a lone male rider (reflecting both the U.S. ideologies of individualism and 'natural' male leadership, and the literary origins of the western in the medieval questing knight), English-speaking and American-born, while the evil that is confronted is usually collective – a gang like the Clantons or Jameses – or both collective and 'alien' – Indian tribes or Mexican armies. The woman's position in this genre is auxiliary – the cavalry commander's daughter, the dancehall girl, the kidnapping victim. The Indian also occupies the role of an Other to be defeated, sometimes noble, wise, and doomed, sometimes a savage sign of white moral superiority, but always a spectator or scout, gazing from distant ridges or camped outside fort stockades or town limits.

In *Caprice* these elements are both present and not present. There is an omniscient narrator, but it is not always sure of the story it is telling, sometimes qualifying it with words like 'probably' (46) and 'somewhere' (82). It shares its task with other eyes and voices and, even more disruptively, hints on numerous occasions that it may have altered the story by including signs associated, not with the nineteenth century and the western, but with the texts of its late-twentieth-century signator, 'George Bowering.' There is a tall lone rider, but she is not only female but, as French-speaking, one of three characters marked as alien, 'Frenchy' and 'Froggie' in the western discourse of the text's other characters. She is also an 'Easterner' – from so far east she rides a Spanish horse and carries a volume of Goethe. In the place of the usual western sign of the 'U.S. revolver' (193) on her hip she carries a Spanish whip and later buys a Luger pistol. This protagonist is not the usual unreflective, morally certain one, but morally troubled, introspective, and conscious of the ambiguities involved in taking power into one's own hands and, as a published poet, introduces her own texts into the narration. The 'evil' she faces is not collective but solitary, the American individualist, the gunman Frank Spencer from Tennessee; collectivity, by contrast, is mostly 'good' and is present in the provincial police force, to whom she 'knows' she should entrust her quest, and in the townspeople, who, by helping her, call her back from the solitudes of hatred and vengeance.

Women are both at the expected margins of the action, farm-wives, and saloon-girls, and also at the centre – not only in the person of Caprice, but also of Gert the Whore, an independent businesswoman whose home sports a basket of captured male weapons. The Indians are also in the expected position, spectators to the action, on various ridges watching the white characters come and go, but they are also at times most unexpectedly the moral filter through which the action is perceived. Rather than speaking in the poetic and symbolic discourses usually awarded them in western fiction, they parody these discourses and speak themselves, rather, in the analytical language of anthropology, to which their role as spectators to another culture suits them. Not only is a convention of western fiction disrupted here, but the usual relationship between white anthropologist and 'native informant' is reversed. Again, such reversals and additions to convention carry with them disruptions, contestations, and qualifications of ideology. The individualist discourse of the western novel is not only altered by being perceived through the individualism-questioning discourse of German romanticism ('Doc, have you ever given any thought to that woman's soul? How long do you reckon she is going to be in possession of it?' [167]) but also by being juxtaposed to the collectivity-affirming discourses of those who advise Caprice to 'leave justice' to the provincial police (64). A cultural construction of Indians as intellectually and discursively incapable, a construction that renders their speech as a halting English, is countered here by a rendering of Indian speech that presents itself as the English translation of a sophisticated discourse. Within this discourse the Indian speakers are depicted as being aware that they have been linguistically constituted as 'Indians' and 'tribe'-members by white discourse – aware that 'Indian' and 'tribe' are 'white' words (4) – and as being capable of pondering metaphysical and anthropological issues.

Such disruptions, repositionings, and overturnings of semiotic codes and individual signs should not be read as merely a postmodern game or even as an ideological assertion of difference and disapproval. Sign and sign-systems do not have stable and eternal meanings which can be differed from and 'disapproved' of, but rather have their meaning, as Saussure demonstrated with linguistic codes, within a fluid field of differential relationships with other signifiers, a meaning which is further subject to the position from which they are perceived within this field. One does not differ from or disapprove of stable signs of solitary patriarchy or marginalized woman when one introduces these into a field that contains both an introspective, questing, Luger-bearing woman on a black Spanish horse and a sagebrush, bushwacker, and stagecoach landscape. Rather one changes the operations of these codes. The individual quester, instead of being defined against an Other of savage gangs and tribes, is defined against moral subtleties of European culture and literature, against a well-meaning if inefficient BC provincial police force, against Indians who ponder metaphysical questions, against ambiguous institutions such as the Indian school in which Caprice's lover Roy Smith teaches. A U.S. sign such as the solitary questing male individual is not so much repudiated as repositioned within a field that includes not only Caprice's solitary 1competence but both Faustus's individual ambition that led to his damnation and Roy Smith's commitment to institutions and teamwork: as a teacher at the Indian school, as second-baseman on the Kamloops baseball team, which includes five 'team-playing' American imports, and as a member of the posse that follows and assists Caprice ('"Let me help you with that," said Constable Burr' [258]) in her last struggle with Spencer. Similarly the meaning of 'western' signs such as *tumbleweed, wrangler,* and *saloon* changes when situated within a 'Canadian' context, or when juxtaposed in the persons of Caprice or the gunman Loop Groulx with Québécois ethnicity (Groulx's name itself punningly merges the whip-wielding Hollywood cartoon character 'Lash Larou' with the legendary Quebec werewolf, the *loup-garou*). The usually closed signs of 'fortress Quebec' alter also when juxtaposed both with the memory of the Northwest Company clerk Antoine Charette, who dies in BC in 1815 (250), and with the wide European and North American travels of the intensely cosmopolitan Caprice.

————————•————————

If you just had ordinary English eyes, you would have seen late-morning sunlight flooding the light brown of the wide grassy valley and making giant knife shadows where the ridges slid down the hillsides, free of trees, wrinkles made in a wide land that didnt seem to be in that much of a hurry ...

But if you had those famous Indian eyes you could look down into the wide valley and see something moving, maybe a lot of things moving, but especially one black or at least dark horse, which meant probably a rider too, and in a little while a rider for certain.

Caprice, 1

The opening paragraphs of *Caprice* emphasize another kind of positioning that influences the meaning of signs – that of the viewer or reader. These rather complex paragraphs not only suggest two different positions – through 'English eyes' or through 'famous Indian eyes' – but in their intradiegetic address to the reader, 'if *you* had those ... eyes,' offer these as possible positions from which to read the text. In addition, however, they mark the second position, 'famous Indian,' as only marginally available. The latter is a textual cliché, too famous to be generally available except perhaps to narrators of westerns and to Indians who, like the two the third paragraph perches above the valley, understand the cliché well enough to make it part of the 'Indian' role they self-consciously play. The reader is left only with 'English eyes' with which to view this valley, although enabled by the narrator's 'western' discourse to imagine and construct an alternate view. Whether 'English' here is presented as a linguistic qualifier (English rather than French) or an ethnic one (English rather than American, for example) is not indicated, and thus both significations tend to be present.

Thirty-two pages later, this antithesis between 'ordinary' and 'Indian' eyes is offered again, but here, instead of 'ordinary English,' the text substitutes 'ordinary eastern,' and instead of 'famous Indian' offers only 'Indian':

> If you just had ordinary eastern eyes you would see a long shallow valley, brown in the honest sunlight, blue on the slopes of the hills, green among the trees on the hilltops ... You would see the enormous quiet bow of blue sky above, and if you were looking actively you might see a hawk up high. If you had Indian eyes you would see the hawk's head bent to look below him with eyes even better than yours. But if you had ordinary eastern eyes you might be satisfied or even transported by the lovely morning light ...
>
> ....
>
> If you have ordinary eyes and a good heart you will stop working or riding for a minute or two and look ahead of you for twenty miles. (33)

'English' has been redefined as 'eastern,' although just as 'English' was not specificed as either linguistic or ethnic, here 'eastern' has not been specified as either eastern-Canadian or eastern–North American. 'Famous Indian' is now merely the less textualized 'Indian.' The you-reader has been renamed as Eastern, although some sub-positions within this will soon be offered – those of 'normal reader' and 'curious reader,' both still alternating with 'Indian.' 'Indian,' like 'famous Indian' before, is marked as preferred and is still available to the reader as a 'gift' from the narrator, whose own access to it remains textual – as a narrator of a text in the western genre, it apparently enjoys free use of the codes 'famous Indian' or 'Indian' eyes:

> If you have normal reader's eyes you will see the Europeans here sitting down to pull the small cactus off their trouser legs. You will see the people in high boots acquiring the skill or habit of looking around the ground and rocks before they sit down ...
>
> If you are a curious reader you will see a familiar crumbling of rock, and look closer, to find ... light blue agate, opal, jasper ...
>
> But if you were an Indian you always knew these things were here ... Curiosity was to be expended on the white men. (34)

One interesting effect of this positioning of the you-reader as English, Eastern, and, within this, as either ordinary/normal or curious, is what is excluded. As well as 'Indian,' all of 'western,' 'American,' and 'French/Québécois' positions – those occupied in the text by the stagecoach driver Charlie Westoby, Frank Spencer, and Caprice, respectively – are left either unavailable or doubtfully available. These positions in turn are evidently to be perceived with 'English' 'eastern' eyes, ordinary or curious. Or are they? For just as the initial naming of 'famous Indian eyes' relativized and textualized that position, the heavy foregrounding of 'English eyes,' 'eastern eyes,' and 'curious eyes,' together with repeated attention to how people are viewed ('there was no scarcity of eyes turned her way as she walked' [25], 'The eyes above the beard were flat with derision' [125], 'Lady, you are a sight for sore eyes' [235]), work to textualize even this widely 'available' position – to name it as relative, constructed, arbitrary, and thus to loosen its 'inevitability' for the named-as-Eastern reader.

Several other elements in the text also operate to unfix the position from which the reader encounters the text. One is the narrator's own identification of itself with 'eastern' and naming of all of twentieth-century British Columbia as 'east':

> But as soon as you get to the Pacific Ocean, with a train or something,

all you have in front of you is the east. A rotting market spilling fruit peels into the harbour, probably. A landlord collecting paper money from people living on bamboo boats.

  The east just keeps coming till it sees the tip of its own tail and begins to wonder what it would taste like ....

...

  The hell with us. We are all Europeans now. Now we can write the books and plays and operas. We just have to look around in the past and find subjects. There we will find a cowboy rather than a business man. The west has shrunk so much we can get it inside us.

  It is awfully dry in there.

  We walk around in our European clothes, carrying our eastern newspapers, and we have a little dry something inside us. (110)

An effect of this pasage is to empty the term 'east' of much of its geographic significance, leaving it a temporally limited spatial concept. Another is to cast irony on the narrator's own self-identification as an Easterner – for it is accompanied by a simultaneous identification of itself as a 'westerner.' 'We are all Easterners now,' it says, implying that at another time this British-Columbia-dwelling 'we' was something else, not 'eastern.' Further, its definition of the condition of being 'eastern' does not quite match the textual activity we are reading. Carrying an 'eastern' newspaper the narrator may be, but looking around in the past and finding a subject it certainly is not. Caprice is a very unlikely historical subject, a poor convent-educated girl from Ste Foy who, during a period when conservative and ecclesiastically controlled Quebec's growing contacts with republican, anti-clerical France were limited to the upper classes, grew up to live in France and marry a wealthy Frenchman, who learned to speak virtually unaccented educated English, to read Marlowe and Goethe in English, at a time when English was rarely taught in Quebec except to the young men of privileged families (there were no colleges for Québécois women until the twentieth century), and who became a skilled horsewoman in a culture in which riding was a mark of power and privilege. Caprice is not merely a mystery within the text, and not merely an emanation from 'Mr. Bowering's sexual fantasies' (as the paperback edition approvingly notes a *Winnipeg Free Press* reviewer has proposed), but a specific ideological construction, indicative of a Quebec dreamed by a distant part of Canada, endowed with both 'western' and 'European' signs, made both familiar and exotic in a dream which has access to the 'western' and yearns for the cosmopolitan: 'A few years ago Caprice had worn expensive rings on both hands. Now she wore gloves that were strong enough to hold a whipstock and tight enough to hold a pistol' (251). The narrator's position, then, with its peculiar construction of a nineteenth-century Quebec woman, its partial draining of signification from 'eastern,' its unlimited access to 'western' semiology, and its ironic remarks about its own activity, both destabilizes its naming of the reader as 'eastern' and implies yet another possible perspective for the reader, a plural one neither 'eastern,' 'Indian,' nor 'western' but able to move, like itself, among these and others.

A second positionally destabilizing element in the narration is the large number of non–North American characters through whom the action is viewed. One of these is the Chinese restaurant owner, Soo Woo, one of the wealthiest men in Nicola, whose gruff kindness accompanies a view of the action as an incomprehensible distraction from daily business. Another is the Austro-Hungarian journalist Arpad Kiss, alias Kesselring, who seeks local colour he can reprocess into romantic and saleable texts that meet European discursive expectations of western North America. As he tells Caprice about her hotel room, 'it may be simply your room as far as you are concerned, Miss Caprice ... but for the literate people of the Empire it will be legend. It will be history. Most important, perhaps, it will be romance' (171). Yet another is Soo Woo's employee, Everyday Luigi, born in Istria, who had 'spent his childhood in Trieste' and whose 'first fourteen years were spent as Lause Martens rather than Luigi Martino' (9). His wanderings have taken him through six languages, and by the end of *Caprice*, his jaw shattered by a Frank Spencer bullet, he is learning a seventh, Indian sign language. Luigi's linguistic wanderings, and his coming from Trieste, which has been in this century Austrian, Yugoslavian, and Italian, further emphasize the arbitrariness of language and viewpoint.

A third positionally destabilizing set of elements for the reader are various allusions the narrator includes in the text that, by invoking the biography of the signator, 'George Bowering,' emphasize the constructedness of the text and its idiosyncratic and personal position within Canadian culture. Various character names in the novel connect in some way with historical people within Bowering's life. Soo Woo's 'Canadian Cafe' carries the same name as the cafe associated with poet Red Lane in Bowering's *The Man in the Yellow Boots* (48); newspaper man Cyril Trump and his cousin Doc Trump carry the same name as Bowering's high school friend Willie Trump. Fairview hotel owner John Kearns appears modelled on the grandfather of Bowering's writer-friend Lionel Kearns, and is described as 'rugheaded' (53) much like the writer himself is described ('mustachioed rugheaded kern') in Bowering's early poem 'Letter to Lionel Kearns' (*Delta* 15 [Aug. 1961], 2–3). An unfortunate young victim of a Frank Spencer robbery is G. Delsing, a character name modelled on 'G. Bower-ing' that appears in early Bowering short stories. Some *Caprice* characters are linked to other Canadian texts. One of Gert the Whore's girls is named Lily Traff, in an apparent reference to Sheila Watson's character Traff, an habituée of the brothel in *The Double Hook*. The homesteader's wife whom Caprice meets on her way to her climactic encounter with Spencer tells her that she is from Lucan, Ontario, home of the historically and fictionally known Donnelly family. The Iroquois poetess who visits Nicola early in the novel is dubbed 'The Belle of Caughnawaga' (70) in a punning invocation of my own early poem 'The Caughnawaga Bell.' These various allusions signal the overall textuality of what the reader encounters, that the constructor of the novel is himself specifically situated within Canadian and British Columbian writing, and that the text of this siting is as much a part the text of the novel as is nineteenth-century British Columbian history or the significations of 'west' and 'east.'

'One thing I found out long ago, Doc – the average outlaw shares one thing with the average lawman. They both think of themselves as acting out a story that's half drama and half history. They love getting their pictures taken. They are both already looking for the sympathy of the audience, even if the audience is going to be watching the story unfold, as they say, a long while after the players are all dead.'

'Players, eh?'

Doc Trump never forgot his own role as the grouchy observer and commentator on the relentlessly passing scene.

Caprice, 168

The destabilization of the reader's perspective on the novel's text is increased by the number, incongruity, and often the apparent arbitrariness of the discourses that it contains. Characters associated with a particular set of signs frequently do not speak in the discourse with which those signs are associated and within which the relationships between the signs have been produced. Instead they attempt to assume what they think is a more attractive discourse. Loop Groulx, the Québécois outlaw, attempts to use a western discourse – 'Aw Frank, if you would of let me ventilate that old coot' (164) – while Frank Spencer, western gunslinger, corrects his usage like an 'eastern' schoolteacher:

> 'I hate this goddamn country,' said Frank Spencer.
> 'Me too,' said Loop. 'I more'n hate it. I abominize it.'
> 'Abominate it,' said Spencer. (198)

While Arpad Kesselring speaks in an inflated, circumlocutional discourse which implies a necessity to erase local difference and conform to a 'high' literary norm, the two Indians speak in the text's most sophisticated discourse, one which can contain and parody others:

> 'Some of the white men from across the medicine line asked me whether they might be permitted to visit a steam house,' said the second Indian.
> 'Did you tell them that it would be difficult because our sacred laws suggest that the red man's spiritual wealth depends on his keeping the mysteries of the divine steam?'
> 'I never heard of that,' said the second Indian.
> 'Well,' said the first Indian, 'it is not strictly true, but I have always found that the white man places more value on our stuff if we can convince him that we are religious about it.' (23)

Like Doc Trump above, these Indians are aware of the role-playing involved in producing oneself through a particular discourse, whether this be that of the 'mystical Indian' above, the 'poetic Indian' ('If a white man asked him how old he was he always replied: many moons. They liked that' [246]), or the 'silent Indian': "... you could forebear talking altogether and just observe," said the first Indian. "Many whites think that is the Indian way" ' (247).

Against the subtle, introspective discourse of the Renaissance and nineteenth-century European poetry favoured by Caprice, the text also introduces and foregrounds a number of other poetic discourses. One is the simplistic, hegemonically masculine discourse of a newspaper poet:

> There are some women on this creek,
> So modest, and so mild and meek!
> ...

> Each one's a mistress, too you'll find,
> To make good folk think that she's joined
> In honest wedlock unto one.
> She's YOURS – or ANY OTHER MAN'S. (135)

Of which the narrator comments, 'The bard was tremendously interested in honesty, and seemed throughout to find it only among the hardscrabble miners. Poets interested in honesty ... always seem to think that poetic skill is basically dishonest' (136). Another is a more skilled, pornographic discourse which, in parodying Pope, positions the woman even more specifically than does the discourse of 'the bard':

> The study of the whip was, to his mind,
> The 'properest study' of all womankind,
> And woman's proper sphere – a boy's behind. (141)

A third is the romantic federalist discourse of the Canadian Confederation and Maple Leaf schools, which enters the text in the person of the Caughnawaga Indian princess Emily Peachtree Guano. Her poems parody both Pauline Johnson's and the vaguely transcendentalist poems of Carman, Lampman, and such imitators as Wilson MacDonald, Marjorie Pickthall, and Isabel Ecclestone Mackay:

> Something so sacred lies upon the ground,
> Like to a blessing to a holy mound,
> A calm we sense but cannot yet propound. (70)

Guano's explanation of her work invokes, in addition to the nationalism of the Canada First movement, the Confederation group, and its Maple Leaf followers, the 1970s nationalism of thematic critics such as Atwood, Jones, and Moss, who also offered a single hegemonic Canada grounded in the 'forest-floors' of Ontario:

> If this nation is to be drawn together and its heart filled with hope, it must
> be with the spirit of democracy and fellow feeling that reigns on the forest
> floor. It may have been my fortunate lot in life to be born with the blood
> of a princess and the breath of a muse in my ear, but I travel this broad
> Dominion secure in the knowledge that its myriad people have the touch
> of their enlightened maker in their hearts. (72)

The theatrical nature of Ms Guano's performances – she travels from town to town and 'clad in feathers and hides she would stand before [audiences] in the Methodist church hall and recite verses about God and the whispering voice of the dark woods' – again suggests this is an assumed discourse, one that is part of a role she has taken upon herself 'of knitting the Dominion together in the face of the Yankee threat of manifest destiny' (70).

Three other discourses of poetry within the text, gathered in a miniature anthology just after the text of Ms Guano's performance, and all associated with Caprice herself, not only contrast with the other poetries but further destabilize the position of the narrator and the narrative perspective. The first of these is an amateurish poem in French, very simply rhymed and in somewhat naïve diction:

> Toujours le bon Dieu reste muet
> En dessinant les lacs et les forêts.
> Les matins frais et lumineux qu'il crée,
> Me font que pleurer les êtres destinés
> A partager les ombres désolées. (83)

This text, which ends in mid-line two lines later, appears to be the poem the narrator reports Caprice to have been writing when her brother was struck by Spencer's bullet and both God and her pen were struck with silence. It is followed by a longer and apparently 'complete' three-stanza English poem in similar line-structure, also dealing with the silence of God, but in an exclamatory syntax and in a much more sophisticated nineteenth-century versification:

> How silent is the God who drew the hills!
> This sky above this rider on her search
> Belies a soul consumed with wondrous hate,
> And almost lulls the nemesis contrived
> To bring some sunshine to a brother's grave. (84)

This seems an answer not only to the French poem but to that of Ms Guano, silencing her mysteriously mumbling deity and gracefully resolving her difficulties with diction and metrics. It merges a discourse of the West ('this sky above') with that of Goethe ('lulls the nemesis contrived') in a manner one might expect of Caprice herself, who elsewhere combines these two discourses in her person. This poem is followed by a longer ten-stanza poem in free verse which not only rewrites once again the two earlier poems but overtly interweaves passages from Goethe with passages from the narration, and combines these with a set of first-person pronouns which appear ambiguously or concurrently to refer to both the narrator and Caprice:

How quiet
the morning breaks
my concentration
on my target.

Is this target the narrative or the killer Frank Spencer? – the narrator's target or the target of the narrative Caprice has entered through her quest?

Ordinary English eyes
would see a flood of light
coursing down the valley
like a ghost of ice

Famous hunter eyes
penetrate the shadows under rocks,

...
Black and beautiful
the shadow in my heart
rides without luck to south,
to north, to a west
too wide. (85)

The 'eyes' of the narrator combine here with the 'black and beautiful' of Caprice's black horse, Cabayo, which becomes the dark shadow that rides in her heart, or the narrator's heart, in search of the ends of narratives. The succeeding stanzas that rewrite Goethe, translating his divine thunder into Frank Spencer's gunfire, and Faust's hubris into Caprice's appropriating the 'speech' of divine retribution, do so, however, from a woman's point of view:

Then did I in creations of my own
(Oh, is not woman in each thing divine?)
build worlds – or bidding them no longer be –
exert, enjoy a sense of deity –
doomed for such dreams presumptuous to atone;
all by one word of thunder overthrown!

Over-throne! The rumble of those words

is my sport, a seizing of His speech
for my dire purpose
and my duty. (86)

The question these poems raise for the rest of the novel is who is
Caprice? – a narrative caprice, and gender alternative to the narrator,
or possibly even a multiple transformation of Western, male, anglophone, North American narrator into Eastern, female, francophone,
both Québécoise and European? If we understand the presence of a
poet to be indicated by textual activity, by the coming into being of
poetic texts, then, in a sense, the presence of Caprice in the novel is
most affirmed by this peculiar series of translations and transfor-
mations, which, by moving from French to English, from nineteenth-
century to twentieth-century poetic forms, also join Western narrator,
Québécoise protagonist, and Goethe into a single resonant and capricious text:

Pete Foster died at four in the morning. While he was doing it he just had
time for one word.
   'Caprice.' (18)

'Caprice' is indeed a word, but is it an exclamation or a summoning,
a comment on life or the name of 'a poet' or 'a sister,' or 'perhaps a
fury' (31)?

A visitor to pioneer Saskatchewan in 1907 remarked at the strange sight
of a sod hut with a big Canadian Bank of Commerce sign on it, open for
business. The essence of the Canadian west is in that image. Organized
society usually arrived with the settlers or ahead of them – not only the
branch bank manager, but the mounted policeman and the railway agent,
the missionary and the Hudson's Bay factor. Dawson City at the height
of the gold rush had its sins and shortcomings, but even here lawlessness
was not one of them. Violence and terror do not yet stalk the subways or
the streets of darkest Toronto. The posse and the desperado belong to the
American wild west, the citizen vigilante to the American metropolis.

William Kilbourn, 'Introduction,' in *Canada: A Guide to the Peaceable
Kingdom* (1970), xv

Near the end of the novel Caprice achieves her encounter with Spencer, disarms him, and – perhaps not surprisingly – not only declines

to kill him but becomes a part of the group that rescues and arrests him. This reversal from fury to rescuer, from pursuit of personal vengeance to acceptance of collective social action, is later marked in the book by the collective purchase by the people of Nicola of a white Arabian stallion to replace Caprice's dead black Cabayo. As they affirm her passage from black to white, they pronounce the horse 'not as valuable as what you have done for this community' (263).

The ambiguous signification of Caprice, both black and white, anglophone and francophone, North American and European, Western and Eastern, is repeated in other peculiar shadings and pairings that occur in the text. Together with her lover, Roy Smith, she forms part of a pair that reverses the usual male-female roles in the western: Roy is sedentary, committed to a steady job and to roles in his community; Caprice is a self-reliant wanderer. The two Indians, the first the tribal instructor of the second, are paralleled by both Roy Smith and his Indian students and by Frank Spencer and his de facto protégé Loop Groulx. Roy Smith, second-baseman, lover, and violence-opposing counsellor to Caprice, is less sophisticated than the first Indian, overwhelmingly less successful as a teacher, and involved through his teaching in a hegemonic colonizing discourse. Roy is a better teacher, however, than Frank Spencer, who has little but anger and contempt for Loop but has an equally intense relationship with Caprice. Roy's relationship with her is in fact dependent on Frank's – it is her passionate hatred of Spencer that brings her to meet Smith, and the resolution of this hatred that occasions her leaving him.

The text's twinning of Roy Smith, schoolteacher and team-player, and Frank Spencer, alias Frank Smith, anti-social gunman, offers another focus on the ideological considerations of the novel. Both, like the narrator, are fascinated by Caprice and her *difference* – her standing outside the text of female submissiveness, outside the text of North America, outside even the vaguely known text of Quebec. Both, however, stand as implicitly hostile to this difference, even while fascinated by it. Roy throughout the novel pleads with her to marry him, to become 'the wife of a schoolteacher, the mother of some of the children in his school one day' (61) – a role which would take her out of Quebec, stop her wanderings, and end her ambitions as a francophone poet. Frank Spencer appears to wish simply to kill her, although paradoxically this wish arises from his fascination with her, from his inability to run from her even as she hunts him, from his compulsively needing to keep himself near her. It is an enormous puzzle to Caprice why this man, whom she considers evil and murderous, neither flees her nor uses his many chances 'to put a rifle shot into her from behind a rock, or confront her on the road' (226). When, armed with only her whip and Luger, she corners him, he declines to shoot her with his rifle, and when he has his revolver aimed at her from ten feet below on a cliff, he delays shooting to let her slash the gun from his grip.

Caprice in effect has two lovers, two men, English-Canadian and American, who seek some irreversible linking with her. Roy Smith, like the good angel of Marlowe's *Doctor Faustus*, calls her to the text of English-Canadian community, Kilbourn's 'peaceable kingdom'; Frank Spencer, like Mephistopheles, calls her to the text of Faustian sin and bloody revenge, calling her to be a killer like himself. A few pages before their last encounter Caprice drops Goethe's text, and it falls open at the passage

> What! shall the poet squander then away,
> For thy poor purposes, himself, his mind,
> Profane the gift, which Nature, when she gave
> To him, to him entrusted for mankind,
> – Their birthright – thy poor bidding to obey ... (240)

Thus does the text ask the reader to perceive Spencer as a Satan, who would have Caprice kill and profane the 'gift' which she holds for 'mankind.' When, rather than striking Spencer from the ledge, she lowers her whip to assist him upward, it is presumably his dismay at her having refused his trap that makes his face 'bright with hatred' (258).

> Spencer got down and flexed his saddle-stiff legs. Groulx decided to sit where he was. For a while they stayed still like that, resembling a sentimental painting such as one was likely to find in an Alberta hotel lobby.

Caprice, 243

The text's relentless parody of the western genre, with its accompanying reminders that the characters are role-players who have become either self-situated or historically situated within particular genres and discourses, offers amusing distraction from the allegorical and ideological implications of the precise field of signs and discourses it constructs and the Western/Québécoise/Indian positions its narrator takes for itself within them. Concealed beneath the rhetoric of parody, and beneath the multiplicity of positions and signs, is an allegorical semiotic which attaches a set of overdetermined meanings to each of three major characters: Roy Smith, man of English-Canadian civilization, team-player, educator, reluctant acculturator of the different; Frank Spencer, Faustian product of American individualism and materialism; Caprice, an idealized vision of Québécois memory, poetry, loyalty, and torment, situated, like the narrator that identifies with her, between domestic and hard-working English Canadians and flashy but lethal Americans. Despite her ahistoricity as a character possibilty, she is in other ways firmly connected to Quebec semiology: to its 'je me souviens' motto in her inability to forget the death of her brother, to twentieth-century Quebec feminism and nationalism in the title of her one published book of poetry, 'L'Ancien Barre du Jour' – an allusion to the once nationalist and currently feminist Quebec literary journal La Nouvelle Barre du jour and its best-known editor, Nicole Brossard. It is into this 'barre du jour' that she rides at the end of the novel, east 'into the sunrise' (266), thereby affirming Quebec, choosing poetry, leaving the Nova Scotia–born Roy Smith, and rejecting and reversing the 'into the sunset' path of the (American) western hero.

Within the textuality that the novel offers as its vision of East, West, Canada, the United States, and Europe, Caprice is both a wishful British Columbian construction and an imaginary alternative self for the narrator – a beautiful, intelligent, five-foot-eleven non-'eastern' Québécoise who carries difficult-to-obtain European culture, the calmness of having a fixed home, 'Ste Foy,' 'Holy Faith,' and who can speak both French and better English than the unilingually anglophone Westerner. She also participates in a more general Canadian idealization – a female Quebec that is recurrently tempted by and rejects the United States, that has a concern about its 'soul' that English Canada ambiguously envies, that has the power to make English Canada feel either loved or abandoned, that says an anguished 'no' to the United States, but both discouragingly and encouragingly gives neither an absolute 'yes' nor 'no' to Roy Smith or English Canadians. Either answer would, in a sense, destroy the Caprice whom Roy loves, and end her narrative:

'Are you going to come back?' asked Roy Smith.

   She let go his hand and lifted her braids from her chest and let them fall to her back. Then she put on her tight gloves.

'That is for history to tell,' she said. (265)

The text ends, not with a marriage, which it implies would erase difference, or with an individual killing, which it has defined after Goethe as an overreaching of the individual, but with actions that affirm both community and difference. Spencer, who dislikes difference, who 'speaks with an accent from Tennessee, and ... shoots people who do not' (158), is executed by the law following a breakfast of 'a pot of British tea' (259). Caprice is given a horse collectively purchased by Soo Woo, Gert the Whore, Doc Trump, Cyril Trump, Arpad Kesselring, the wealthy Briton H.P. Cornwall, and Charlie Minjus, town photographer. The two Indians teach Everyday Luigi sign language. Roy Smith stays at his Indian school, while Caprice returns both to the East and sunrise and her own language. ' "*Couple, adieu; je vais voir l'ombre que tu devins,*" ' she quotes Mallarmé, as she rides into her own future and Roy's past. But the narrator's last words are paradoxically about the end of difference – 'She rode eastward through the west that was becoming nearly as narrow as her trail' (266) – and returns to a fear it declared earlier: 'the future of the west was going to be the east' (108). Caprice survives as woman, francophone, and poet, but 'western' difference, 'Indian eyes,' are threatened by well-meaning Easterners like the schoolteacher she abandons. The narrator's last act of destabilization here constitutes Caprice, and with her Quebec, as a nostalgic lost Western 'difference,' a future that is now the West's past, a text that is not properly a 'western' but only a caprice.

This Land That Is like Every Land
Obasan

The first reaction of the people that I experienced was in Kaslo. And there, the girls told me that they thought there would be little monkeys coming out of the train. They went to greet the first train that arrived with the Japanese evacuees, and they thought that all would be slant-eyed and bow-legged and real short, so they hid in the bushes to see what we'd look like. That was their first experience with the Japanese. Anyhow, when the girls came off, boy, they were just like fashion models and they all looked pretty, and they said, 'Gee, we expected something very different.' But this was later when we got closer and they confided in us.

> Tom Oikawa, in Cassandra Kobayashi and Roy Miki, eds., *Spirit of Redress* (1989), 127

The five novels considered to this point have all in some way viewed Canada under the sign of difference. They have offered various grounds for this difference and attached various idealizations to these grounds. Native people have been an important reference point in at least four of these: the source of a utopian, North American vision of nature in *The Temptations of Big Bear*; a model for community and for inter-ethnic cooperation in *Caprice*; the ultimate mark of liberality in the anti-hierarchical values on which *The Diviners* would implicitly found its Canada; and in *Slash* inadvertently the one trans-provincial community able to imagine Canada as a single, dynamic political field. The idealizations offered have been expansive in *Slash*, in which the field of a potentially successful politics grows throughout; fearful and defensive in *Nights below Station Street*; nostalgic in both *Nights below Station Street* and *The Temptations of Big Bear*; and cautious in *Caprice*, in which the ideal of local communities of difference must still negotiate its relation to a surrounding field of international, potentially homogenizing signs. In each novel a community or people has been implicitly offered as a microcosm for a possible nation: the nearly lost rural New Brunswick of Joe Walsh and Allain Garret in *Nights below Station Street*; the spiritual, anti-instrumental, ecologically aware 'North American' aboriginal culture of *The Temptations of Big Bear*; in *The Diviners* the laissez-faire relationship Morag establishes with Jules (a relationship which encodes models for both English-French and aboriginal-white interactions); in *Caprice* the community of Nicola with its implicit model of a Canadian polis of diversities.

In Joy Kogawa's 1981 novel *Obasan*, however, this perception of Canada as characterized by difference is replaced by an emphasis on harmony, and the figurations of Canada as in conflict with, or conflicted by, ideologies and practices imported from other nations and cultures are replaced by emphasis on the shared experiences and desires of humanity.

If I could take all the cooked rice in all the rice pots in the world, dump them into a heap and tromp all the bits to glue with my feet, there would be enough to stick anything, even Humpty Dumpty, together again.

Obasan, 115

At first glance the political role of Joy Kogawa's *Obasan* seems straightforward enough – to rewrite the story of Canada's Second World War persecution of its citizens of Japanese origin from the point-of-view of those citizens, and to inscribe this retelling into Canadian memory and literary history: as the cover of the Penguin paperback edition summarizes, 'A moving novel of a time and a suffering we have tried to forget.' The book shrewdly repositions newspaper articles and government communications concerning the internment of Japanese Canadians within the story of a small child's loss of parents, home, and self-esteem, so that the blindness, arrogance, and cruelty of those discourses can be illumined. Within the text of that child's story, however, lurk conflicts – about how that story might best be told, how best to explain the oppression the Japanese Canadians have suffered, what cultural strategies might best suit them, and what kind of Canada they should work towards.

Throughout the novel these conflicts complicate and problematize its narration and make difficult a reader's assignment of viewpoint to characters, the text, or the text's signator. As in the case of many first-person narratives the boundaries of this narrative are unclear. The text opens with a biblical epigraph (Revelations 2:17), continues with an author's note that acknowledges the 'use' of 'documents and letters' from the Public Archives of Canada, begins a first-person narrative on the final preliminary page, continues with a long first-person narration by Naomi Nakane that may or may not continue the initial narrative, and concludes with a three-page excerpt from a 1946 memorandum by 'The Co-operative Committee on Japanese Canadians to the House and the Senate of Canada.' Although this excerpt is not tagged or framed so as to assign its selection and quotation to Naomi's or another narrative, its three page numbers extend the page sequence of Naomi's story.

Among the questions a reader must ponder is who 'writes' Naomi's first-person narration? – that is, is this narration a written public discourse in which Naomi herself breaks some of the social silence that has surrounded the Japanese internment or is it a private discourse, an 'interior narrative,' Naomi speaking to herself, converted into written form by the public discourse of Kogawa's novel? Who selects the biblical epigraph – is it Naomi's interpretation of her own experience or an authorial comment on the narrative to follow? Who verbalizes the first-person paragraph that concludes the preliminary pages – the author, or one of the characters, most likely Naomi, from the narrative that begins on the facing page? Who appends the excerpt from the 1946 memorandum – is it part of Naomi's narrative, or is it added by another narrative agent to generalize the novel's focus? Such questions address relationships among signator, character, and narrative. Although all of any text is ultimately 'devised' by its various constructors, in a first-person narrative much of the narrative construction – the manner in which its events are verbalized, the sequence in which they are presented – operates as character-construction and can be read as being relativized or ironized by the frame of this character's narrating activity. In *Obasan*, for example, the narration's revealing of Aunt Emily's diary only when Naomi reads it, its frequent slipping between past and present tense in its flashbacks, and its particular selection of incidents and documents can be attributed to Naomi's narrating presence, her individual perspective and interests. But the selection of Naomi as focalizing character, the use of a first-person perspective, the giving to Naomi of particular experiences – being molested as a small child by a white next-door neighbour, being saved from drowning by a white recluse – can be attributed only to a narrative constructor who selects and places these elements in the fiction.

At a thematic level a variety of points of view on Japanese-Canadian culture are offered by *Obasan*. Many of these are associated with the three generations of immigrant experience perceived by the culture: the first-generation Japanese-born *Issei*, the second-generation Canadian-born *Nisei*, and the third-generation *Sansei*. The novel presents the Issei, particularly in the persons of the title character and her husband, as inclined towards silence and forgetting, as hoping not for full social participation in their new country, but merely to be harassed as little as possible. It presents the Nisei as more activist – eager to participate in Canadian society, angry and indignant about their wartime treatment, and naïvely trusting that protest and appeals to law will bring redress. The foremost character here is Emily, to Naomi 'Aunt Emily, BA MA, ... a word warrior ... a crusader, a little old grey-haired Mighty Mouse, a Bachelor of Advanced Activists and General Practitioner of Just Causes' (32). For over thirty years Emily has gathered documents, written to government commissions and officials, and compiled her personal record of the internment and its consequences. Her indignation is echoed by that of other Nisei characters – the newspaper editor Tom Shoyama, the student nurses Eiko and Fumi. Emily's motto from Habakkuk, 'Write the vision and make it plain' (31), is itself somewhat echoed in the publisher's cover copy, which terms Kogawa's text a 'powerful, passionate ... novel [that] tells ... the moving story of Japanese Canadians ...' Emily's vision is positivist and idealist; it relies on facts, documents, and universal principle; it trusts the institutions of the nation to eventually 'get the facts straight.' 'What's right is right. What's wrong is wrong,' she tells Naomi (183). Although this is indeed an activist vision, its reliance on 'rightness' leads it away from careful political analysis or pragmatic political action. The Sansei, dispersed geographically as a consequence of internment, deprived by it of a Japanese-speaking community, and vulnerable to assimilation into other communities, are as a group unrepresented in the novel. The two Sansei characters, Naomi and her brother Stephen, are constructed as individuals who lead dissimilar lives, have little if any contact with other Sansei, and thus little opportunity or motive to act socially or politically.

The novel affiliates itself decisively with each of these groups, and yet by affiliating itself with all three subverts the strength of each affiliation. Its title character is an Issei, its point-of-view character is a Sansei, and the character whose research activities focus its action and whose idealist philosophical views inform the lengthy quotation with which it concludes is a Nisei. Many critical responses to the novel have seen it as a Nisei text which, like Aunt Emily herself, directs attention to the documentary record and seeks just and rational redress for factual wrongs.[1] There are considerable difficulties, however, with any reading that would reduce *Obasan* to Emily's activist, positivist, Nisei position – despite the text's ending with one of the documents on which she has based her faith. The novel's title character remains an Issei, one who embodies the modesty, unassuming kindness, and self-effacement required by what the text presents as the traditional Japanese concept of *yasashi* (51). This *yasashi* perspective is reinforced by the text's disapproval of those who are *wagamama*, who 'try to meet [their] own needs despite the wishes of others' (128) and by the prominence its opening and closing chapters give to Obasan's husband and to his yearnings for 'natural' harmony. The novel's focalizing character continues to be the Sansei Naomi, who early in the novel questions Emily's positivism, saying that 'the truth for me is more murky, shadowy and grey' (32), and whose 'Mighty Mouse' characterization of Emily carries at very least some ironic reserve. The most powerful document among Emily's papers, a letter from Naomi's Issei grandmother from the ruins of Nagasaki to her husband back in Canada, works to subvert Emily's positivism. The letter is foregrounded as an Issei text, *yasashi* in tone, and framed by apology – ' "For the burden of these words, forgive me" ' (236).

Further subverting affiliation with any of the Issei, Nisei, and Sansei generations is the prominence the novel gives within each of these to female characters. Although their inherited Japanese culture is one of male privilege, Naomi's Issei grandfathers are portrayed by the text as faltering in confusion at the sudden onslaught of events the Second World War unleashes; her Issei uncle retreats into nostalgia for his old way of life; her Nisei father becomes disheartened and increasingly vulnerable to the TB from which he suffers; and her Sansei brother Stephen openly rejects Japanese culture in hope of becoming a raceless international musician. In contrast, the characters made to 'speak' most forcefully within the novel are women, who thereby break with the Japanese woman's traditional confinement to silence or unprovocative discourse: Grandmother Sato, who writes to her husband of the horrors of Nagasaki; Emily, who publicly questions government policy; and Naomi, who finally pronounces the

1 For example, Marilyn Russell Rose, 'Politics into Art: Kogawa's *Obasan* and the Rhetoric of Fiction,' *Mosaic* 21, nos. 2–3 (Spring 1988), 215–26; Mason Harris, 'Broken Generations in *Obasan*: Inner Conflicts and Destruction of Community,' *Canadian Literature* 127 (Winter 1990), 41–61

'wordlessness' of herself and her mother to have entailed their 'mutual destruction' (243). Within the context of Japanese culture *Obasan* thus offers itself as a feminist novel, in which women occupy the major narrative roles and in which its two major narrative agents, Naomi and Emily, are single because of an apparent lack of worthy men.

Between the river and Uncle's spot are the wild roses and the tiny wildflowers that grow along the trickling stream. The perfume in the air is sweet and faint. If I hold my head a certain way, I can smell them from where I am.

Obasan, 247

Framing Naomi's narrative are her descriptions of a small coulee near the southern Alberta town to which she and her aunt and uncle were eventually exiled. The coulee is the favourite place of Naomi and her uncle, a place which her descriptions invest with permanence and beauty. 'The coulee is so still right now that if a match were to be lit, the flame would not waver,' she begins her story (1). The coulee is primitive, primordial. 'Everything in front of us is virgin land. From the beginning of time, the grass along this stretch of prairie has not been cut.' It telescopes history: 'About a mile east is a spot which was once an Indian buffalo jump ... All the bones are still there, some sticking right out of the side of a fresh landslide.' It affiliates, or is made by the text to affiliate, the two Japanese Canadians with aboriginal North Americans. 'Uncle could be Chief Sitting Bull squatting here. He has the same prairie-baked skin, the deep brown furrows like dry river beds creasing his cheeks. All he needs is a feather headdress, and he would be perfect for a picture postcard – "Indian Chief from Canadian Prairie" – souvenir of Alberta, made in Japan'(2).

The images given this coulee – ancient, natural, aboriginal – announce a movement throughout the text to 'naturalize' the Japanese Canadians by associating them with organic signs familiar to readers of Western literature: the North American native, the natural landscape that transcends time and politics, the Wordsworthian refuge that compensates for social cruelties:

The first time Uncle and I came here for a walk was in 1954, in August, two months after Aunt Emily's initial visit to Granton. For weeks after she left, Uncle seemed distressed, pacing back and forth, his hand patting the back of his head. Then one evening, we came here.

It was a quiet twilight evening, much like tonight. His agitation seemed to abate as we walked through the waving grass, though his eyes still stabbed at the air around him and occasionally at me. (2)

This affiliation with nature, together with an insistence that Japanese Canadians are part of a universal nature and universal humanity, involve only Issei and Sansei characters. As here, it excludes Aunt Emily, whose focus on the social rather than the natural is made to appear responsible for the agitation which Naomi's uncle has come to the coulee to heal.

Naomi's return to the coulee in the final paragraphs of her narrative to seek relief from the pain she has felt at learning how her mother died, to seek comfort in the coulee's affirmations of universality and continuity – 'the underground stream seeps through the earth' (247) – repeats a persistent pattern in her life of retreat from the social to the natural: from the sexual aggression of Old Man Gower to seasonal certainties of her backyard peach tree, from the pain of separation from her father and loss of her Vancouver home to delight in the 'oilcloth ... with tiny daisies and blue flowers' and the 'bright flowered curtains' with which Obasan has alleviated the shabbiness of the shanty to which they have been temporarily assigned.

Repeatedly Naomi seeks to be reassured about the unity of existence and the universality of human experience. Her reflections on her past are structured around images of unity and fracture, of community and diaspora – a group photograph of her family (17), a 'family of dolls' she was forced to leave behind on internment (52), recurring thoughts about the Humpty Dumpty story and of reassembling its broken hero. The musical abilities of several members of her family suggest to her family harmony, a family harmony punctuated with 'natural' images of eagle, crane, fern, and goldfish:

Here they are in the music room in the evening, before dark, Mother in her chair beside Stephen who sits on the piano stool with its eagle-claw feet clutching three glass globes.

...

Stephen's practice time each night is half play. Father, with his violin bow raised dramatically, bobs in time to the music ... Everything about Father is precise and graceful as the milk-white porcelain crane, its beak pointing straight up from its long smooth neck.

I am sitting in my nemaki on the wicker chair beside the fern, eating a tea biscuit and watching the goldfish with their little round mouths puckering open and closed endlessly. We three, the goldfish and I, are the listeners in the room, as Mother sings and Stephen and Father play. (51)

In another combination of images from nature and music Naomi's fantasies about the Indian myth of the 'King bird' envision it as a master musician holding the world from dissolution: 'Perhaps, I am thinking, the King bird was a conductor that called all the birds together to some auditorium in the woods where people couldn't go. Perhaps they sang together, a great bird choir, each bird adding its part to the melody, till some catastrophe happened and the song disappeared into chirps and tweets' (142).[2] Such an image of harmonic synthesis later becomes the basis for her praise of her internment community of Bayfarm, a community

alive and kicking like Ezekiel's resurrected valley of bones, the foot bones connected to the ankle bones, the ankle bones connected to the leg bones, and all them bones, jitterbugging in the Odd Fellows Hall ... There are craftsmen carving ornaments and utensils from tree stumps, roots and driftwood, making basins, bins, spoons, flower stands, bowls, building wooden flumes, bathhouses, meeting halls.

...

One place that we meet regularly is the public bathhouse. It smells of wet cloth and wet wood and wet skin. We are one flesh, one family, washing each other or submerged in the hot water ... (160)

Again the impression of social unity is linked to images of nature, as the craftsmen transform stumps, roots, and driftwood into the halls and bathhouses in the 'wet wood' of which the community members can become 'one flesh.'

Such images of social harmony, together with images that suggest

2 Evidence that this music image for the harmony of Japanese-Canadian culture may have been part of the wartime discourse of their community is contained in journalist Laura E. Jameson's merging of music and concepts of communal sharing in her August 1941 article 'Where White and Brown Men Meet' when she writes: 'Walking through the Japanese quarter in the evening, one invariably hears music, usually a piano. Sometimes classical pieces are being played, sometimes scales. There are not many pianos, one serving several families. Little girls take their turn going to a neighbour's house after school to practice' (*Canadian Forum* 21, no. 247 [1941], 146).

both the unity of nature and Japanese-Canadian participation in Wordsworthian nature, combine in a passage in which Naomi offers her personal political analysis of Canadian cultural structure and the Japanese Canadians' place in it:

> Where do any of us come from in this cold country? Oh Canada, whether it is admitted or not, we come from you we come from you. From the same soil, the slugs and slime and bogs and twigs and roots. We come from the country that plucks its people out like weeds and flings them into the roadside. We grow in ditches and sloughs, untended and spindly. We erupt in the valleys and mountainsides, in small towns and back alleys, sprouting upside-down on the prairies, our hair wild as spiders' legs, our feet rooted nowhere. We grow where we are not seen, we flourish where we are not heard, the thick undergrowth of an unlikely planting. Where do we come from Obasan? We come from cemeteries full of skeletons with wild roses in their grinning teeth. We come from our untold tales that wait for their telling. We come from Canada, this land that is like every land, filled with the wise, the fearful, the compassionate, the corrupt. (226)

The passage posits a universal nature, an 'every land,' within which the Japanese Canadians, 'sprouting,' 'rooted,' can claim membership and thus make a further claim to membership in universal humanity similar to that made by the reminiscence of Tom Oikawa at the beginning of this chapter. The plenitude represented by this figure of universal humanity ostensibly compensates the Japanese Canadians for the loss of their social community, much like that of Morag's mysterious river is made to appear to cancel out all the social injustices of *The Diviners*. The founding of the figure on a view of the physical world as organically whole and harmonious distinguishes it from Emily's positivist appeals for political redress on the basis of rational justice.

> Once they were reconciled to the uncertainties, the singular existence of ghost town confinement did not need to be unbearable nor restricting. On the contrary, most, both young and old, readily adapted to the life in limbo which might be agreeable so long as they ignored the realities of the 'outside world.' The spirit of 'we're all in the same boat' drifted through the camps as they schemed ways to whittle away the time, of which there was plenty. A flurry of planned activities – weekly dances, regular movies,

concerts, baseball in summer, skating in winter – awakened the sleeping ghost towns.

Toyo Takata, *Nikkei Legacy* (1983), 134

Naomi's yearnings for a return to 'natural' unity, dramatically enacted in her various returns to her uncle's beloved coulee, firmly mark the structure of the novel. The hermeneutic of the narrative concerns what happened in the past, specifically Naomi's question 'Why did my mother not return?' (26). The direction of the narrative is to recapture the 'wholeness' of her life before her mother's departure and her family's destruction – to recapture a family that was 'the original "togetherness" people,' to become the 'leaf in the wind restored to its branch' (170). Its fulfilment is not specifically Naomi's recovery of the documentary materials gathered by Emily, but her achievement of the mythical union of uncle's coulee, mother, earth, and sky which these documents enable:

> Gradually the room grows still and it is as if I am back with Uncle again, listening and listening to the silent earth and the silent sky as I have done all my life.
> I close my eyes.
> Mother. I am listening. Assist me to hear you. (240)

The chapter which follows, the second-last narrative chapter, addresses the mother in the same terms of organic unity with which the lost family 'harmony' had been described: 'You are a tide rushing moonward pulling back from the shore' (241); 'Your leg is a tree trunk and I am branch, vine, butterfly. I am joined to your limbs by right of birth, child of your flesh, leaf of your bough' (242–3).

Elsewhere Naomi's narrative is punctuated by various passages in which a wounded nature struggles against a militarized positivism, represented by a British soldier (29, 61) or doctor (158), and by recurrent references to European fairy tales. Like the coulee or the natural images associated with Naomi's mother these dreams and fairy tales – 'Snow White in the forest' (64), Goldilocks 'in the middle of the woods' (126), Chicken Little for whom 'the sky is not falling after all' (170) – operate to inscribe Naomi's experiences within universal humanity. Although the child Naomi is perplexed by inconsistencies between these tales and Canadian social practice during the Second World War – the yellow Chicken Little, which resembles the 'yellow peril' of war rhetoric (152), the Goldilocks story, in which she is not sure she is the title character or smallest bear (126) – she clings to the possibility that the general meanings of these stories can include her:

> In one of Stephen's books, there is a story of a child with long golden ringlets called Goldilocks who one day comes to a quaint house in the woods lived in by a family of bears. Clearly, we are that bear family in this strange house in the middle of the woods. I am Baby Bear, whose chair Goldilocks breaks, whose porridge Goldilocks eats, whose bed Goldilocks sleeps in. Or perhaps this is not true and I am really Goldilocks after all. In the morning will I not find my way out of the forest and back to my room where the picture bird sings above my bed and the real bird sings in the real peach tree by my open bedroom window in Marpole? (126)

Located in a book owned by Stephen, the most colonized member of Naomi's family, the story invites interpretation as an allegory for the displacement of Naomi's family by white Canadian culture, for the seizing of the family's property, and its dispersal at token prices to white buyers. Naomi here seems on her way to recognizing this, but in the fourth sentence she abruptly denies the 'Clearly' with which the second began and settles on the less likely ('perhaps') hypothesis. From a parable about her own oppression Naomi transforms the story into one of identification with her oppressors. In the process she writes herself into a hope and power which actual circumstances seem always to refuse her. 'No matter how I wish it, we do not go home' (126).

Goldilocks, Chicken Little and the yellow peril, and Naomi's dreams of abuse by the British officer and the British doctor offer Naomi opportunities to interrogate the racism which has disrupted her life and ended its ostensibly 'natural' harmonies. They also offer the novel opportunities to examine the textual grounds of bias and power, to seek the social causes of the Japanese-Canadian internment. However, both the novel and Naomi decline these possibilities. Naomi clings to notions of universal humanity: 'Greed, selfishness, and hatred remain as constant as the human condition,' she says to herself, in rebuttal of Emily's 'speech-making and story telling' (199). 'Father, Mother ... we have come to the forest tonight, to the place where the colours all meet – red and yellow and blue,' she thinks as she broods over her mother's terrible death (246). The novel, by ending not with the conclusion of Naomi's narrative in her return to the coulee, but with a document from Emily's archive, qualifies Naomi's humanism with an affirmation of the 'speech-making' activism she so sceptically mistrusted: 'the Orders-in-Council [for the deportation of Canadians of Japanese racial origin] are wrong and indefensible and constitute a grave threat to the rights and liberties of Canadian citizens ...' (248). By doing so, however, it does not so much posit a social sphere, such as that of *Caprice*'s Nicola, within which a diverse citizenry may construct justice, as modify one universal explanation, universal nature, with another, universal justice and law.

Obasan never really chooses between the Issei and Nisei positions it foregrounds in its title and concluding document. Its choice of the Sansei Naomi as its narrator and focalizing character reflects its indecision. Naomi is unadventurous, trusts in 'natural' process over personal action, and repeatedly resists Emily's invitations to become a writer and join her 'crusade.' She ties herself instead to the *yasashi* values of the Issei generation, particularly in her attachment to her uncle, to his coulee vision of a prairie landscape that merges with the sea, and to the commitment of her aunt Obasan's generation that its children 'endure' (245). It is through the making of Naomi's story 'public' in the form of the novel that the text moves towards endorsing Emily's call to 'write the vision and make it plain' (31). But there is no evidence in the text that Naomi herself 'does' this making public, that she has been moved by Emily or by her grandmother's painful narrative to construct her own autobiography and thus challenge the received inscriptions of the Japanese Canadian in Canadian textuality. The placement of both the final document and the brief preliminary first-person narration outside of Naomi's narration implies the presence of a textual constructor other than her. The chronological structure of her narration, its series of flashbacks ostensibly triggered by events in an ongoing present, and its lack of reflection on how it should be narrated, all suggest it to be a private interior narrative rendered into the public discourse of the novel through the efforts of the constructor, whose presence is elsewhere indicated. By not making Naomi the writer of her own narrative, the novel discreetly reinforces the *yasashi* values of modesty, self-effacement, and consideration for the feelings of others; by writing this narrative itself, it also endorses Emily's call to 'write the truth.' By writing the narrative in the framework of a universal nature within which a Japanese humanity can be located, it offers a frame that can accommodate both Issei reticence and Nisei activism. The result, however, is a novel that also implicitly accepts the injustices done to Japanese Canadians during 1940–7 as part of the 'human condition' its universalizing strategies have constructed, at the same time as it asserts the equal standing of Japanese, native Indian, and Caucasian ethnicities as parts of an undifferentiated human community. Ideologically it enacts a polite, conciliatory Issei gesture of acceptance towards the white Canadian community which in 1942 supported internment policies, while simultaneously making a Sansei affirmation that a discourse of humanism should replace a discourse of rights and difference. In terms of possible discourses of multiculturalism *Obasan* offers a model in which cultures co-prosper because their commonalities are acknowledged – a model that conflicts considerably with models offered by *Slash*, or even *Caprice*, in which cooperation is only possible if differences are acknowledged and possible divergence (where *Caprice's* leaving of Roy Smith can be read as Quebec's leaving of Canada) accepted. That *Obasan's* model appears to have had some political success, in terms of both federal offers of redress and renewed Japanese-Canadian cultural activity, may have something to do with how its endorsement of universal humanism echoed the 'official' Canadian cultural arguments of Frye and Jones. It may have much to do also with how decisively the internment period transformed the Japanese Canadians from a coherent community, like Canadian aboriginal and Caribbean communities today, into a diaspora people more conscious of commonality than of difference, as well as with how directly the novel has echoed the most powerful discourses of that dispersed community.

Homoerotic Capitalism
The Wars

The whole language of football is involved in sexual allusions. We were told to go out and 'fuck those guys'; to take that ball and 'stick it up their asses' or 'down their throats.' The coaches would yell, 'knock their dicks off,' or more often than that, 'knock their jocks off.' They'd say, 'Go out there and give it all you've got, a hundred and ten per cent, shoot your wad.' You controlled their line and 'knocked 'em into submission.'

Over the years I've seen many a coach get emotionally aroused while he was diagramming a particular play into an imaginary hole on the blackboard. His face red, his voice rising, he would show the ball carrier how he wanted him to 'stick it in the hole.'

David Kopay and Perry Deane Young, *The David Kopay Story*, (1977), 53–4

The First World War has usually been constructed in Canadian history and culture as a national rite of passage. Historians such as Morton (1963), Lower (1946), Brown and Cook (1974), and Finlay and Sprague (1979) have emphasized the national government's success in maintaining the Canadian Expeditionary Force as a separate unit, rather than as merely a source of manpower replacement for British units, and in becoming a separate signator of the Treaty of Versailles. As a result of the war Canada is 'no longer a colony in fact or in image' but 'a nation among the others' (Finlay and Sprague, 303). Popular historians like Pierre Berton have attempted to develop theses that the Canadian units had specific fighting qualities, and that these qualities – whether tenacity, courage, or tactical ingenuity – were significant in giving Canadians a sign of their own distinctness. Some of these theorists, like Daniel Dancocks in 1986 and 1987, emphasize a Canadian recognition of the futility of the tactic of frontal assault favoured throughout the war by most British and French commanders and hint at a contrast between Canadian pragmatism and European traditionalism – that is, between a textually creative culture and a textually determined one. Among the academic historians Lower also makes this argument.

One of the major focuses of dispute over this conception has been the figure of Billy Bishop, the most successful Canadian pilot of the war, with seventy-two confirmed kills and a celebrated solo raid on a German aerodrome. Until recently accounts of Bishop's exploits, like his son's 1965 biography (*The Courage of the Early Morning*), had focused on his individual daring and his extending the text of aerial combat, not only by surpassing the number of 'kills' by other Allied pilots but by conceiving his unauthorized but destructive raid on a German aerodrome. John Gray's 1981 play *Billy Bishop Goes to War* rewrote Bishop somewhat, in terms not of his exploits but of his person. Bishop was constructed by Gray as someone who could have been successful only in wartime, whose restlessness and uneasiness with social convention found expression in individual aerial combat which they could have found neither in civilian life nor in the war's highly ritualized ground combat. Gray's Bishop enjoys war, in part because it is the only thing he does well. On entering combat, in a sense he risks losing nothing since it is only combat which gives his life value. Gray's rewriting of Bishop caused little debate, possibly because its satirical portrait was paradoxically congruent with earlier idealizations and, from the perspective of those who idealized Bishop, imperceptible as satire. However, the 1985 National Film Board *The Kid Who Couldn't Miss* was another story. In this text the anti-social elements evident in Gray's Bishop were extended, so that Bishop becomes not merely someone who disobeys military conventions, but someone who lies – who claims credit for other airmen's kills and whose celebrated aerodrome raid is a cynical fantasy. Public response to this film included attempts by Conservative politicians to reduce National Film Board funding and pressure from veterans' associations which eventually caused the Board to restrict showings of the film and to commission a second Bishop film from a more favourable perspective. The controversy over Bishop arose, to some extent, from his having 'become' Canada in the public imagination – the rebellious youth who understood strategy better than his elders, the colonial who outfought the privileged aristocrats who are popularly believed to have populated the air corps on both sides, the young airman who rises to be a general in the country's own Royal Canadian Air Force by the Second World War.

It is into this construction of the war that Timothy Findley inserts his protagonist, Robert Ross, in writing his 1977 novel *The Wars*. Ross, however, is no 'wild colonial boy' – he is the son of a privileged Toronto family whose affluence is based on the industrialization of southern Ontario, an affluence that will be increased during the war by its sale of tractors to the British army. This family, and its social relations, are already highly textualized, particularly in their gender patterns. In fact the 'innocent' or 'restless' Canadian, unfamiliar with authority and resistant to it, as constructed in the early biographies of Bishop or later in Birney's Second World War novel *Turvey*, is not to be found anywhere in *The Wars*.

The narrative strategy of *The Wars*, like that of realist fiction, attempts to divert the reader from awareness of the constructedness of the text and its characters. The topos of the novel is that of archive, interview, and documentary research. The novel offers two narratives, one of the search of an unnamed narrator into the history of the unfortunate Robert Ross, and the second that narrator's hypothetical reconstruction of that history. Behind this reconstruction is the implication that there was a 'real' Robert Ross, that the events near Magdalene Wood that day on the 16th of June in 1915 'really' happened, despite their survival only in 'stories' and 'mythology' (181). The novel's inclusion of characters from 'history' – Siegfried Sassoon, Virginia and Leonard Woolf, Sir Sam Hughes – rather than creating an effect of metafiction, in which the historical is recast as fiction, serves to further anchor the Ross story in seemingly 'actual' events. In one sense the narrative structure of the book involves three layers of construction[1] – a text

---

1 Simone Vauthier (16–26) argues a somewhat different set of narrative layers: an implied author (indicated by the signing of the text), a scriptor (indicated by the arranging and repetition of elements within the text), an I-narrator (indicated by an intradiegetic 'you' which she reads as this narrator's addressing of the character who researches Ross's story), and an impersonal narrator who narrates the events of Ross's life. Her locating of a separate I-narrator and impersonal narrator allows her to posit an undermining of narrative authority in the text, since these two both have access to the interviews the researcher has conducted, and since the boundaries between the two narrators frequently blur. In my reading the 'you' employed by the I-narrator does not address the researcher specifically, but is a familiar replacement for 'we,' having a similar weight to that of the French 'on.' It indicates that the I-narrator is the researcher and wishes to invite the reader to share his or her own research position. The impersonal narration can be read as a second narrative voice of the I-narrator.

which constructs a researcher who in turn constructs the Ross story from archival records and from a third level of construction in which two aging women, in interviews, recall their encounters with Ross. The distinctness of these layers, however, has little effect on the text overall, which, if anything, affiliates itself with the perspectives of the researcher and the two women. The only constructions subject to irony in the novel are the archival photographs, annotations, and newspaper clippings, which are pointedly relativized by the narrator.

———————————

It is the heavily scripted character of Canada of 1914 which *The Wars* posits and emphasizes:

> Here is the Boys' Brigade with band. Backyard minstrels, got up in cork, bang their tambourines and strut across a lawn on Admiral Road. Every parlour has its pianos: here are soldiers, arm in arm and singing, *'Keep Your Head Down, Fritzie Boy!'* Tea-Dance partners do the Castlewalk to orchestras of brass cornets and silver saxophones. Violins have been retired. (6–7)

From the beginning of the novel Robert Ross is subject to this scripting and yet also puzzled by it:

> Robert was supposed to be 'interested' in Heather Lawson but the fact was it was she who was interested in him. Not that Robert didn't like her – only that he wasn't interested. 'Interested' led to marriage and this is what Heather Lawson wanted. So did her parents. Robert was a fine catch for any girl. He was a scholar and an athlete. Besides – he had money. (10)

Robert is particularly puzzled when Heather Lawson tells him that someone else was in love with her and that he 'ought to fight him':

> 'Because he *loves* me,' she said. She spoke as if Robert were stupid. It all made perfect sense to Heather, but Robert thought it was idiotic and said so. Heather wailed out loud at that. Wailed and railed and paled. And fainted. In short – she made 'a scene' of the sort then popular in the books of Booth Tarkington. (15)

The text ties together in these passages the social rules of eros and of war. Men are expected to desire and love women, and to express this love through violent interactions with men. The close relationship between love and violence is repeated a few pages later when, after his hydrocephalic sister has died in a fall, his mother orders him to kill her pet rabbits. He must do this, she tells his father, 'BECAUSE HE LOVED HER' (20).

The implication here is that war itself is textually determined and produced, an implication that is made explicit elsewhere in the book. When an Atlantic storm strikes his troopship, Robert is called upon to shoot an injured horse but is unable to figure out how until he recalls 'that somewhere in *Chums* – as a boy – he'd seen a picture of a cowboy shooting his horse behind the ear' (68). On that voyage one of his fellow officers is described as so 'deadly serious' about the war that 'every night before he went to sleep he stood at the bridge with Horatio – brought the news from Aix to Ghent and smiling, fell dead. He said "you're damned right" a lot, and spent a good deal of his time in the bathroom, secretly tilting his hat and his grin at the mirror' (60). Robert's expectations about an ocean voyage are also textual – 'by way of Joseph Conrad and *The Boy's Own Annual*' (58). The inappropriateness of these expectations foreshadows how the war in which he is going to participate will transcend its textual causes – whether these be *Boy's Own Annual* romanticizing or the rational analyses of von Clauswitz favoured as battlefield reading by Lieutenant Levitt. The war that is textually anticipated and caused also renders books themselves silent and useless; after the novel's central battle and the destruction of the Canadian trenches and dugouts, Levitt's books are 'piled beside him – scorched almost beyond recognition. Certainly, they could never be read again' (153).

While the script for men emphasizes adventure and carefree death – the researcher comments about one of Ross's solemn army portraits that it says 'death is romantic ... the hero sighs his way to death while linen handkerchiefs are held against his wounds. His wounds are poems' (49–50) – the society's preferred script for women is passivity. The sign of women in *The Wars* is Robert's hydrocephalic sister Rowena, with passive body and useless head. Women's principal functions are to join men together and to provide men the role of looking after them. Their role is only indirectly sexual – as a socially accepted site for the concealed autoeroticism and homoeroticism of men. Rowena's last social action is to be passed by Robert to his brother Stuart, so that Robert can go to his room to masturbate.

Women's position in this culture is peripheral, on the sidelines of parade squares or battlefields, admiring soldiers or assisting doctors, or on the edges of attractions between men. As Heather Lawson's wish that Robert fight for her suggests, they are dependent on men's quarrels for both entertainment and significance. In London, when Barbara d'Orsey takes her present lover Taffler to visit her mortally wounded lover Jamie Villiers, it is Taffler who speaks to him, while Barbara remains detached and silent. Robert's mother's principal infatuation has been her debonair brother Monty Miles Raymond – 'everyone's favourite young man' (70) – who had been killed by a streetcar, and whose death has left her crippled with self-pity and unable to love her husband or son. 'Birth I can give you – but life I cannot,' she tells Robert. 'I can't keep anyone alive. Not any more' (25).

The marriage between her and Robert's father has united her late father's machine shop and her husband's carriage-making business, creating the farm machinery firm 'RAYMOND/ROSS Industries.' Although she has married Thomas Ross after the trauma of the deaths of her brother and father, not for love ('being loved' put 'all you had in life ... in jeopardy' [157]), but for security, the novel's foregrounding of the 'RAYMOND/ROSS' trade mark suggests that, in effect, this has been a male marriage, one between the Raymond and Ross businesses, in which she has merely been the locus of the transaction. This suggestion is reinforced by the number of occasions in the text in which women serve as homoerotic links between men. Barbara d'Orsey's first lover, Jamie Villiers, is her brother Clive's best friend. When she persists in 'tagging along' with them, Clive tells her 'she was mucking up a friendship,' and her sister clarifies, *'Don't you know anything about boys at all? They're in love with each other'* (113). Later Barbara becomes involved with other pairs of men, with Robert and Harris, and with Taffler and Jamie. At the army training camp it is the nearby brothel, 'Wet Goods,' which initiates the soldiers into male comradeship – 'If you didn't go, you were peculiar. It was that simple ... Either you "do" or you "don't" and if you "don't" you face a kind of censure most men would rather avoid' (36). As with marriage and war the brothel exists within a firmly written social script.

The covert homoeroticism of the brothel is made overt at the end of a long narrative when Ella allows Robert to peek into the adjacent room, where his friend Taffler, 'lying on his back' and pretending to be a 'bucking,' ridden horse, sodomizes his eager rider, the 'male mute' bouncer, Swede. Robert's extreme reaction, smashing Ella's mirror and a water jug one by one with his boots, the leather of which suddenly seems to have a 'human feel' (45), suggests that he may not be unfamiliar with such desires himself, as well as suggesting what can happen to women who get entangled in violent passions between men.

One of the principal questions of *The Wars* is what roles are open to men in such a deeply scripted and covertly homoerotic society, and what becomes – actually or symbolically – to the penis/phallus. One possible role is looking after the woman, as Robert looks after Rowena and his father looks after his mother. The advantage of this role is that by identifying with the woman he looks after, the man can indirectly provide himself with the love not given by any woman. Rowena is 'the first human being' Robert remembers seeing. 'When she smiled, he thought she was his mother. Later, when he came to realize she couldn't walk and never left the chair, he became her guardian. It was for her he learned to run' (9). The text here blurs the distinction between the physically and mentally crippled Rowena and the emotionally crippled Mrs Ross. In guarding Rowena, Robert both guards his mother and replaces her, not merely with Rowena but with his affection for Rowena – becoming in a sense his own mother. But this relationship leaves the penis unaccounted for and leads to his entrusting Rowena to his brother Stuart, so that he can go to his room to masturbate.

While Robert is masturbating, and while Stuart is elsewhere teasing the family pony by whirling a phallic 'baseball bat above her head' (18), Rowena falls to her death from her wheelchair. The penis that is unaccommodated in heterosexual relationships in *The Wars* is dangerous, becomes an instrument of death, and ultimately becomes the guns and flame-throwers of the war. When the text next shows Robert masturbating, it positions him a few miles from the front. 'Bang-bang-bang! went the guns ... He slept with his fist in its place and the cold wet blooming of four hundred thousand possibilities – of all those lives that would never be – on his fingertips' (193–94). Here, in the place of one death, there are now four hundred thousand; this four hundred thousand is in turn linked by the guns' 'bang-bang-bang' which accompanies it to another figure, the 557,017 the text has told us a few pages earlier have been killed in the novel 'so far' (185).

The penis in these scenes is figured as a misfiring gun, a weapon that kills unpredictably and indiscriminately. It is similarly characterized when Robert and his companions visit the brothel; Robert cannot perform and ensure that his partner Ella receives her payment

from the madam because he 'had ejaculated coming up the stairs'
(42). The guns of the text are in turn phallicized. When Robert must
shoot the injured horse in the hold of the troopship, his gun fires
weakly, like his penis at the brothel:

He took his aim ...
   He fired.

  ...

   The air in front of him was filled with little fires but the horse was not
dead ...
   Robert forced his eyes to open: aimed – and fired again. This time the
horse was hit on the withers. Robert sank to his knees. He could hear
himself breathing. He held the gun in both hands ... He began to squeeze
the trigger and he squeezed it again and again and again ...
   ... Robert ... walked away with the gun dangling down from his finger.
(68–9)

Two major portions of the text make this equation of gun and
phallus explicit. The first is the scene in which Robert encounters
Taffler on the open prairie hurling stones at bottles lined up on a
board. 'He didn't miss once' (31). Taffler comments bitterly that the
war pits 'one little David against another,' which leads Robert to
speculate that Taffler appears to be seeking 'a Goliath,' a worthy
enemy, that for him 'war wasn't good enough unless it was bigger
than he was' (33). When Robert later sees Taffler having intercourse
with Swede, he identifies Swede as Goliath. In terms of the textual
structure David and Goliath become an additional homoerotic pair,
worthy enemies, linked by the phallic gun that joins Taffler to Swede.
The second major part of the text that links gun and phallus is the
scene in which Robert is raped by a group of fellow soldiers in the
baths at Bailleul, in a cell which he associates with the dugout that
collapsed upon him at the front. Here one sees sexuality transformed
by the war into mere aggression – his legs 'forced apart,' his body
'probed,' 'poked,' and 'entered' with a 'terrible strength ... of force.'
Robert's main thoughts here concern emasculation – he has just lost
his handgun, misplaced with his pack on his way from England; his
first response to the attack is to 'cover his scrotum' with his hand;
his third thought afterwards is 'he wanted his pistol' (200–1).
   The pistol Robert has lost is the focus of another important part
of the text in which the symbolic authority with which this society

invests the phallic gun is made clear. Robert is not provided with a sidearm by the Canadian army but must obtain one from his father. The passing of the gun from father to son takes place in the railway yards of Montreal, and without the participation of Robert's mother, whom railway tracks paralyse with memories of her brother's death. The father comes here in his private Raymond/Ross railway car, symbol of his own authority. He sees giving the gun to Robert as almost ceremonial: 'He had brought Robert down a hamper of food as well as the Colt revolver in its wooden box. He wanted these gifts to pass from hand to hand' (73). He had handed him the box and 'cautioned him not to open it until the train had started moving' (51). But it is the wrong gun – not one of the .455 Webley Mark I automatics that are 'wonderful to fire, and ... kill at fifty yards' (70) but a Colt .45 revolver that on the troopship is not 'wonderful' to fire and cannot kill a horse at one yard. Eventually Robert does obtain his Webley .455, not directly from his father's hands, but through the Raymond/ Ross representative in London. These events suggest not only the replacement of the personal by the industrial, but also a breakdown in the handing on of male sexuality and authority from father to son. The penis Robert has inherited goes off prematurely at the brothel or inadvertently causes the death of his sister; the gun he receives from his father is the wrong one and fires only weakly into the injured horse. The gun the father wants to give him is a 'Colt,' a young horse, and distantly related to the organic. But the powerful phalluses of this society are unambiguously industrial – the 'Webley .455 Mark I,' twelve-inch howitzers dragged by 'RAYMOND/ROSS steam-driven tractors' (195), and field guns that 'probed with deeper and deeper bursts into the heart of the marketplace and railway yards' (214–5). They are carried by men 'specially trained in "liquid warfare,"' 'carrying tanks of fire on their backs,' who 'spread the fire with hoses' (151). As industrial objects these weapons are linked with the father's private railway car and with the streetcar that emotionally crippled Robert's mother by killing her dashing brother.

Deploying a violent and implicitly misogynous discourse that can be found throughout contemporary North American entertainment and sports – as in the remarks of National Football League running back Dave Kopay at the head of this chapter – *The Wars* constructs all authority as male, homoerotic, and savage. Although there is a suggestion in many of the most vivid passages that the phallus is misused in war, the text offers no construction of its non-violent use.

The only heterosexual union that is portrayed, between Robert and Barbara, is framed not only by her habitual involvement with pairs of affectionate men but by Juliet's strained account of it:

> I knew in a cool, clear way at the back of my mind that this was 'making love' – but the shape of it confused me. The shape and the violence. Barbara was lying on the bed, so her head hung down and I thought that Robert must be trying to kill her. They were both quite naked. He was lying on top of her and shaking her with his whole body ... Robert's neck was full of blood and his veins stood out. He hated her. And Barbara's hand was in her mouth. (183)

The scenes of homosexual union are even more violent – Robert's rape in the bathhouse, Taffler on his back 'lifting the weight' of Swede 'with his shoulders and his knees – and bucking, just like the mustangs Robert and others had broken in the summer.' 'The rider ... using a soldier's stiff-peaked cap, beat the horse on the thighs – one side and then the other' (44). The one suggestion of the 'good phallus' in *The Wars* is the officer Rodwell, who has a young daughter he writes to and who cares for toads, birds, rabbits, and hedgehogs he has rescued in the trenches. But this phallus is also problematical – its love is paternal rather than sexual and can operate only in unequal rather than equal relationships. The only sexual possibility constructed by the novel remains an immensely destructive homoeroticization of society which excludes women from both power and adult male affection, and condemns men to self-destructive sado-masochistic violence among themselves.

> [Robert] spent a good deal of time in the hold and – oddly – found it was a marvellous cure for seasickness. He became intrigued with this world of horses, rats and bilge that had been consigned to his care. It took on a life entirely of its own – presided over by the booming B.S.M. and watched from its towers of hay by the pale and looming faces of the pickets in their masks. Robert soon became completely disengaged from the other life on the upper decks. He even went below off duty.
>
> *The Wars*, 63

The alternative to homoerotic phallic authority offered by *The Wars* is a relationship to an animal. This is the alternative to which Rowena and Robert both turn in caring for her rabbits, and which Robert chooses in preferring the companionship of the horses stabled below decks to that of his fellow officers above. In the first months of his army experience Robert encounters a coyote while jogging alone across the Canadian prairie. The coyote leads him to a small hidden lake and valley, where it drinks and leaves him to bathe – 'it looked directly at him – right at Robert, with its tail slightly lowered – and barked ... Now it was telling Robert the valley was vacant: safe – and that Robert could proceed to the water's edge to drink.' Robert is late returning from his run. 'His punishment was that he was confined to barracks for two weeks. In the evenings he sat on the roof and stared and stared across the prairie – wishing that someone would howl' (30). The contrast the text proposes here is one between the pastoral valley and confinement to barracks, between water and punishment, between safety and arbitrary regulation.

This contrast is similar to that which informs the climactic event of the novel: Robert's attempt to save from enemy shelling some thirty each of horses and mules he has just delivered to the battalion stables, despite being forbidden to do so by his commanding officer, Captain Leather. Prevented from freeing more than half of them before incoming shellfire destroys the stable area, Robert looks at the crippled and dying horses and thinks 'if an animal had done this – we would call it mad and shoot it and at that precise moment Captain Leather rose to his knees and began to struggle to his feet. Robert shot him between the eyes' (212). In a sense here Robert changes sides, from the masculine disciplinary side of Captain Leather (whose name offers its own hints of sado-masochism, plus a sign of the industrial exploitation of animals) to that of the animals. It is in the animals' name, so to speak, that he shoots Leather.

An intertextual invocation of Swift's Gulliver among the Houyhnhnms certainly is active here, and in the subsequent episode in which the fleeing Robert, his pistol hanging 'down from his fingers between his knees,' encounters a black dog and a 'fine black mare,' already saddled, seemingly waiting for him beside an abandoned train loaded with one hundred and thirty horses. As Simone Vauthier has noted, Robert moves here 'to secede from the insane world of men and join a new community':

Almost providentially, he comes across a mare and a dog: 'It was as if both dog and horse had been waiting for Robert to come to them' (182). And because the mare whinnies to the horses she smells in the cars, as the little company goes to the station yard, Robert Ross takes the decision to release the animals. 'Then we shall all go together' (183) ... this assuming of new bonds is Robert's undoing. When he is summoned to surrender, his renewed use of the pronoun 'we' ('We shall not be taken') 'dooms' him: to the pursuing officer it signifies that the renegade has one accomplice or more. So, Mickle has his men set fire to the barn where Ross and the horses have sought refuge. (13)

Robert's identification with the horses rather than his fellow troops, and his attraction to the black mare, confirm elements that have been in the text from the beginning. Although the hydrocephalic Rowena can be read as the sign of the socially crippled woman, she can also be seen, together with her rabbits, as the site – perhaps the only site in Robert's childhood – of non-violent affection. The semiotic system of this affection reaches from Rowena, her rabbits, the pony Meg, through the coyote, the horses on the troopship, Rodwell's toad, hedgehog, and rabbit, the horses at the battalion stables, to the black mare, dog, and horses of Robert's last adventure. This system implicitly constructs its opposite – the industrial, the military, and the homoerotic and sado-masochistic which inform the industrial and military. Robert's position throughout the novel has been somewhere between these systems – 'on the sidelines' of the parade square with Rowena, 'half admiring – half reluctant to admire' (8), on the roof of the barracks listening for the coyote, or on a troopship but with the horses. Despite his attraction to the animal he makes a strong effort to join the industrial: enlisting for war, visiting the brothel, acquiring the Webley pistol, becoming Taffler's friend and Barbara's lover. His rape by 'his fellow soldiers' or by 'his brother officers' (201) repositions him, however, with those to whom violence is done – the horses, Rowena, the prostitutes of 'Wet Goods,' the rabbit and hedgehog.

The Wars intervenes in late-twentieth-century Canadian culture with a narrowly focused reconstruction of the First World War text, a reconstruction that violently condemns the phallic authority on which nearly all the 'official' transactions of that culture are conducted. The novel's semiotics gathers together under the homoerotic sado-masochistic phallus not only the artillery of the First World War and the politicians and generals on both sides who deployed it, but also such basic contemporary institutions as capitalist business practice ('RAYMOND/ROSS' tractors with their echoes of Massey-Harris), the church (the bishop's sermon about 'holy wars' [54]), education, marriage, heterosexual and homosexual relations, and literature. The only spots of value the text can offer are among those virtually barred from power because of their exclusion from the human phallus – animals, the hydrocephalic Rowena, or women who remain on the sidelines of phallic activity, like the nurse Marion Turner or the unmarried spectator Juliet d'Orsey. The ground of this analysis is small, not even Central Canada or Toronto, but a socially and geographically small part of Toronto. The Ross family lives in Rosedale and travels regularly to England, where Robert, who attends boarding-school, affiliates naturally with the minor aristocracy in London. Considerations of class, region, and ethnicity are hidden within the text by the weight it accords to the binary opposition it develops between aggressive, homoerotic culture and passive nature. The 'brawling, husky lot of men ... mostly out of lumber camps and factories' that Robert proudly describes to his father (52) are marked by the same violence that moves his father to build factories, or Taffler to enjoy sexually both the Swede and Barbara. The legendary Indian runner Tom Longboat enters the text as both a model of triumphant male toughness for upper-class boys (48) and as kin of the coyote that runs with Robert from his barracks.

There is an enormous silence in the novel about what a culture might do once it had moved from the violently phallic norms presented here. There is no Captain Mendez here to follow the voyage to the land of the Houyhnhnms. There are no instances of even remotely fulfilling heterosexual or homosexual relations. The only 'good phallus,' Rodwell, kills himself in despair. The most successful relations in the book are Robert's to Rowena and Juliet's to the wounded Robert, with Rowena hydrocephalic and Robert burned over most of his body and unable to 'ever walk or see or be capable of rational judgment again' (224). This silence can also be read as an absence of a sufficient number of positively marked signs to allow the text to enter into the social debates of the culture it condemns. The novel paradoxically constructs itself outside the structures (Clarke Irwin and Co., Penguin Canada, Webcom Limited) that publish it, and outside the authority of the educational and critical institutions that will receive it. Seeking to speak to these institutions from the position of someone outside sexual exchange as well as from that of someone who would escape the human community, it risks being recuperated as an ingenious narrative (Vauthier), or as a critique merely of war (Thompson). The concluding utterance of the narrator of the novel and researcher into Robert Ross's life is his agreement with Ross's one documented utterance, his notation on the back of a photograph of *'Robert and Rowena with Meg'* – " 'Look! you can see our breath!" ' (226). The question both researcher and reader are left with is what, given one's own reading position within a sexually active and phallicly defined culture, and within the rational discipline of archives and archivist, can the 'breath' of a female horse, a female hydrocephalic, and a young man who has identified himself with them signify? Is 'breath' and its implicit romanticizing of the organic and the 'natural' the only gesture that the codes of their society and ours permit them? That 'breath,' along with the 'commotions' of the birds outside the archives' windows, should signify is perhaps the only statement the text can enter into contestation.

Masculinity is a doubly *defensive* structure, fortified against the return of the pre-Oedipal maternal relation as well as the inverted Oedipal homosexual relation to the father.

John Fletcher, 'Freud and His Uses: Psychoanalysis and Gay Theory' (1989), 106

In terms of its actual signs of Canadian culture, the Canada of *The Wars* is minute – geographically focused on Rosedale, socially focused on the wealthiest classes, chronologically focused on the years around the First World War. But in defining Canada as part of a violent, patriarchal, latently homosexual and misogynist Western industrialism, the novel's range is large. Far from marking the beginnings of Canadian nationalism, as Canadian history has often argued, the First World War in *The Wars* marks Canada's full entry into a huge transnational arena in which official heterosexuality masks a violent homosexuality which drives almost all activities – business, sports, courtship, and war. All considerations of nation, family, region, ethnicity, or race, on which a national polis might be argued – in fact all social and political considerations – are erased here by this monolithic, ubiquitously textualized force of misdirected sexuality. *The Wars* can see no social/textual alternative to this force; the only 'remedy' that it offers – the 'innocence' of animals – is nowhere nearly as available to humanity as is the similarly extra-social power of universal nature in *Obasan*, or even the 'Green Grass World' of Big Bear. This 'innocence' lies not only outside the social order (which is perhaps why Robert must die) but also, as Swift suggested some two hundred years earlier, nearly outside human experience: an illusion of breath in a fading sepia photo.

A Farewell to Politics
Joshua Then and Now

On the field, they watched a milling group of scrawny girls in green-and-white tights, their teeth chattering, their noses running. The Riderettes. Pimply sex kittens of the prairie. Fortunately, a thoughtful bandmaster had provided them with woolies, sadly loose-fitting, to wear over their stockings. The girls bobbed up and down, running in place, to keep warm. Suddenly, a TV camera came into play, the drums went boom, and the intrepid girls, after one last wipe of the nose with chapped hands, flashed radiant smiles and began to strut across the frozen field.

'Get 'em, get 'em,' the Riderettes chanted. But the Riders were down 17–0 at half-time.

Joshau Then and Now, 322–3

This is the most extended image *Joshua Then and Now* offers of Canada outside the Montreal setting of most of its events. In a novel in which pretension is a major paradigm, particularly pretension to glamour, power, and sophistication, the Saskatchewan Roughrider cheerleaders are marked as especially failed pretenders, their radiance subverted by their running noses and chapped hands, their claims as 'sex kittens' belied by their 'scrawny' bodies and pimples, their 'Get 'em' command to conquer belied by the half-time score. Their failure occurs in the context of the Canadian Football League's annual Grey Cup game, a match between 'West' and 'East,' the significance of which is in turn subverted both by the lacklustre performance of its participants and by the 'freezing' weather which sends Joshua and several of his companions back to their hotel to watch on television. The role the media play in allowing and requiring pretension is signalled by the Riderettes' smiling and strutting only when the TV camera comes 'into play' and by Joshua's preference for the game's televised image.

Although Joshua Shapiro, Canadian journalist and national television personality, and focal character of the novel, travels extensively, the Riderettes paradoxically provide one of very few glimpses of Canada outside of Montreal's anglophone community and its Eastern Township retreats. The geography of Joshua's travels, and of the signs of the book, extends from English Montreal to Ottawa, to Britain, France, and Spain, to Hollywood, and to a small extent into the northeast United States. In addition to the scene above the Prairies appear also as a place where the 'meek' are rumoured to have sex with their daughters ('they go in for [that] a lot out on the prairies, where the winters are long,' Joshua's father jests [199]), as the home of 'Rocky Mountain University' (ostensibly the University of Calgary), the only institution sufficiently 'provincial' to wish to purchase Joshua's papers, and as the birthplace ('born in a sod hut' [69]) of 'The Flopper,' a mediocre NHL goal-tender who now tends bar in Montreal. British Columbia and the Atlantic provinces are virtually unmentioned. Ontario is represented by Cornwall, a place for a Montreal bank robber to conceal his loot, by Toronto's comfortable Jewish community of Forest Hill, which hopes not to be disturbed by Jews emigrating from an independent Quebec, and by the corrupt politics of Ottawa. Overall, the novel's array of Canadian signs is only slightly larger than that of *The Wars*.

While the action of the novel focuses on Joshua's childhood, adolescence, and marriage to the Westmount princess Pauline Hornby ('Joshua Then'), on his adult struggles against family disaster and on his comic crusade against pretension ('Joshua Now'), the events which pervade the novel morally and politically are the Spanish Civil War and the Holocaust. These in turn help define the novel's geographic field and the kinds of significance it awards to its geographic signs. Joshua, born like Richler in 1931, and thus old enough to participate imaginatively in both the Spanish Civil War and the Second World War, but not old enough to fight, has been fascinated by republican Spain for most of his life and eventually writes a modestly successful book about the international volunteers who fought alongside its soldiers. This obsession renders Joshua 'colonial' throughout most of his life, in that it has caused him to view his own history, in which he is Canadian rather than European, and in which he can only write about the war rather than fight it, as less meaningful than the histories of those more directly involved. It has caused his response to the

Spanish Civil War, and to Nazism in particular, to become the measure he feels continually impelled to invoke to judge himself. The novel constructs him as feeling required not only to imagine himself as Robert Jordan waiting stoically for death at the end of Hemingway's *For Whom the Bell Tolls*, but also to accuse every German he meets with complicity in Jewish genocide. This obsession eventually causes him to see less value in his family and marriage than in his ambiguous relationships to the various war survivors he encountered in Ibiza some thirty years before, and thus to nearly lose his beloved Pauline.

Joshua Then and Now is narrated in the third person, in a manner that often seems merely to disguise a first-person narration by Joshua himself. On only three or four pages of this 435-page novel does the narrator clearly dissociate its process of focalization from that of Joshua. Throughout most of the narration the narrator moves to blur the distinction between its observations and those of Joshua by framing its statements as potentially focalized by both parties. For example, the following paragraph begins as if an 'impersonal' history of the Spanish Civil War, but is transformed by the concluding sentence into a recollection by Joshua:

> A few evenings later, when Almeria was choked with refugees, some forty thousand people having reached what they believed to be a haven, the city was heavily bombed by German and Italian airplanes. The airplanes made no attempt to hit the government battleship in the harbor or bomb the barracks, but deliberately dropped bombs in the very center of the town, where the exhausted refugees were gathered. While I, thought Joshua, was learning to play polo and cheering on Boston's Kraut Line: Milt Schmidt, Bobby Bauer, Woody Dumart. (125)

The external narrator that offers the framing 'thought Joshua' has apparently relativized the earlier historical observation by assigning it to Joshua and thus making its reliability subject to his characterization. What has seemed at first a discourse of fact ('the city was heavily bombed') has been revealed as one of interpretation ('deliberately dropped bombs ... exhausted refugees'). Or has it? Perhaps the reverse has happened – a discourse of interpretation has been passed off as one of fact. Since the qualifying 'thought Joshua' comes so late in the paragraph, a reader has already 'read' the earlier sentences as the focalization of an external narrator; the temporal priority of that reading continues to give it power over the revision signalled in the concluding sentence, thus creating an implication of agreement between narrator and character. Even the introduction of documentary texts, such as Paul Johnson's comment on the Suez War (257), is done in a way which creates ambiguity about whether it is cited by Joshua or by the narrator alone.

This blurring of the distinction between what Mieke Bal calls 'character-bound focalization' and 'external focalization' (105) is extremely significant in a novel as satirical as *Joshua Then and Now*, since it exempts Joshua and those he loves from being targets of satire. The novel can caricature only those people and institutions that Joshua is willing to caricature – his wife's first husband, her upper-class Westmount friends from college, his own upwardly mobile friends from high school, his best friend the alcoholic Britsh novelist Sydney Murdoch, North American universities, and Canadian nationalism. It invests Joshua's cynicism with a credibility that rests on its being contradicted by neither narrator nor writer. It renders his gradually evolving views on the Spanish Civil War, on Marxism, on what constitutes hypocrisy and pretension, and on what parts of the world are culturally most significant the dominant views of the novel. It leaves Joshua subject only to occasional dramatic irony (for instance, in his failure to link Mueller's characteristic unhappiness to the bombing of Dresden [359]) and to a recurrent self-criticism which invariably returns narrative authority to Joshua himself.

The narrative structure of the novel rests not on any visible motivation of its narrator but firmly on this recurrent self- criticism. For the fabula of *Joshua Then and Now* is above all the story of Joshua's self-interrogation, as he lies in bed attempting to recover from a serious automobile accident, from his wife's nervous breakdown, and from widely published stories that he is homosexual. 'Look at me now, Joshua thought,' the novel begins, and very soon he is looking at himself both Then and Now: 'Joshua could still remember' (13); 'he didn't remember much ... but he did recall' (16). By moving in a fragmentary way among the stories of his childhood, his first visit to Spain, his wooing of Pauline, and his most recent actions, this structure above all constructs Joshua as a moral person, one concerned about what he should have perceived and how he should have acted – whether towards his parents, his wife, or towards the Germans, Spaniards, and Jews of Ibiza. Rather than subverting his perceptions, his self-questioning tends to aggrandize them as coming from an ethical source.

The self-questioning basis of the narrative also gives it a strong hermeneutic push, in that its questions promise answers, posit causes, and suspend the announcement of important narrative detail. Three major questions are suspended for much of the novel: What happened at Ibiza? How did Joshua's accident occur? and Will Pauline recover from her breakdown and return to him? The answering of these questions in turn promises a wholeness: to the novel, to Joshua's life, and to his and its vision of human relations. That is, the strong hermeneutic dimension of the novel is ideological: it promises answers on which ultimately Joshua, the external narrator, and the writer who implicitly constructs both of them will ostensibly agree.

The field of signs offered by Joshua – his sense of a Montreal that opens onto Europe rather than North America, of an Ottawa that is merely an extension of Montreal high society, and of a Hollywood that is a mere sidebar to European history – is thus very much also the field offered by the narrator and the text itself. The grand politics of the fight against fascism during the Second World War is the central political event for the text as well as for Joshua. For both, this politics effectively trivializes any politics outside that struggle. There are numerous cultural and class conflicts in the Canadian episodes of the story, but few of these are inscribed by the novel as *political*. The bad feeling between the wealthy Leventhal family of Joshua's mother and the Polish-Jewish immigrant family of his father is readable as a sign of class conflict within the Jewish community, but is constructed by the novel as a conflict among eccentric individuals. The anger which the working-class Jack Trimble expresses by eventually marrying the privileged and sophisticated Jane Mitchell in order to 'get his dirty finger-nails under [her] skirts' (431) is similarly presented by the novel as specific to Trimble's character. The profound differences between the wealthy anglophones of Westmount and the upwardly mobile Montreal Jewish community are kept by the novel from being explicitly political by the simple expedient of minimizing contact between the two groups. The various cultures and classes of the novel – wealthy Montreal anglophones, wealthy and poor Montreal Jews, Québécois, Spanish fishermen, upper-middle-class British – coexist but rarely intersect or negotiate. Contact at an individual level – as between Joshua's 'gangster' father and Senator Hornby, his wealthy father-in-law – may result in amusing perceptions and accommodations, but fails to challenge general social structures. Despite several references in the novel to a possible exodus of Jews from Montreal because of the 1976 Parti Québécois election victory, francophone/

anglophone conflict is virtually invisible because the Québécois themselves are invisible. In the absence of Québécois characters even this election loses its social and political character and becomes merely an environmental given – an empirically noted but ideologically unexamined stage prop for Joshua's European concerns.

However, although the novel has very little to say about Canadian politics, it has a considerable amount to say about Canadian politicians. Joshua and his fellow alumni from Fletcher's Field High School hold annual meetings of the 'Mackenzie King Memorial Society' to mock and satirize the Liberal prime minister's mysticism and obsession with his mother. Periodically, Joshua meets in Ottawa with Pauline's father, a Liberal senator, and their conversation turns sardonically to ballot-rigging and influence peddling. The portrayals of politicians implicit in these scenes emphasize sameness rather than difference, and corrupt administration rather than a clash of ideologies. The politicians are similar in their corruption and pragmatism, not different because of regional, class, or linguistic loyalties. Mackenzie King is ridiculed not for his policies but for his manner of articulating them. His anti-Semitism is constructed not as political but as part of a cultural style in which even Jews who anglicize their names participate. Even more remarkably, despite the novel's narrative inquiry being situated in Montreal and Ottawa during the 1970s, during one of the most intense periods of francophone-anglophone conflict and Western dissatisfaction with Central Canada, almost none of this politics enters the text. Federal Canadian politics is presented simply as an unequal conflict between evil and good, between corruption and honesty, with the clear implication that elimination of such corruption should result in a process of governance that is unproblematical and conflict-free.

A system of world order based upon cooperation between states may be said to be 'political' in nature, in that it is brought about through negotiation between governments acting on the basis of their respective national interests. By contrast, a system of international order based on the direct cooperation of the peoples of the world may be termed 'economic,' in the sense that it comes about through the development of an ever-tightening web of commercial transactions which gradually bind the world into a single community. A system of 'political' order is concerned essentially with power and security, with the ever-delicate balancing of rival state interests. A system of 'economic' order, in contrast, is concerned with the unification of peoples of the world and the promotion of their prosperity.

Stephen C. Neff, *Friends but No Allies* (1990), 2

The ideological presuppositions evident here in Stephen Neff – that an unregulated transnational economy is synonymous with the interests of individuals or 'peoples,' that, in contrast, a world economy regulated by treaties between national governments places undesirable limits on both individual freedom and 'prosperity,' and that 'economics' is an apolitical social concept and should replace 'politics' in human organization – have circulated widely in recent decades under such names as 'Thatcherism' or 'Reaganism' and constituted as well a major part of the Canadian pro–Free Trade argument in 1988. In *Joshua Then and Now* these presuppositions operate in the novel's general suspicion of both national governments and political movements as corrupt, oppressive, and constraining, and its endorsement of transnational travel and movement of goods as the sign of both individual freedom and the possibility of individual prosperity. In the place of a socially declared politics in *Joshua Then and Now* one finds individualism. Joshua's cynicism about organized politics, about Liberal party bagmen and Communist writers clubs, is founded on a belief in the primacy of self-interest that drives his own actions and informs the novel's views of others. Those who affiliate themselves with national or international political movements do so because of personal motivation. Colin Fraser becomes a Marxist, and later a strident Canadian nationalist, in rebellion against his wealthy parents. Mackenzie King enters politics to indulge his fantasies and line his pockets. Senator Hornby becomes an MP for the Liberals because that party offers easy access to the positions of governmental power he covets. Even Joshua's view of the Spanish Civil War tends to underestimate the organized and ideological dimensions of republican resistance and construes the struggle as one between an organized oppression and tragic individuals. 'Ah, but once there was Spain. Once writers had been committed to revolutionary change, not their own absurdity. Instead of *Catch-22*, there was *La Condition Humaine*; rather than Portnoy, Robert Jordan' (234).

Throughout *Joshua Then and Now* there is an implicit politics, a kind of laissez-faire internationalism in which group affiliations are seen to interfere, as in Neff, with individual liberty. Although the Spanish Civil War is the event that haunts the novel, the conflict the

book foregrounds among its own characters is between those of hum-
ble beginnings who build successful lives through their own efforts
and those who have money and status given to them by inheritance.
This conflict recurs throughout the book – between Murdoch, 'the
council school boy from Bradford' unwilling to 'stand in queues'
(121–2), and the other Cambridge students who, like Joanna, smell
'of old money and country houses' (122); between the charming Kevin
Hornby and the 'fierce driving' Jewish students he meets at McGill
law school, 'each one hollering "me, me, me"' (208); between the
well-bred children of Westmount and Joshua Shapiro, who trains
himself as a journalist by studying a thesaurus and imitating prose
styles in a public library. The novel associates the privileged with
signs of indolence and waste – Kevin with his MG and tennis skills,
his school friends Tim Hickey and Dickie Abbott with country clubs
and summer places on Lake Memphremagog; it associates the poor
with signs of energy, passion, and penetration – the Jewish law students who 'interrupted you in mid sentence,' 'dark men with heated
black eyes' (209); and Jack Trimble, who yearns to have Jane Mitchell
take his 'barber boy's Point St. Charles cock into [her] well-bred mouth
and choke on it' (432).

The ambitious and energetic are all individualists, self- made, who
must offend and transgress in order to succeeed. The privileged com-
placently rely on tradition and social convention to protect their rank
and privilege. Thus the novel uses repeated images of theft and penetration to characterize creative energy – Trimble's desire to penetrate
Jane Mitchell's skirt and mouth, Pauline's joke about needing to wear
'another layer of panties, even barbed wire' when near Jewish students (208), Joshua's intrusions into Pauline and Colin's apartment
to leave seductive bourgeois gifts in her bed and lingerie drawers.
Political conflict here is replaced by the figure of burglary. Joshua
sneaks into Spanish-language classes at McGill; he crashes a McGill
dance and, when identified and ejected, in rage smashes open an
athletics locker, appropriates a hockey uniform, and bluffs his way
into a practice, where he violently assaults most of the players. Later
in England, unsuccessful in seducing 'a fetching Girton girl' (122), he
steals her pearl necklace in order to finance his first trip to Spain. In
Ibiza, convinced he has been photographed and compromised by the
German Dr Dr Mueller, he breaks into Mueller's house and smashes
his camera and much of his record collection.

The horror that drives Joshua in his later life as a successful journalist in Montreal is that anyone might give up a transgressive self-

reliant life for one of bourgeois comfort and group affiliation. He is particularly disturbed that most of his old classmates from Fletcher's Field have tried, by concealing their origins beneath signs of wealth and pretension, to represent themselves as born to high social standing. Joshua readopts his burglar persona to invade some of their West-mount mansions and vandalize these specific signs. In the home of Pinsky, who has come to wear 'Persian lamb, a black cashmere over-coat, a silk scarf, kid gloves, suede fur-lined boots' (126) and collect hundreds of vintage wines, which he keeps in a thermostatically con-trolled cellar, Joshua soaks the labels off each bottle and randomly rearranges them on their racks. At that of Yossel Kugelman, who has changed his name to Jonathan Cole, monogrammed his sterling silver JC, and become an art collector, Joshua removes the signature from a prized A.Y. Jackson landscape and signs it: 'this copy by Hershl Sugarman' (312). Each of these assaults is directed at the new sign that the former classmate has attempted to adopt. In the Kugelman burglary Joshua attempts to literally reinscribe Jewish words that have been concealed beneath the adopted 'Jonathan Cole' and its Christian 'JC' monogram. Joshua has a similar distaste for wealthy Jack Trimble's concealment of his origins as a Quebec barber's son by pretending to have been born in England.

The general figure of criminality operates throughout the novel as the renegade individual's answer to a culture of greed and hypocrisy. The criminal appears produced here by despair of society's ever achieving honesty and justice. Joshua's inspiration is his father Reu-ben, a moderately successful professional boxer who, on retirement, worked as a gambling-debt and loan enforcer, in Prohibition-era boot-legging, in ration-coupon forgery, and possibly from time to time in protection rackets and bank robbery. Reuben is portrayed as a loyal father, am amateur theologian, witty, unpretentious – the 'honest' bank robber. He both retains Joshua's respect and wins that of the senator and Pauline. His positive portrayal by Joshua and the narrator offers a further endorsement to the implicit approval the book gives to Joshua's various criminal acts. The implication is that those who have amassed undue wealth, inherited undue advantages, or pros-pered because of deceit and pretension deserve whatever thefts, frauds, and tricks can be perpetrated on them. Universities that seek prestige by purchasing the papers of famous writers deserve to have writers like Sydney and Joshua create fakes of early manuscripts. Kugelman deserves to have his A.Y. Jackson re-signed. Joanna perhaps should be ready to sacrifice her pearl necklace to the cause of Joshua's Spanish research.

———————— • ————————

We should – in the constitutional reshaping of Canada that lies ahead – plan with an eye to the world's interests as well as our own, bearing in mind that the day of the old nation-state is almost ended and Canada is in a uniquely favorable position to present a genuine alternative, a working model of a confederalism that will minimize central administration and promote local self-government. And in cultural terms we should put an end to artistic protectionism. It is our right to have the artistic productions and the artists of all countries as freely available to us as books are in our libraries. And if our artists are as good as we boast they are, there is no need to impose handicaps on outsiders. The flow should be free.

George Woodcock, 'The Mirror of Narcissus' (1978), 29

The discourse of Thatcherism has been translated by George Woodcock, John Metcalf, and others into a Canadian discourse of artistic 'right' and 'freedom'; this translation itself had a prominent part in the pro–free trade argument, in the proposition that Canadian artists were 'not fragile' and in need of 'protectionism.' In Woodcock's argument here, as in that of the pro–free traders, artistic quality has no contingency to local context but is transcendent and unproblematic: '... if our artists are as good as we boast they are ...,' they will be able to compete against 'outsiders.'

Near the mid-point of *Joshua Then and Now* Pauline's failure to purchase liquor for a weekend party before the Memphremagog store has closed sends Reuben, her father, and Joshua to the Quebec-Vermont border in search of Prohibition-era liquor Reuben once helped to bury. Several images of transgression operate here – defiance of liquor excise laws, national and provincial politics, the provincial liquor monopoly, and international borders. In the comedy of the scene various social questions resonate: Should a national polity have the power to prohibit or regulate a commodity like alcohol, cocaine, tobacco? Or to 'protect' a liquor industry that may not be 'as good as we boast'? One is reminded of the irrelevance of such borders to Joshua's career – how the sales of his Spanish Civil War book, *The Volunteers*, spilled across borders, how much of his income came from British and American royalties, how the book itself addressed a transnational subject, and how the 'volunteers' themselves came to Spain's international brigades as individuals from numerous countries. As the individualist 'Robin Hood' dimension of Joshua's burglaries implied despair that a local politics could ever address social injustice, so too the 'Robert Jordan' aspects of his father's rum-running and of his own vision of the Spanish war as a war against nationalisms imply a despair that a nation-based politics can ever accommodate human desires for full lives. Several times in the novel the narrator notes that it was national armies that led the fascist defeat of republican Spain – 'mechanized Italian units,' 'German cruisers,' 'German and Italian airplanes' – and national governments in Spain and Portugal that organized various Renaissance massacres of Jews. Although a simple dichotomy evades Joshua – there were Russian planes supporting the republican cause, and republican Spain also had a national government – a sense that human energy and diversity breach and trivialize national boundaries pervades the book.

A major characterization in creating this effect is that of the German Dr Dr Mueller, whom the young Joshua in Ibiza insists on reading as a stereotypical Jew-killing German and Nazi. Mueller enters the novel bearing a large and contradictory assemblage of signs:

> ... a tall sorrowful man leaning against the deck railing, biting into an ivory cigarette holder ... Suitcases, saddle, a rifle in a canvas case, and what appeared to be a furled teepee ... a handsome brown stallion. (151)

> Tall, lugubrious, with grieving blue eyes, a prominent broken nose that hadn't been mended just right, and a long thin mouth pulled downward at the sides, Dr. Dr. Mueller favored a white linen suit, the jacket slung over his shoulders continental-style. He hiked through the village each afternoon, hands clasped behind his back, slit of a mouth biting angrily on that ivory cigarette holder, and wherever he drifted he commanded a deference that infuriated Joshua .... Officers saluted him on the road and peasants stepped aside to make his passage easier. (186)

Signs of grief, anger, and arrogance, of the blue-eyed Aryan, the aristocrat, and the North American Indian jostle together. Joshua later discovers the Dr Dr to dress up both as a North American cowboy and as Marlene Dietrich, to use the name 'Gus McCabe' to author a series of western novels in German, to collect recordings of *Carmen* and Roy Rogers, and to be a well-read student of North American Indian wars, including the Canadian Northwest Rebellion. He served in France, but not, as Joshua suspected, as a soldier but as a journalist.

He is wanted in France, not for war crimes but for having 'tried to scalp' a prostitute in postwar Nice (362). He keeps a photograph of 'an elegant lady with coiled blonde hair seated on a sofa beside two plump boys,' inscribed 'Dresden, 1943' – a photo which Joshua seems unable to connect with the British fire-bombing of Dresden in 1945. Neither the German national stereotype nor the Nazi stereotype can accommodate all these signs. Joshua's assumptions that they do lead him into bizarre acts of aggression which leave him vaguely embarrassed and dissatisfied, and haunted by a belief that he has somehow failed. The 'evil' of Nazism here may be multinational rather than specific to the historic, economic, and cultural context of interbellum Germany, and 'good' and 'evil' themselves are blurred – in the Dresden bombing and in the wide variety of the Dr Dr's interests.

Canadian-born, he sometimes felt as if he were condemned to lope slant-shouldered through this world that confused him. One shoulder sloping downwards, groaning under the weight of his Jewish heritage (burning on the market square, crazed Cossacks on the rampage, gas chambers, as well as Moses, Rabbi Akiba, and Maimonides); the other thrust heavenwards, yearning for an inheritance, any inheritance, weightier than the construction of a transcontinental railway, a reputation for honest trading, good skiing conditions.

Joshua Then and Now, 190–1

Ultimately, however, Joshua does return to 'honest trading' – not on the national level suggested here, but within the bounds of his marriage, and metaphorically within the bounds of his wife's garden at Memphremagog. Canada remains a site of banality – of quick wealth and shallow success. The value that, for him, finally eclipses his image of Ibiza and of himself triumphing over Nazis and their self-styled 'nationalism,' and of avenging Jewish wrongs, is that of domestic intimacy – marriage as the private garden that he stocks with 'bales of peat,' 'rose bushes,' 'sacks of leaf mold,' in an attempt to lure back his absent Pauline. The figure recalls the domestic intimacy of Mueller's photo of the woman and children on the Dresden sofa. As the archetypal resonance of 'garden' suggests, the immediate family is an even more transnational figure than the fight against Nazism, potentially beyond all politics except those of the couple. The novel concludes with Pauline having been lured back to that garden, and Reuben's affirmation of the appropriateness of her return:

> The two old men continued down the road, the kids trailing after, and everybody piled into the Jeep. Reuben could see Joshua and Pauline in the vegetable garden. They weren't embracing. He was touching her hair. Then, watching from the rear window of the moving Jeep, Reuben saw them start back for the house. Joshua wasn't leaning on his cane. Pauline was supporting him. Well, yeah, right, he thought. (435)

Here Joshua and Pauline's marriage stands against the fractured and ruined marriages of their parents, of the Murdochs, and of their various Fletcher's Field and Westmount friends, as well as in mystifying relationship to Joshua's renegade impetuousness and Pauline's troubled youth. Beyond the marriage resonates the friendship and support of the two grandfathers, who are driving off with the children in search of ice-cream. And beyond still further rages the disorders of human society, with its deals, betrayals, revolutions, and hypocrisies, from which Joshua has concluded that only one's close family can be worthy of loyalty.

In the pastoral image of the garden are hints of the faith in a transcendent nature that underlies the suspicion of politics implicit in the framing imagery of *The Diviners*, *Obasan*, and *The Temptations of Big Bear*. But Joshua's is a much smaller garden and carries none of the hopeful suggestions of the interrelatedness of humanity that the images of the other texts carry. The loyalty of the family is less a sign of human good than a defence against a politically incapable humanity outside the garden walls.

Art over History
In the Skin of a Lion

... still photographs cannot convey the motion, the kinetic energy, that envelops the city. It is something like the swarming of flies, like Brownian motion, but not as random. There is chaos in the whole, but there is order in the components: pedestrians passing on sidewalks, cars starting and stopping at lights like the coils of a Slinky Toy and flowing around interchanges like corpuscles in capillaries. It can be comical or it can be mesmerizing, but the motion is always present, and always in the foreground.

Montreal and Toronto together account for a fifth of the nation's population. These cities are to the Canadian urban landscape what the St. Elias Mountains are to the natural landscape: they fill the senses and perplex the mind. They are built by man but are beyond human proportion.

Bo Curtis and J.A. Kraulis, *Canada from the Air* (1981), 50–1

Michael Ondaatje's 1987 novel *In the Skin of a Lion* is built around three major Toronto historical events: the disappearance of theatre entrepreneur Ambrose Small in 1919, and the building, under city commissioner Rowland Harris, of the Bloor Street Viaduct in 1917 and of a new city waterworks in the early 1930s. In the public discourse of Toronto the constructions given to these major institutional events have emphasized their wealthy and powerful protagonists and the monumental public structures they built – Small's Grand Theatre and Harris's waterworks, viaduct, and St Clair reservoir. Ondaatje's reconstructions of these events bear some similarities to the treatments of official history by Wiebe in *The Temptations of Big Bear*, Kogawa in *Obasan*, and Laurence in *The Diviners*, in that all four texts offer views of historical events from the positions of participants hitherto unable to speak 'officially' about them. *In the Skin of a Lion* tells Small's story primarily from the perspectives of his mistress, the young actress Clara Dickens, and her infatuated admirer, Patrick Lewis. It narrates the story of Harris's monumental buildings from the positions of two workers who helped build them, the high-rigger Nicholas Temelcoff and tunnel-worker Lewis.

In the Skin of a Lion's most prominent character is not Small or Harris but Lewis, with whom the book begins and ends, and who, through a highly problematical frame, is made to appear to focalize and partly narrate its action. Patrick Lewis is emphasized by the book as a character who lacks advantage, privilege, or beneficial social or geographic background, and who along with others of the immigrant and economic underclasses is oppressed by the dominance the wealthy possess over official names and socially legitimate language:

> He was born into a region which did not appear on a map until 1910, though his family had worked there for twenty years and the land had been homesteaded since 1816.
> In the school atlas the place is pale green and nameless. (10–11)

He is the motherless son of a landless farm worker and self-taught dynamite technician, who works with his father until the latter is killed in a mine explosion. Yet he also has advantages over many other characters in the novel. He has an English name, unlike most of his co-workers at Wickett and Craig's tannery or the waterworks project, and easy access to spoken English. Despite lacking apparent formal education, both he and his father are literate. Literacy enables his father to write 'away for books' (15) about high explosives and teach himself how to employ dynamite with precision in order to break up log jams on rivers or uncover ore deposits, and thus enables him to abandon the hard labour of farm work for the skilled job of contract blasting. Literacy enables Patrick to find work as a 'searcher' for Ambrose Small on first arriving in Toronto, to develop friendships with actresses like Clara Dickens and Alice Gull, and to develop a political perspective on the various large enterprises that employ him.

While Patrick is undoubtedly alien to the world of public wealth and success of Small and Harris, others in the novel are alien even to Patrick's unmapped birthplace and small linguistic privilege. Every winter the woods of his home region are visited by Finnish loggers, who sleep in the shacks behind the Bellrock Hotel and have little connection with the town ... No one in the town of Bellrock really knows where the men have come from ... The only connection the loggers have with the town is when they emerge to skate along the line of river, on homemade skates, the blades made of old knives. (8)

In Toronto Patrick will meet other non-English-speaking workers – Finns, Macedonians, Italians, Poles, Lithuanians – who struggle against political marginalization in a city whose police chief 'has imposed laws against public meetings by foreigners. So if they speak this way in public, in *any* language other than English, they will be jailed. A rule of the city' (133). He will slowly come to see their struggle to acquire language and recognizable names, and to have their stories enter into the acknowledged stories of their new culture – to be 'sewn into history' (149) – as key parts of any fight for social justice.

In the Skin of a Lion is presented in a third-person narration that contains few internal clues as to the identity of its narrator. All of its characters are constructed in the third person, and thus have equivalent syntactic relationships to the narrator. The narrator enjoys limited omniscience; it has access to most of Patrick Lewis's life, including his childhood and adolescence, but only to the present lives and recollections of other characters. It has access to some of the experiences of Nicholas Temelcoff and the thief Caravaggio which occur without Patrick's participation, but for the other characters has access only to events which occur while they are with Patrick. It has access also to wide historical perspective:

In 1938, when Patrick Lewis was released from prison, people were crowding together in large dark buildings across North America to see Garbo as Anna Karenina. Everyone tried to play the Hammond Organ. 'Red Squads' intercepted mail, tear-gassed political meetings. By now over 10,000 foreign-born workers had been deported out of the country. Everyone sang 'Just One of Those Things.' The longest bridge in the world was being built over the lower Zambesi and the great waterworks at the east end of Toronto neared completion.

At Kew Park a white horse dove every hour from a great height into Lake Ontario. T.S. Eliot's *Murder in the Cathedral* opened in England and a few weeks later Dr. Carl Weiss – who had always admired the poetry of the expatriate American – shot Huey Long to death in the Louisiana capitol building. Just one of those things. (209)

It has access to a variety of complex discourses, the authoritative historical one above, detailed, intimate narrations of interpersonal relations, and intricate poetic discourses that aestheticize action:

> The animal from the nightmare bares its teeth. Caravaggio swerves and its mouth rips open the boot to the right of his neck. Water is released. He feels himself becoming lighter. Being swung from side to side, no vision, no odour, he is ten years old and tilting wildly in a tree. A wall or an arm hits him. 'Fucking wop! Fucking dago!' 'Honour your partner, dip and dive.' His hands are up squabbling with this water creature – sacrificing the hands to protect the body. The inside of his heart feels bloodless. He swallows dry breath. (185)

It also can introduce literary humour dependent on a time period long after the action of the novel – humour such as the reference to novelist Sarah Sheard's father on page 209 ('Judge Sheard's Best Jokes'), or the cameo appearances of Al Purdy as the Trenton boy who helps Caravaggio escape prison (181–2) and of Anne Wilkinson as the wealthy young poet whom Caravaggio encounters while hiding in cottage country north of Toronto.

A brief italicized framing passage that follows the table of contents and precedes the numbered narrative sections purports, however, to attribute all of the narrative to the joint efforts of two characters:

> *This is the story a young girl gathers in a car during the early hours of the morning. She listens and asks questions as the vehicle travels through darkness. Outside, the countryside is unbetrayed. The man who is driving could say, 'In that field is a castle,' and it would be possible for her to believe him.*
>
> *She listens to the man as he picks up and brings together various corners of the story, attempting to carry it all in his arms. And he is tired, sometimes as elliptical as his concentration on the road, at times overexcited – 'Do you see?'* ([1])

The reader learns at the end of the book that the two are Patrick Lewis and his sixteen-year-old stepdaughter Hana, driving to Marmora, Ontario, to meet Clara, Hana's dead mother's best friend and Patrick's erstwhile lover. But on this final page it is Hana, not Patrick, who is driving.

'Who is speaking' is an extremely important question in a novel that claims to call into question the large numbers of people – women, workers, immigrants – who are silenced by the 'official histories' (145) of Canadian culture. The novel explicitly argues that it is Patrick who takes up 'the skin of a lion' and assumes responsibility for the narration of the lives of those whom official history leaves nameless and silent. On numerous occasions it shows Patrick finding language – a name for the Finnish loggers, a square-dance song to save Caravaggio from a knife attack – or saving or 'giving' the stories of others. At the same time the complexity, wit, and range of references of the novel suggest strongly to a reader that very closely behind Patrick 'speaks' and names the signator of the novel, Michael Ondaatje, immigrant from Sri Lanka, canonical Canadian poet, university professor, younger brother to financier Christopher Ondaatje – 'You don't want power. You were born to be a younger brother,' the novel slyly has Alice Gull remind Patrick (124). Does the text manage to affiliate its narrator more with its characters than with its signator, to transfer to them any large portion of its narrative capability? The answer that seems to be argued by the text is that it has delegated this capability to Hana Gull, daughter of the socialist Alice Gull and of the murdered union organizer Cato, who in turn enables Patrick, as her informant, to speak, narrate, and name indirectly through her – that is, that it has delegated its narrative to representatives of the marginalized and silenced.

But the force of this answer is subverted not only by the complexity of the novel's discourses but by the very framing elements themselves. If Hana drives the car to Marmora, can she be the non-driving young woman who the prologue says 'gathers' the story? The reliability of both this young woman and her informant is also specifically cast into doubt by the frame. She is hinted to be ingenuous – she might believe 'in that field is a castle'; Patrick is said to be 'tired ... elliptical ... overexcited'; only a 'faint light' illuminates his narrative. How either this excitable man or his sixteen-year-old listener could gather a story into the elaborate and varied discourses of *A Skin of a Lion* remains exceedingly unclear. Without the framing passage, however, responsibility for the narrative moves entirely to its signator; it becomes a text, not of Hana and Patrick's 1938 consciousness reconstructed in 1987, but entirely of one in 1987; it represents, not the experiences of a disempowered Patrick Lewis, narrated in part on behalf of his less-articulate fellow workers, but the selections and inventions of an urbane, highly educated late-twentieth-century professional writer.

The contradictions implicit in the brief frame narrative of *In the Skin of a Lion* suggest that the text is struggling with problems of representation similar to those evident in *The Diviners* and *The Temp-*

tations of Big Bear: how can one use a widely published novelist's powerful position to 'represent' both artistically and politically those who are excluded from power, without appearing both to be in a custodial or paternal relation to these and to be making 'use' of the unempowered to create bourgeois art? In terms of the explicit politics of these books it is essential that Big Bear's vision re-enter the public record, that the Métis songs of Jules Tonnerre become circulating texts, and that *In the Skin of a Lion* be Patrick and Hana's narrative. But in each text various structural and discursive signs remain to remind the reader that the constructor of these texts has remained the more textually empowered – has assigned words, deployed literary convention, and commanded knowledge far beyond the ken of the characters.

> Patrick ate most of his meals at the Thompson Grill on River Street where the waitress, through years of habit, had reduced to a minimum the action of pouring coffee or flipping an egg. He could spot the oil burns on her wrists, the permanent grimace in her eye from the smoke.
>
> *In the Skin of a Lion*, 111

Canada is represented in the novel through the metonymy of Ontario, and constructed as a battlefield of class interests. While the Canadian geographic range here is as limited as in *The Wars* or *Nights below Station Street*, the novel's marking of nearly all of its conflicting elements as 'Canadian' creates the illusion that its overall field of signs is both larger and more nationally representative. At one extreme in this field are the mill and mine owners, 'the aldermen and the millionaires' (238), and entrepreneurs like Ambrose Small who set the economic agenda of the country and, through a complicit media, establish its social significances. At the other are the anonymous foreign workers forbidden to organize publically or speak, murdered by their bosses if they seek to unionize, allowed only the temporary identities of their work, as exemplified by the tannery workers who must assume the colours of the dyes their job requires them to plunge into, who must lose their 'skins' as they have each lost language:

> And the men stepped out in colours up to their necks, pulling wet hides out after them so it appeared they had removed the skin from their own bodies. They had leapt into different colours as if into different countries.
> (130)

Close to these in status are the workers of British origin like Clara Dickens's father, who spends his life working at 'Wheeler Needle Works' – with 'Wheeler' suggesting the capitalist 'wheeler-dealer,' the relentless wheels of assembly-line industry and the closed-circuit world of the labourer trained for one industry and one site-specific task. Patrick's father is one of these who, despite managing to educate himself out of a dreary job as a farm labourer, ends up killed by the greed of mine owners:

> – He got killed setting charges in a feldspar mine. The company had tried to go too deep and the section above him collapsed. There wasn't an explosion. The shelf just slid down with him into the cave and drowned him. He was buried in feldspar. I didn't even know what it was. They use it in everything – chinaware, tiles, pottery, inlaid table tops, even in artificial teeth. (74)

Patrick follows his father into similarly dangerous and exploitive jobs, working at the tannery, where the men who work as dyers 'last in that job [no] more than six months' and where they and 'the hide-room workers' and the workers on 'the killing floors' are all 'left ... invisibly with tuberculosis and arthritis and rheumatism' (131); working on Harris's tunnel, where 'no record was kept' of the number of workers killed. As Ambrose Small's mistress, Clara Dickens follows her father's career at Wheeler Needle Works somewhat differently, although the text emphasizes the similarity: 'She had been the lover of Ambrose Small, had been caught in the slow discreet wheel of the rich' (72).

While Patrick's experiences with a labourer's life in a class-structured economy – directly through his own employment and indirectly through the consequences of his father's death and Clara's seduction by Small – construct the social parameters of the novel, it is Alice Gull, who, as actress-turned-social-activist, gives them clearest articulation. The novel offers little of Alice's early history – her father died when she was fifteen, she became a nun, she left the Church after being blown by a gust of wind from the Bloor Street viaduct during its construction and being miraculously caught by Nicholas Temelcoff and renamed by him Alicia. How her father died, why she became a nun, or why she eagerly assumed a new identity when officially presumed to have died beneath the viaduct is left obscure. She marries Cato, the Finnish logger who is murdered while trying to unionize the loggers in Patrick's home region, and after his death turns her energies to improving the political rights of Toronto's immigrant workers. In various discussions with Patrick, Alice offers what appear to be the social propositions of the novel:

'I'll tell you about the rich,' Alice would say, 'the rich are always laughing. They keep saying the same things on their boats and lawns. *Isn't this grand! We're having a good time!* And whenever the rich get drunk and maudlin about humanity you have to listen for hours. But they keep you in the tunnels and stockyards. They do not toil or spin. Remember that ... understand what they will always refuse to let go of. There are a hundred fences and lawns between the rich and you.' (132)

In these discussions Patrick characteristically questions the effectiveness of collective social action, preferring to act as an individual: 'I don't believe the language of politics, but I'll protect the friends I have. It's all I can handle' (122). Alice responds that something more public must be done: 'You must name the enemy': 'You name the enemy and destroy their power. Start with their luxuries – their select clubs, their summer mansions' (124–5).

In terms of the kinds of resistance to capitalist oppression the novel chooses to represent, it appears to favour overwhelmingly Patrick's individualist course over Alice's collectivist one. Alice and Cato are its only extensive characterizations of collectivist resistance, and even these are less than unqualified endorsements of a collectivist model. Cato, despite his loyalty to the union for which he organizes, and the network of workers who pass on his letters, works and dies alone. Alice's work with the immigrant community appears to be done outside any formal political organization. Her death, in the explosion of an 'anarchist's' bomb that she had been mistakenly given, is caused by such an organization and, in the context of Patrick's assertion that he loves her because she doesn't believe herself *big enough to put someone in a position where they will hurt another* (160), operates in the novel as an argument against both violence and group political action.

The other remedies the book offers against the power of the wealthy are individual ones that involve the assistance of others only through voluntary acts of kindness. Nicholas Temelcoff acquires the capital necessary to open his own bakery by becoming 'a solitary' (34), 'lost to community' (39). Hazen Lewis, Patrick's father, finds relative freedom through self-improvement, teaching himself dynamiting skills, and going into business as a small blasting contractor. His son enacts his anger against the wealthy through solitary acts of sabotage; he burns down a Muskoka resort hotel and later attempts to dynamite, or dreams of dynamiting – the novel insists on this ambiguity – Harris's water filtration plant. In this real or dream venture he is helped by the thief Caravaggio, whose life he had once saved, and Caravaggio's wife, Giannetta. Caravaggio's own numerous and precisely executed burglaries of wealthy homes stand as a metaphor for such individual resistance; the language in which they are narrated emphasizes his solitariness, the artistic precision of his movements, and his insertion of himself among the art objects his victims have collected:

> ... all those libraries he had stepped into in Toronto homes, the grand vistas of bookcases that reached the ceiling, the books of pigskin and other leathers that fell into his arms as he climbed up the shelves looking for whatever valuables he imagined were there, his boots pushing in the books to get a toe-hold. And then from up there, his head close to the ceiling, looking down on the rectangle of the rooms, hearing his dog's clear warning bark, not moving. And the door opening below him – a man walking in to pick up the telephone and dialing, while Caravaggio hung high up on the bookcases knowing now he should move the second he was seen up there in his dark trousers and singlet, as still as a gargoyle against Trollope and H.G. Wells. He could land on the leather sofa and bounce into the man's body before he even said a word into the phone. Then go through the French doors without opening them, a hunch of his body as he breaks through the glass and thin wood ... (198)

Caravaggio the thief, and the Italian Renaissance painter his name invokes, in fact appear to stand at the centre of the problematical ideological position of *In the Skin of a Lion*. He insists on working alone: 'I can never work with someone else, you know that!' (203). He prefers to work in shadow, or in the play of light and shadow – 'a sliver of new moon that gave off little light' (180). The Renaissance painter Michelangelo Amerighi da Caravaggio was an immigrant to Rome, as Ondaatje's Caravaggio is an immigrant to Toronto. He too came into legal conflict with authority, over fourteen times in six years, in offences ranging from slander and assault to murder in a 1606 gambling dispute (Moir, 31). His paintings were distinguished by their extraordinary detail and their dramatic contrasts of light and shadow – features which play large roles in the descriptive discourse of *In the Skin of a Lion*.

Both Caravaggio and Patrick are presented as being obsessively aware of the minute, sensuous surfaces of experience, and particularly so in darkness faintly punctuated by light. Caravaggio trains himself to work 'in unlit rooms' (189), meets his wife-to-be in the 'minimal light' (190) of a mushroom factory, and later makes love to her in 'the half-lit kitchen' (204) of her brother's house. Patrick also is presented in successive scenes of fine detail and abrupt juxtapositions of light and shadow. As a small boy he scrutinizes insects:

> Up close they are prehistoric. The insect jaws munch. Are they eating something minute or is it subliminal – the way his father chews his tongue when in the fields. The kitchen light radiates through their porous wings; even those that are squat, like the peach-green aphid, appear to be constructed of powder. (10)

Throughout the novel he is shown repeatedly moving in dark, dimly lit scenes, watching the Finnish loggers skating by torchlight on a river; swimming underwater to plant dynamite charges for his father; blindfolding himself so that he can move 'immaculate and magical' (79) around a room whose topography he has memorized; set on fire in 'the dark night' beside the Depot River by Ambrose Small (94); tunnelling by lamplight in the darkness beneath Lake Ontario; swimming 'in darkness, just the pull of this water to guide him' (230) through this tunnel years later; and finally driving 'through darkness,' 'by the faint light of the speedometer,' to Marmora to retrieve Clara (1). In most of these scenes the action is aestheticized by a shift of attention away from the human drama to the movement of forms, textures, and shadows:

> So Patrick moved in this darkness, the eye of the flashlight swallowing the colours, the room turning under his gaze like a jewel.
>
> ...
>
> The light moved down her arm to the bowl, illuminated her hand which wet the cloth, squeezed it, and moved forward to give it to him. She saw his right hand reach to take it from her. His hand began to wipe her neck. He removed the brown paint, turned her around and slowly wiped the vermilion frown-mark by her mouth, the light close on her face. (120–1)

This discourse of darkness, small detail and faint light – 'darkness' is the text's most frequently occurring noun – reinforces the narrative's emphasis on individual action and mistrust of collective politics. It assumes a single perceiving consciousness, ascribes value to a sharply limited field of vision, to a social space that can contain no more than two or three people. The discourse is also used in the one large narrative segment that concerns neither Patrick nor Caravaggio, the narrative of Nicholas Temelcoff's virtuoso high-steel work on Harris's Bloor viaduct. While the solitary and resourceful Temelcoff is solving his political problems by earning money through his adroit trapeze-artistry beneath the viaduct, and teaching himself English by mimicking the actors at live theatre, the chapter which presents him is punctuated with fiery tar pots being trucked through 'passing darkness,' 'flares along the edges of the bridge on winter's nights' (28), the 'flickering light' of workers rushing to be the first to cross the completed bridge. By sharply limiting and intensifying the visual field of the bridge worksite, the chapter is able to depict Temelcoff as knowing this site so intimately he can work at night 'swinging up into the rafters of a trestle holding a flare, free-falling like a dead star.' Like Patrick blindfolded in a room he has memorized, or Caravaggio gathering valuables in a darkened house,

> he does not really need to see things, he has charted all that space, knows the pier footings, the width of the cross-walks in terms of seconds of movement – 281 feet and 6 inches make up the central span of the bridge. Two flanking spans of 240 feet, two end spans of 158 feet. He slips into openings on the lower deck, tackles himself up to bridge level. He knows the precise height he is over the river, how long his ropes are, how many seconds he can free-fall to the pulley. It does not matter if it is day or night, he could be blindfolded. Black space is time. (35)

The discourse of light, shadow, darkness, sharp detail, and precise measurement is that of the overall narrative rather than of one character. It marks both how the major male characters – Patrick, Temelcoff, and Caravaggio – experience the world and how the narrator recurrently imagines and frames the narrative. It effectively allies the text with the three major male characters; how they experience the world is also how the novel constructs it; the value they implicitly attribute to the texture of phenomena becomes the prime value endorsed by the text overall. Intense intimate experience – Caravaggio and Giannetta's love-making in the shattered glass and pottery of her brother's dark kitchen, Temelcoff's rescue of Alice while swinging on a rope beneath the dark bridge, or even the illusion of sensuous intimacy offered by the text of the novel itself – are given precedence here over any quest for political justice or systemic social change.

One important effect of this discourse is to introduce a third term into what in its rough narrative outlines seems to be a bi-polar story that opposes exploitive businessmen and big government, on the one hand, against exploited and silenced workers, on the other. This third term is the sensuous and includes both art and intimacy: the solitary performer – the acrobatic Temelcoff in his ropes and tackle, the amorous couple encountering through tastes, smells, textures, and darkness. The scale and sightlines of this third term are small, no more than the limits of a room and often no more than fractions of inches between lovers. Its values are precision, economy, and emotional focus on a single object or person. Its human model is Patrick's devoted but 'taciturn' (19) father, who calls square dances without moving a muscle in his body, and when working with dynamite is said to wear 'no metal on him, not a watch or belt buckle':

> He was a man who with his few props had become self-sufficient, as invisible as possible ... He left a track of half-inch holes in the granite all down the Depot Lakes system and along the Moira River system where he sometimes was hired. But these were as modest and minimal as they could be. (18)

The sensuous, with its goals of intimacy and self-sufficiency, not only becomes a third possibility alongside the anonymous worker and the wealthy employer, but also obscures any sharp division between these; while offering an illusion of harmony between men and women socially in conflict, it also impedes and mystifies the political action necessary to end this conflict. The immigrant Caravaggio, the poor native white Canadian Patrick, the self-made man of power Harris, and the arrogant entrepreneur Ambrose Small can all achieve its precisions and minute intensities. Harris becomes so intimate with the filtration plant he is building that 'he could *smell* the place before it was there, knew every image of it as well as his arms – west wing, east wing' (109). Small 'choreographs' his business schemes like Temelcoff measures and plans his rope-end journeys or Caravaggio plans his escapes. He buys 'houses under different names all over Ontario.' '"I'm a thief," he'd say, "all thieves must plan their escape routes"' (58). 'A rich man who escaped from a rich shoe' (99), he exchanges the 'grand' (as in his Grand Theatres in Toronto and London) for the small and intimate – for a reclusive life with Clara Dickens beside the river on which small-town Patrick Lewis spent his boyhood.

Small's blatant capitalism had clarified the gulf between the rich and the starving.

In the Skin of a Lion, 59

The contrast *In the Skin of a Lion* constructs between the powerful and the powerless, in such pairs as bridge builder Harris and bridge worker Temelcoff, or Ambrose Small and Patrick Lewis as sexual rivals for Clara, argues indeed for clear demarcations between rich and poor, the privileged and the disadvantaged. Whenever confrontations occur between the two, however, the 'gulf' between them tends to lose clarity. A text which has appeared to offer indignation at the disparities of a capitalist society becomes one which charitably views both entrepreneur and workman equally as potential artists – painters, choreographers, dreamers, people of imagination. When Patrick confronts Ambrose Small at the old Rathburn estate and is ambushed and nearly killed by him, both Clara as idealized love-object and 'clarity' falter. The mysterious Clara remains kind and loving to both men. The balance between her feelings for the two becomes especially evident when she reaches the halfway point in her return from Patrick's hotel to Ambrose's house and the text comments: 'she felt somehow deliriously happy between the two points of this journey' (100).

In the episode in which Patrick appears to attempt to dynamite Commissioner Harris's filtration plant (220–42) a similar blurring of conflict occurs. The very ambiguity that frames the episode – conflicting evidence that it is a dream (Patrick goes to sleep just before its narration begins and is awakened by Hana from the same sleep as it ends) and that it is a flashback to something that actually happens (Patrick's arm which he injures at the filtration plant is in a cast before and after the narration) – suggests the novel's reluctance to admit to class divisions. The events of the episode, which constitutes the last major narrative sequence of the novel, are constructed, as in the Patrick–Ambrose Small confrontation, as a conflict between rich and poor – exploiting boss and exploited worker. Patrick 'dreams' that he reaches the filtration plant by collaborating with Caravaggio and Giannetta to steal a yacht from the opulent Royal Canadian Yacht

Club and by swimming through the plant's 'servant's entrance,' its water intake tunnel beneath Lake Ontario. Harris waits in his lavishly adorned waterworks, with its brass elevator, marble walls, and mosaic-tile floors. His desk, inlaid with feldspar, recalls the death of Patrick's father in the callously run feldspar mine. Patrick enters Harris's office with his left arm hanging broken, as Temelcoff's had hung fifteen years before, after his rescue of Alice beneath Harris's viaduct.

In the argument that occurs between them, however, Harris manages not only to prevent Patrick from detonating the dynamite charges he has planted but also to construct himself as a 'poor boy' artist and Patrick as potential exploiter and killer. He claims that his mother was a City Hall caretaker, that he 'worked up' to his present position of power in the city administration. He recounts his dreams of monumental parks and structures throughout Toronto and declares that his filtration plant will be admired for its 'excess' in fifty years time. He persuades Patrick to recount Alice's death at the hands of 'an anarchist.' In remembering that scene, Patrick recalls his anger and his being calmed by Nicholas Temelcoff. Structurally this memory transforms Patrick from bomber to bomb-victim, from someone angry and aggressive to someone aggrieved and comforted. Rather than detonating the charges he has planted he falls asleep.

Throughout the episode the novel creates a Harris who refuses to be constructed as Patrick's opposite. Harris not only claims the same working-class origins as Patrick but argues that they have a similar relationship to political power. Patrick 'move[s] around in it all the time' (236) even though he rejects it. Harris claims that he himself – like Patrick – doesn't have 'real power'; that 'those with real power ... didn't carry a cent. Harris was an amateur in their midst. He had to sell himself every time' (242). When he realizes that Patrick has swum into the filtration plant through the intake tunnel, he applauds him silently in the same terms as he had, a page earlier, praised his own imaginings of the 'wonderful' Toronto that might have been: 'What vision, what dream was that?' (241). When he discovers that Patrick has fallen asleep, he responds mercifully, like Temelcoff at Alice's death: 'Let him sleep on ... Bring a nurse with some medical supplies here, he's hurt himself' (242).

Whether a dream or a recollection of fact, the episode appears to constitute Patrick's unconscious resolution of his anger at Alice's death and the concentration of wealth and power she opposed, as well as the text's resolution of one of its major ideological questions. Its placement close to the end of the novel and immediately before the text's narrative resolution leaves the episode's constructions of power and artistic process uncontradicted and seemingly endorsed by the happiness with which Patrick leaves for Marmora. The narrative resolution, in fact, encloses the ideological resolution within a traditionally patriarchal comic structure; wealth and poverty are reconciled within the ethic of individual responsibility articulated by Harris ('You must realize you are like these places, Patrick. You're as much of the fabric as the aldermen and the millionaires' [238]), and a symbolic marriage, the recreation of an archetypal father-mother-child triad, is about to be accomplished in Marmora.

Contained within southern Ontario, Canada here is made up of waves of predominantly male immigrants and structured by uneven and intractable distributions of wealth. Immigrants arrive and become workers or thieves, and the wealthy amass property and power oblivious to other parts of Canada or to other cultural claims within the nation. An implicit socialist critique of capitalism ('Ambrose Small had been the jackal of Toronto's business world. ... He was bareknuckle capitalism. He was a hawk who hovered over the whole province' [57]) is abandoned to its own self-parodying phrases, dissolved into angry, incoherent anarchist acts – random bombings, individual acts of arson. Gradually replacing it is a humanist construction of the male individual as artist – bridge builder, lover, choreographer, or dreamer – who must progress like Nicholas Temelcoff from 'a solitary' acrobat to a 'citizen,' a baker whose 'breads and rolls and cakes and pastries reach the multitudes in the city' (149). One general ahistorical model of Canadian society – rich and poor, exploiter and exploited – yields to an even more general but implicitly patriarchal one in which all men appear to have some access to sensuous visionary experience which can link them with a universal human fabric (the women do not focalize any of the action or artistic vision of the novel and remain in the conventional auxiliary roles of patriarchy, Clara overwhelmed by love, Alice assisting Cato and later the Macedonian workers, Hana driving Patrick to Marmora). This is a significantly different humanism from those of *Obasan* or *The Diviners*, based on a concept of the aesthetic rather than on ones of general humanity or transcendent Nature, based entirely on male 'artists,' and emphasizing the ability of these artists to actively participate in the aesthetic rather than enter into the kinds of 'negative capability' suggested in the Kogawa or Laurence novels, but it is nevertheless one equally indifferent to political process.

On the final page of *In the Skin of a Lion* the immigrant worker, the absent dog, 'seemingly tamed' raccoons, and the hedges, steps, and porches that testify to human creation all come together into a 'comfortable' narrative of beauty. Although this coming-together is rendered in a more subtle language than is the touristic text which heads this chapter, its eliding of meaningful social conflict beneath figures of pattern, beauty, or artistic construction is similar:

> The second-floor balconies curved out to the street. Odours from each hedge. Mr. Rivera hosing his garden at three A.M. having just returned from a night shift, private as they passed him. A dog's chain hung off a step railing. They were off to guide Clara back to this street. He found it most beautiful, felt most comfortable at this hour when they often saw raccoons pausing on steps, seemingly tamed, as if owning the territory of the porch. (244)

Conflicts resolved or forgotten, cooperatively driving their car, Hana and Patrick drive off to reintegrate Clara into this community, which, even if it exists only in Patrick's imagination, affirms thereby the power of imagination to transcend or harmonize human difference. The car, however, is not imaginary. That a sixteen-year-old orphan and a labourer newly released from jail can acquire it late in the Great Depression speaks volumes about the text's preference for art over history, economics, and cultural contest.

Canada as Periphery
Fifth Business

Critics of the works of Robertson Davies have on numerous occasions associated his novels with conservative and elitist social positions. Elspeth Buitenhuis wrote of his 'insistence on Apollonian restraint' (70) and a 'vision ... that we are now in a fallen world' (77). Robert Cluett concluded a study of Davies's syntax and lexis with a suggestion that he wrote in a 'Tory mode'; Stephen Bonnycastle argued that Davies's narrative constructions are monologic and authoritarian, that even when they employ more than one voice these voices are hierarchically arranged to minimize conflict and ambiguity. In the case of *Fifth Business*, however, such arguments appear at first glance to face some difficulty. Although the novel does associate itself closely with conservative institutions and their discourses – the Roman Catholic church, private school education, big business, and Jungian psychology – all are to some extent subject to irony. The novel's narrative structure is indeed monologic in the sense that all of its voices and discourses are contained within the autobiographical and self-apologetic discourse of a letter by narrator Dunstan Ramsay, but none of these voices nor even Ramsay's own is marked as reliable. The duplicity and uncertainty of Buitenhuis's 'fallen world' undermine the narrative, so that finally all motivation and characterization in the novel are rendered uncertain and ambiguous.

Fifth Business is narrated by its main character, history teacher and hagiologist Ramsay, in the letter he writes to the headmaster of the private boy's school, 'Colborne College,' in which he taught for some thirty years – a letter which the headmaster is to open only after his death. The text thus offers a regression of 'authors': a signator, the public 'Robertson Davies,' actor, journalist, master of University of Toronto's Massey College, and author of numerous plays and novels;

a scriptor, someone within the novel who has retrieved the dead Dunstan Ramsay's letter and made it available within the fictional context of the novel; and the I-narrator, Ramsay himself. It is the I-narrator that appears to fill most of the space of the novel, controlling the sequence and pace of narration, controlling its characterizations, and commenting interpretively on all actions including Ramsay's own. The scriptor gives no direct indication of his presence, apart from contributing an epigraph from the Danish dramatist Thomas Overskou; the signator confines indication of his presence to the cover and title page, and to the selection of characters, incidents, structures, and discourses he allows to his narrator. It is on this selection, however, that any reading of the novel must rely.

Four of the five principal characters of *Fifth Business* come from the small turn-of-the-century southwestern Ontario town of Deptford and from moral certainties the I-narrator and his text work steadily to belie. Ramsay is the son of Presbyterian Scots immigrants, a newspaper publisher and his intensely pragmatic wife, whose firm social and moral views dominate the family. His nemesis, 'Boy' Staunton, is the son of an even more pragmatic and prosperous doctor, who avoids illness and amasses wealth by gradually subordinating his medical work to real estate speculation. Leola Cruikshank, courted by Ramsay and Staunton and 'won' by the latter, is the carpenter's daughter who 'always smelled of fresh ironing' (70). Paul Dempster, who at age ten runs away with a circus and eventually becomes a master illusionist, is the son of a Baptist minister whose theology is characterized as strict, unimaginative, and soul-constraining. Although there are disputes within the community which these families and their neighbours form over what may constitute piety and good sense, the community is united in its assumptions about the systematic nature of morality and the relatively easy compatibility of moral and material goals.

The text allows the community only a few, but very strong, signs of rupture or dissent. On its boundaries is a gravel pit where transients sometimes camp, and to where the town teenagers often repair for sexual experiment. Ramsay recalls that the Presbyterian minister occasionally compared the pit to 'Gehenna, the hateful valley outside the walls of Jerusalem, where outcasts lived, and where their flickering fires, seen from the city walls, may have given rise to the idea of a hell of perpetual burning' (47). Ramsay's father frequently, although not too successfully, disputes his wife's hysterical defences of her moral universe and is known to have been 'pro-Boer in 1901' and to have dissented from his village's 'romantic' view of the First World War, having 'serious doubts about the justice of any war' (69). In the village library the teenage Ramsay discovers a hidden cache of forbidden books on sexuality, stage magic, and Roman Catholic saints. And Paul Dempster's mother, Mary, not only dissents from village practice of frugal and diligent home management by neglecting her housework to wander from house to house, offering gifts of wilted vegetables to her neighbours, but dissents from its moral and sexual code by being caught in the pit offering sexual solace to a tramp because 'he was very civil' and 'wanted it so badly' (49).

The novel thus sets up two constrasting discourses about what constitutes morality and knowledge – a positivist discourse of moral certainty and pragmatic materialism, and a counter-discourse of dissenting and banished voices. Most of the action of the novel – Mary Dempster's psychological collapse, Paul's running away with the circus, Ramsay's rejection of his family to join the army, and his lifelong contempt for Boy Staunton – stems from these counter-discourses. A general binary opposition, between social pragmatism and materialism, on the one hand, and spiritual adventurousness and generosity, on the other, is built upon these and made to qualify nearly every event and character. Characters are either cautious, conventional, and essentially self-serving – Ramsay's mother, Paul's father, Paul himself, and Boy Staunton – or they are generous, adventurous, mythmaking, and selfless – the eccentric Jesuit Ignatius Blazon, Paul's enigmatic patron Liesl Vitzipuetzli, and the profligate Mary Dempster. This opposition, and not Dunstan Ramsay's narrative per se, is responsible for the monological effect of the novel. For while Ramsay's own discourse is filled with pomposities, contradictions, and unconscious ironies, the general opposition between the pragmatic and the selfless runs consistently through the novel from first page to last. Even Canada is subsumed within this opposition when Liesl comments that Paul had to get 'out of that dreadful Canada and into a country where big spiritual adventures are possible' (256).

The terms of this opposition operate throughout the novel to disvalue public discourse and debate, and to valorize eccentric, private, and specialized discourses that have partitioned themselves from public life. In particular, the public institutional life of Canada – its village politics, its public libraries, its newspapers, its federal politics – are subjected to condescension and irony while secretive, transnational institutions and knowledges – Deptford's 'cupboard of banished books'

(36) – are celebrated. In contrast to novels like *The Diviners, Obasan, Slash, Caprice,* or even *Nights below Station Street* which, despite their specific ideological differences, attempt to enlarge human community and to expand the field of affiliations of their central characters, *Fifth Business* progressively diminishes and encloses Dunstan Ramsay's social field. From being a boy in touch with the entire life of his village – its various churches, its newspaper, its varieties of wealth and poverty – Ramsay moves steadily into more restricted and specialized discourses. His university years are in many ways a retreat from the public sphere: 'it was a pleasure to be inside and warm, instead of wallowing in mud ... I made no close friends and never sought popularity or office in any of the student committees ...' (124). He chooses to teach in a private rather than public school. He immerses himself in the study of saints – in 'the wonderful enclosed garden of hagiology' (142). At the same time the novel relentlessly contructs the public realm of Canadian politics and business as nonlegitimate by repeatedly associating it with the callow and manipulative Boy Staunton.

———————

Because Ramsay is portrayed as slowly moving from the Canada/ Deptford/philistine side of this dichotomy to its European/transcendent/generous opposite, his own position within the opposition is often ambiguous. It takes Dunstan the entire novel to come close to outgrowing his selfish, 'Canadian,' instrumentalist origins. The text frequently constructs him as smugly deceiving himself that he is possessed of taste and learning, that he has lifted himself above the mere practicality and materialism of Deptford. He may be contemptuous of Leola's inability to understand his research into saints and of Boy's obsessions with money and power, but his own attitudes are themselves far from being unworldly or idealistic. He is overly proud of his secret visits to the ostracized Mrs Dempster, of his marginally useful but encyclopaedic learning, and of his eccentric books on the history and psychology of saints. He is overly proud also of his strange beliefs that the eccentric Mrs Dempster brought his brother Willy back from the dead during a childhood illness and later saved Ramsay himself from death by appearing to him as the Virgin Mary on the Passchendaele battlefield. The text also emphasizes that in many of Ramsay's most important decisions his conviction that he is someone who rejects 'Canadian' pragmatism and embraces mysticism and selflessness appears to be hypocritically forgotten. When a lawyer's embezzlement leaves Mrs Dempster penniless, he declines the opportunity to sacrifice his European research-vacations in order to pay for her hospitalization in a private facility, instead committing her to an impersonal public ward where he knows she will be miserable. And when Leola, grief-stricken at having been betrayed by her husband, begs Ramsay to make love to her – asking him even more 'civilly' than the tramp once asked the same favour of Mrs Dempster, he refuses, thinking mainly of his own emotions:

> It had been at least ten years since I had thought of her with anything but pity. I had made my bed and I intended to lie on it, and there was no room for Leola in it ... I was not to be a victim of her self-pity. The emotional upheaval caused by her disappointment about Boy's unfaithfulness had sharpened her sexual appetite; that was all. (219–20)

Not even considering any principle of self-sacrifice or compassion, Ramsay invokes what the novel has argued are the puritan and pragmatic discourses of Deptford; he construes his own past as moral destiny ('had made my bed and I intended to lie on it'), Leola's need as 'sexual appetite,' and the possibility of his own generosity as exploitation ('I was not to be a victim'). The terms in which she expresses her desire to him – 'Kiss me *really*' – recall another instance of his using her for his own aggrandizement: on her engagement to Boy he had kissed her publicly with feigned passion in order to show the village that 'there had been a contest and that I had been a near winner myself, and had shown some speed in the preliminary heats.' Ramsay's main thoughts then, as later, were not about Leola but himself: 'It was a good moment and I enjoyed it thoroughly' (113).

Immediately after Ramsay fails, so to speak, the Mrs Dempster test by declining to make love to Leola, she attempts suicide, and once again his thoughts are mainly for himself. She leaves a note addressed to him, which concludes, 'I always loved you.' His response appears not even to notice her declaration of love, or to give any thought to her own plight:

> Fool, fool, fool! Thinking only of herself and putting me in an intolerable position with such a note. If she had died, how would it have sounded at an inquest? ... I was furious with Leola, poor idiot. No note for Boy. No, just a note for me, which would have made me look like a monster if she had not made a mess of this, as of so much else. (221)

This ambiguous position of Dunstan Ramsay within the novel's

opposition of pragmatic self-interest and selfless generosity operates,
however, to confirm rather than interrogate this opposition. The text
never questions his intellectual affirmation of Mrs Dempster, and of
the world of mythical and irrational sainthood he believes her to
symbolize. What it does question is his ability to do more than admire
selflessness, to recognize his own narcissism, to cease being the Canadian 'moral monster' who, Liesl tells him, despises 'almost everybody except Paul's mother': 'No wonder she seems like a saint to
you; you have made her carry the affection you should have spread
among fifty people' (255). When the text shows Ramsay at last gaining
an ability to care for others more than for himself, this change confirms the text's endorsement elsewhere of the spiritually generous
over the selfishly pragmatic. The crucial incident in this change is a
quarrel with Liesl, who, like Leola before, has asked Ramsay to make
love with her. After a short but violent physical quarrel, he overcomes
his perception of her physical 'ugliness' (243), feels unexpected so-
licitude towards her, and accepts her love. The text then has him
declare he has 'never ... known such deep delight or such an aftermath
of healing tenderness' (267).

'Mary, what made you do it?'

Fifth Business, 49

Although most of the major incidents of *Fifth Business* concern sexual
intercourse, not as an act of passion or lust but as a test of charity or
selflessness, the incident to which the text gives most prominence is
the throwing of a stone-cored snowball in the novel's opening chapter. In this incident Boy Staunton, enraged by the speed of young
Ramsay's sleigh, hurls the snowball at him, which the latter evades
by ducking behind the Reverend and Mrs Dempster. The snowball
strikes and fells Mrs Dempster, causing Paul's premature birth and,
in the view of some observers, the apparent 'simpleness' of her later
behaviour. The text, however, is careful to qualify such an explanation, offering in addition the suggestion that she was fragile and over-
protected before her marriage and, through Ramsay's mother, the
observation that after the snowball incident 'Mrs. Dempster was really
no different from what she had been before, except that she was more
so' (21).

Two possible teleological chains are established by the incident.

In one the snowball creates a gap in the social code of the village, making Mrs Dempster mentally incapable of obeying its practices and injunctions. It leads to her carelessness as a mother and housewife, her casual granting of her body to the tramp, and from there to her son Paul's being taunted in the schoolyard as the son of a 'hoor' and to his leaving with the circus. In the other it creates a gap in the village's social code for Dunstan Ramsay, a gap through which he can distinguish himself as both opposite to Boy Staunton and as linked by guilt to the eccentric Mrs Dempster. These two teleological chains echo the general opposition between the material and spiritual that structures the novel. The first is anti-spiritual, offering a scientific explanation for Mrs Dempster's ignoring of social convention: a stone has injured her brain and made her incapable of judgment which would be 'natural' to an unimpaired individual. The second is anti-material; despite the presence of a chain of causality there is no necessary physical connection between the trajectory and velocity of the stone and Mrs Dempster's kindness to the tramp, or between the stone and young Ramsay's construction of his own relationship to its possible consequences. While the second chain appears to deny the first, it is, however, in some ways also dependent upon it and interwoven with it. The stone does appear to contribute to Paul's premature birth, small size, and odd appearance. This in turn does add both to Mrs Dempster's afflictions and to the stock of events for which young Ramsay may experience responsibility.

Within the self-preoccupation of Ramsay's narration it is the second chain which gains precedence; the snowball gradually appears to have had more impact on Ramsay, whom it did not hit, than on Mrs Dempster, whom it did. His assumption of guilt for having ducked, and responsibility for the various social disasters that later befall Mrs Dempster and Paul, lead him to visit and assist her when her husband is not home, to teach elementary magic tricks to Paul, and, through his contact with apparently simple generosity, to idealize her as a saintlike incarnation of goodness. These developments in turn will lead not only to his assuming care of her when he is an adult but also to Paul's becoming the professional magician who will introduce Ramsay to Liesl, and later to Liesl's attempts to 'free' Ramsay from his obsessions with Mrs Dempster. And, in the final chapter, they will culminate in Boy's visit to Paul Dempster's magic show, the reappearance of the stone, and Boy's murder.

In so elaborating the consequences of a single impetuously thrown snowball, *Fifth Business* constructs a complex network of determinations and contingencies, an elaborate and encompassing teleology, an implication that all events may be enmeshed in meaning- systems so vast and complex they exceed the ability of any individual to unravel them, or of a society to construct its own meanings. One of the two governing topoi of the novel is *mystery* – the mystery of Mary Dempster's 'saintly' behaviour, the mystery of the extent of Boy's knowledge of his role in the shaping of so many lives and events, the mystery of the madonna Ramsay encounters on the battlefield at Passchendaele, the mystery of Boy's death. This topos assumes cause, plan, teleology. The accompanying topos is *research* – Ramsay's conviction that the mystery of his relationship to Mrs Dempster can be solved through his obsessive scholarly research into images of the madonna and the lives of saints. Like the novel's sharp dichotomy between secular and transcendent discourses, this topos of mystery is again politically disabling, in effect positing an autonomous category both privileged within and sequestered from a community's other social practices. This privileged and politically disabling position is similar to the positions given to the aesthetic in *In the Skin of a Lion* and to nature and chance in *Nights below Station Street*.

In *Fifth Business* the mystery that is repeatedly returned to is that of the 'saintliness' of Mary Dempster, ostensibly rendered 'simple' when struck by the stone in Boy Staunton's snowball. Mary Dempster is the largest instance of 'goodness' in the novel; beside her most of the other characters appear rule-bound and self-serving, or at the very least unmindful of the needs of others. Her goodness, however, is circumscribed by the story of the stone, and by the complex pattern of causations within which the stone exerts its force. That is, Mary Dempster's goodness is not a social goodness, and perhaps not even a human one. It is produced by aberration, by an unconventional upbringing or by a mysterious blow; its activity involves transgression of social norms and codings; the complex pattern in which the blow to her head occurs implies transcendent or chance causation. She is Mary Dempster, linked to the holy mother through the Passchendaele madonna whom Ramsay mistakes as bearing her face and constructed through her last name as a redeemer. The touchstone of goodness in the novel is thus placed outside the social, in a mystery which can be, as Ramsay is told by Ignatius Blazon, only 'mythologically' (207) understood.

So Leola ... sat between us while Boy showed the pictures, telling me what lens apertures he had used, and how he had arranged the lights, and how he had achieved certain 'values' which, in fact, made Leola's rose-leaf bottom look like sharkskin and her nipples glare when they should have blushed.

Fifth Business, 182

As well as beginning a complex and seemingly inevitable teleological chain, the stone-in-the-snowball operates also in the novel to join Boy Staunton and Dunstan Ramsay as a necessary pair. From this event onward Ramsay recurrently measures himself in relation to Boy, initially in terms of their contrasting responses to Mrs Dempster's injury, later in terms of their different interests in life and their different relationships to Leola. Immediately after the snowball incident Ramsay experiences guilt for Mrs Dempster's injury, but Boy appears to feel no responsibility, 'would fight, lie, do anything rather than admit what [Ramsay] knew' (18). The incident leads Ramsay to construct Staunton and himself as black and white twins, one pragmatic, acquisitive, and selfish, the other idealistic, mystical, and generous. This construction, like the two explanations of Mrs Dempster's eccentricity, again echoes the general and overdetermined dichotomy the text assumes between the pragmatic and the spiritual. Although the novel does make clear that Ramsay's construction of himself and Staunton is inaccurate – Ramsay is in his own way as selfish and pragmatic as Staunton – it allows it to stand for Ramsay as a kind of ego-ideal. It is this compassionate alternative to Staunton that Ramsay is still struggling to be when, late in the novel, he makes love to the 'ugly' Liesl.

In contrast to Ramsay's smug distinguishing of himself from Staunton the novel itself often portrays his life as parallel to that of Staunton. Both are shown to intervene through the snowball into Mary and Paul Dempster's lives. Both are attracted to Leola Cruikshank, both fight in the First World War, both invest successfully in the stock market, and both become administrators – Boy as chairman of the board, Dunstan as acting headmaster – of Colborne College. The role the novel gives Ramsay, however, is usually a lesser or shadow role. Staunton throws the snowball, whereas Ramsay merely evades it; Staunton obtains an officer's commission before going to war; Ramsay runs away to war, enlisting as an under-age private; Staunton actively courts Leola, whereas Ramsay appears attracted to her mainly because Staunton is, seems relieved to have Staunton marry her, and later,

when Staunton loses interest in her, loses interest too; Staunton suc-
ceeds as a major player of the stock market; Ramsay invests only on
Staunton's advice.

Throughout, the text offers hints of an unconscious homosexual
attraction between Ramsay and Staunton, for which Leola serves un-
wittingly as the bridge. Ramsay's most vigorous courting of Leola
occurs when she is perceived by Deptford as Staunton's 'girl.' During
most of her marriage to Staunton she serves as the occasion for the
two men's interaction. In one notable instance it is Staunton who
initiates an apparent sexual exchange, taking nude photos of Leola,
asking Ramsay to develop them in his darkroom, and then positioning
Leola between them on a couch while he discusses the photos with
Ramsay and argues their aesthetic merits. Later that evening Boy and
Leola conceive their first child. The episode structurally repeats the
snowball incident, in which an action between Staunton and Ramsay
engages a female third party who must substitute herself for the unavailable male.

Through this pairing of Staunton and Ramsay the text indirectly
attacks social discourse by emphasizing the subservience of both of
them to codes of propriety and conventionality and the 'spiritual' self-
knowledge that this subservience denies them. The text also employs
the pairing to imply that the considerable ideological differences between the two men – Staunton's belief that a person's worth lies in
material accomplishment, Ramsay's that it lies in that person's relationship to transcendent process – are individual and psychological
rather than political. The text portrays both as believing they are in
love with Leola, when they are in love only with themselves and the
self-reflections they see in each other. Both are shown to view themselves as unusual men, Staunton as a bold entrepreneur, Ramsay as
a bold eccentric and important scholar, when in fact they are merely
living, in slightly larger contexts, the cautious and pragmatic lives of
their Deptford forebears. Their perception of themselves as paired is
shown also to contribute to Ramsay's unwillingness to grant Leola's
request that he make love to her. Rather than seeing his situation as
a relationship between himself and Leola, he can see it only as a
contest between 'Gyges and King Candaules,' a contest which must
result in the death of one of the males. Through the mythic parallel
the text offers a Jungian explanation of Ramsay's refusal: he is not
only selfishly unwilling to honour her emotions in place of his own,
but also psychologically unwilling to trade his narcissistic relationship
with Staunton for the relationship between two separate selves which

Leola is offering. In so doing, the text ignores the latent political implications of the refusal: that it might equally encode a preference for narcissistic self-love over a selfless entry into the social order announced by a freely offered 'other.' It also blurs the political difference between an entrepreneur for whom power lies in his ability to manipulate money, wife, and friend and a Protestant mystic for whom it lies in a narrowly conceived individual integrity and in privately gained knowledge of transcendence.

... she was a woman whose life and interests were entirely external. It was not that she was indifferent to things of the spirit; she sensed their existence and declared herself their enemy ... All her moral and ethical energy, which was abundant, was directed towards social reform. Easier divorce, equal pay for equal work as between men and women, no discrimination between the sexes in employment – these were her causes ...

Fifth Business, 282

The only character in *Fifth Business* whom the text allows to perceive political and social relations as sites for general human amelioration is Denyse Hornick, a woman Boy Staunton marries late in the novel some years after the death of Leola. Dunstan Ramsay finds her hostile and quarrelsome and, accusing her of attempting to limit his relationship with Staunton, gives her a less than sympathetic portrait. Within the governing dichotomy of the novel he links her with the unimaginative and pragmatic citizens of Deptford who banished books on magic and saints to locked cupboards in the village library: 'The whole notion of saints was repugnant to her, and in her eyes I was on a level with people who believed in teacup readings and Social Credit' (283). He hints that she made Boy 'think it was his own idea' (275) that they marry and suggests that her main goal is to manipulate her political contacts into making him lieutenant-governor of Ontario. Although the text gives Ramsay enough spitefulness and general unreliability to suggest that this may be an untrustworthy portrait, there is nothing in the text to suggest that the values on which this portrait is made – a profound preference for the 'spiritual' over the secular and pragmatic – are to be cast into doubt. The unreliability of Ramsay – his inability to love unselfishly, although admiring that in others, and his inability to perceive others except in terms of what they can do for him – is constructed by the text to indicate, not any deficiency in his ideals, but merely a deficiency in himself. The text itself endorses its narrator's caricature of feminist activist Denyse Hornick, not only by omitting any detail that might indicate her to be other than manipulative and self-serving, but also by preferring other models of virtue, notably Ignatius Blazon and Liesl Vitzipuetzli.

The latter portraits endorse highly individualistic people who urge Ramsay to enact his intellectual preference for actions that affirm 'spiritual' causes and ignore social codes of propriety and practicality. Blazon is, in many respects, an offence to the Jesuit order – 'obviously, indeed theatrically, a priest, which is contrary to Jesuit custom':

> Most of the priests smoked, moderately, but he took snuff immoderately, from a large horn box. His spectacles were mended with dirty string. His hair needed, not cutting, but mowing. His nose was large, red, and bulbous. (198)

He counsels Ramsay to stop being a 'Protestant,' to 'stop whimpering about the cruelty,' to 'get on with [his] own life,' 'to forgive [him]self for being a human creature' (207–8). Liesl also is characterized through signs of size and vitality – 'tall, straight, and obviously very strong ... big hands and feet, a huge, jutting jaw' (240–1). When she comes to make love to Ramsay, she threatens to 'drag' him into her 'arms and crush out [his] boyish modesty' and engages him in an almost even battle before he repels her. Her counsel to him is also to stop being such a Calvinist, to 'make a real life for himself,' to 'do something inexplicable, irrational, at the devil's bidding, and just for the hell of it' (266).

The semiotic map of *Fifth Business* is almost as limited and extra-Canadian as that of *Joshua Then and Now*. This field extends geographically from the small Ontario town of Deptford eastward to Toronto and Europe. The text contains little mention of any place in North America outside of Toronto and southwestern Ontario. From Toronto and Deptford the field moves at once to Europe, to Britain, the Low Countries, France, Germany, Italy, Switzerland, Portugal, Czechoslovakia, and Austria, with a brief tour of Mexico and 'the shrines of South America' (243); within both the text and Ramsay's life these countries are virtually interchangeable. Epistemologically the map extends from the magic books (J.E. Robert-Houdin's *The Secrets of Stage Conjuring*, Louis Hoffman's *Modern Magic* and *Later Magic*) which Ramsay finds as a child in the Deptford Library, through the Roman Catholic iconography of sainthood Ramsay makes his life's work, and into the *mysterium conjunctionis* of alchemy, magic, psychology, and theology of Jung's *The Psychology of the Transference*. This epistemological field is closely related to the geographic, which consists mostly of the Roman Catholic countries of Europe and South America which have nourished the Christian mystical beliefs on which the meaning-systems of magic, sainthood, and Jungian psychology have been founded.

The use of these fields and meaning-systems locates the significant events of *Fifth Business* outside of North America, and thereby places North America on the margins of world events. The books Ramsay finds 'banned' in the Deptford Library come from Europe (Hoffman's *Modern Magic* and *Later Magic*, first published in London in the 1870s; Robert-Houdin's *The Secrets of Stage Conjuring*, first published in French in the 'great and sophisticated capital' [31] of Paris in 1868). The explanations he seeks for Mary Dempster, and for her battlefield apparition at Passchendaele, lead him to repeated summer visits to Europe, to which his winters spent teaching in Toronto become mere interludes. Although the puzzles which activate Ramsay originate in Deptford – the effect of the snowball, Mrs Dempster's generosities, her appearing to save the life of his older brother – the meaning of these puzzles is located in Europe. The touchstone characters of his story become Blazon, a Spanish priest, and Liesl, a Swiss ogress. The text's emphasis on the transnational cultural history of Europe as the potential source and guarantor of Ramsay's spiritual awakening into full humanity has no correlative within his Canadian experiences. Deptford, Leola Cruikshank, Boy Staunton, Colborne College, together with their struggles, practices, and politics, are all joined under the signs of the secular, pragmatic, and spiritually unenlightened. The dichotomy of the pragmatic and the spiritual which governs the book ultimately becomes a North America/Europe opposition with Dunstan Ramsay its only possible exception. The text of *Fifth Business* is itself marked as European in origin – Ramsay writes it from Switzerland as a long autobiographical letter to his Toronto headmaster.

Elspeth Buitenhuis structured her reading of Davies's plays and novels around a distinction between the satiric and the romantic, arguing that Davies's combination of these modes has given his writings a 'double view of the world' (76). In terms of the semiotic fields and systems of *Fifth Business* the satiric mode is associated with the North American while the romantic is associated with the European. That is, North American meaning-systems – Mrs Ramsay's pragmatic piety, Deptford's views of culture and elegance, Boy Staunton's materialism, Ramsay's narcissistic homoerotic infatuation with Boy, Denyse Hornick's aggressive and rationalistic feminism – are all presented by the text with gently condescending humour, while the European are presented with respect, awe, reverence. All instances of the social and political occur in Canada, and thus under the sign of satire, while change and enlightenment are offered in Europe, under the sign of romance, and are individually gained and transcendently offered. Even European social units like the Jesuit Order play no more than an unwitting role in assisting Ramsay in his various quests. 'Politics' in *Fifth Business* remains an obscure secular realm where limited and shallow people like Boy and Denyse pursue short-sighted personal or social goals.

North of Culture
The Tent Peg

The question of whether women that men respected could be brought into that country was one of perpetual discussion. Nowhere does one see so plainly as in districts of new settlement the need of woman as a home-maker. The majority of the men in the Klondike, excepting, perhaps, the very young, were in the literal sense of the term, 'home' sick. They wanted a place as much as a person, but it needed a person to make the place, someone to minister to the common needs of life ... to wash the clothes, to cook the food, to give to one's fireside a human interest ... The rougher the man the more imperative the need appeared. The absence of homes in such a place as Dawson explains to a great extent the existence of saloons; and in noting the contrast between the splendid qualities exercised in the effort to acquire gold and the utter folly displayed in the spending of it, it was impossible to avoid the reflection that in the expansion of the Empire, as in other movements, man wins the battle but woman holds the field.

> Flora L. Shaw, 'Klondike,' *Proceedings of the Royal Canadian Institute* 30 (1898–9), 113

When the drilling crew moves in the chips are down. For these are the men who get the oil, if it's there, or spend as much as $1,000,000 before finding it's not.

They move with the split-second timing of a professional backfield in one of the fastest, toughest, most exciting jobs anywhere. The machine they use looks like a giant windmill with the blades removed. Actually it's a 15-story-high [*sic*] derrick, supporting a long steel pipe with a drilling bit at the bottom. When they are not babying the bit into the hole, they're snaking pipe out to change bits, uncoupling in a matter of hours enough plumbing for a respectable skyscraper. They drill wherever the geologist's clues and the land man's leases take them. And the oldest never outgrow the excitement of the last few hours of drilling before the big question is answered: is it another well – or a dry hole?

Charles Parker, *The Oilman* (1952), 24

Flora Shaw's account of Klondike life follows a familiar discursive pattern of associating women with culture – with 'home,' 'common needs,' 'food,' and 'fireside' – and men with 'want,' 'battle,' and 'Empire.' The discourse of geological exploration, however, as Charles Parker indicates, can offer an equally familiar association of the female with nature and of the male not only with empire but also with magnified toughness, a hyperbolic phallus, and cataclysmic sexuality. For the implied women of these passages the figure of the frontier saloon and its dancing girls can change radically from substitute 'home' to 'well' and 'hole.' Aritha Van Herk's 1981 novel, *The Tent Peg*, set in the Yukon, engages and seems attracted to both these notions of womanhood – the culturally different woman who accepts the supportive, auxiliary, and guiding 'home-making' role offered by empire-building patriarchy, and behind it a more primitive conception of woman as the powerful fertile ground on which men play out their phallic obsessions. Both these conceptions appear to limit the novel's historical and political understandings of Canada or of a woman in Canada.

———————

Near the middle of *The Tent Peg* J.L., a young woman who has managed to become camp cook for a Yukon prospecting crew, is visited by a female grizzly. 'She reared herself up beautiful and wild and strong and she said, "Wait. Don't let them drive you away."' The bear is one of only three female characters that appear directly in the novel, and J.L.'s only female acquaintance other than Deborah, a folksinger who became her friend in a university city somewhere to the south some years before. Like the bear Deborah is envisioned by J.L. as both beautiful and strong, with a 'lush' 'profane body that is underneath as cold as steel' and 'a brain that's as uncompromising as her body seems inviting' (38). In a sense the novel maps the 'character' of the bear over that of Deborah, maps Deborah over the powerful biblical prophetess of the same name to which the title alludes (Judges 4 and 5), and both in turn over that of J.L. All three are isolated in a world that appears overwhelmingly and aggressively masculine

– the solitary bear, mistrusted and feared by the prospectors and pilots, J.L., mistrusted and sexually hunted by the crew. When J.L. first attempts to speak to Deborah after one of her concerts, she has to push her way through male admirers attracted by her gender rather than her singing: '... the circle of admirers with eyes fixed on her face, men with no ears. I had to push my way through them to get to her, elbow my way between the tweed jackets and the monogrammed shirts' (112). This mapping of the female characters over each other, so that each can be read as a metaphor for the others, and so that their oral orientation is repeatedly contrasted to the ocular orientation of the men, is given such prominence that it takes precedence over both the geographical and social maps the novel carries. J.L., the grizzly, the two Deborahs, and the Yukon landscape into which J.L.'s male companions gaze, probe, and dig become to a great extent a single listening and singing female body, a body beyond culture, with much larger significance than the brief search of a prospecting crew for an investment-quality ore deposit. It is to reach this female body, to reach some 'silence' beyond the demanding and presumptuous sexuality of men ('they behave as if there has been another man immediately before, preparing my anticipation and response' [64]), that J.L. has schemed to get to the Yukon – 'all I wanted to find was silence, a relief from the [male] cacophony of sound, of confession that surrounded, that always impinged on me' (57).

The action of *The Tent Peg* involves a journey from 'the outside world' (57) to 'the Wernecke mountains' (33), from outside to inside, from down to up, from town to field, from a context complex in its social and cultural structures to one dominated by raw nature and ritualized and simplified by severe limitations on time, number of people, and supplies. Since at least the overland expeditions of Hearne and Franklin this has been the usual structure of white-perspective narratives of the Canadian North – the North as a place to visit, explore, or prospect in a brief 'season.' As here, in a reflection by the crew-boss, Mackenzie, such a perspective involves a polarization of 'north' and 'south':

> Nothing but tundra and lakes, lakes and tundra. Once you're out there, in amongst the moss and the occasional outcrop, you melt right down into the barrens. Not a dot of anyone anywhere ... I should be in management, shirt and tie, shave my beard off, jog at lunch to keep the pot away. But

> Janice always took the kids to the coast for the summer and even now, I
> can't seem to break the habit. (10)

This structure is affirmed rather than contested by most characters in
the novel. From the young geologist Thompson, who experiences his
town life with his fiancée and his summer fieldwork as 'separate,
different' and who fears he may have to 'trade' her 'for the mountains
or the barrenlands' (88), to the pious Mennonite farmboy Milton, who
feels 'farther away' from God (63) in the Yukon, all the male characters tend to construct the North in a simple opposition to urban
complexity. Hudson, the English geology student, makes only a slightly
different distinction – tending to draw his line between a civilized
'home' in England and an entire Canada he increasingly defines in
terms of the barrenness of the Yukon:

> God, I wish I was home. I should have taken Papa's offer, the airfare
> home and the summer at Bath. Instead, I decide I want to be adventurous
> and see some real geology in the Canadian north. Mad. There's nothing
> here for anyone. We're in the middle of the bloody wilderness and we
> could just as easily never get out again ... I could as well have stayed in
> Edmonton and read my textbooks for next year. (67–8)

The male characters also tend to associate women with 'home' and
thus with culture, and to want women to conform to this view. Dis-
appointment that his wife was once not 'home' when he returned
constitutes Mackenzie's grievance with life; fear that his fiancée may
not be 'back home' waiting for him similarly haunts Thompson. At
the same time the men appear unaware of the extent to which their
heavily phallicized geologic work treats nature as if it were woman's
body, and of how the goal of this work – to convert nature into culture
– provides an ironic parallel to their fears that the women in their
lives may someday refuse culturally defined sexual codings.

Although the insertion of a female cook into the usually male world
of the Northern prospecting crew challenges this conventional mapping of Canadian South and North as separate realms of culture and
nature, it does not challenge the culture-nature opposition itself. J.L.'s
presence at the camp certainly disrupts the usual nature-culture coding of North and South by placing a female whom the men associate
with Southern culture (with home-cooked meals, with 'womanly' advice and compassion) within a Northern nature they have traditionally encoded as the alien and often uncooperative recipient of their

bullets, tent-pegs, and claim-stakes. The response of many of the men is to attempt to force J.L. to one side of the dichotomy or the other – to either commit to culture by showing she can shoot a gun or acquiesce to being part of nature by allowing them unrestricted sexual use of her body. But J.L.'s own experience of the camp is that it is merely a different version of her life in the South. For her there is no sharp dichotomy between North and South, but there is a continuing one between men and women. The North is not distinct, but merely a place in which the male-constructed domination of culture over nature, and with it of patriarchy over women, is weaker. Here a woman can encounter the female bear, or listen to the rumblings of mountains, without always hearing also the 'static' of male voices.

Overall, J.L.'s construction of the North is based on difference rather than opposition. Like the men she too contrasts North with South, experiences the Yukon as 'out here, away from town' (56), as a 'silence' that is somehow radically different from the male noisiness of the South, but she locates in this silence elements she was also aware of in the South in the songs of her university friend Deborah. In search of this silence she constructs the North as one alternative to over-civilization, as a place of escape from the social demands that greet anyone who enters even a semi-intimate relationship. As the emotions of the male crew members press upon her, although she does not abandon this construction, she does abandon the possibility of living within it. Just as in Edmonton she could always 'hear' something ineffably female beneath the 'cacophony' of male voices, in the Wernecke mountains she cannot step entirely out of culture. What she can enter, however, is a more profound sense of female difference than was available to her before – a deeper awareness of the female grizzly that confounds male fears and expectations, of the singer who sings for women but is seen by men.

Implicit in this vision of a timeless female difference that pervades at varying strengths all human contexts is an assumption that this difference also informs the cultural codes of womanhood. J.L.'s friend Deborah sings to men, like the biblical Deborah before her, because her calm wisdom is needed by aggressive and visually obsessed men. J.L. cooks, advises 'with loving wrath and bestows ... respite, peace' (227) on men because only a woman can make this needed contribution to humanity.

Hudson is one of very few characters in *The Tent Peg* whose geographic or ethnic origins are specified. The others are relatively minor characters – Zeke the Dene bouncer in a Yellowknife bar, and Milton the Mennonite teenager. Most of the others have British-sounding names – Bill, Roy, Jerome, Thompson, Hearne, Franklin, Cap Kane. None is differentiated according to the part of Canada he may have come from. The characters who are known by their surnames all carry those of explorers of the Canadian North and West – Henry Hudson, David Thompson, Samuel Hearne, John Franklin, Elisha Kane, and Alexander Mackenzie. These names accomplish a further mapping of seventeenth-, eighteenth-, and nineteenth-century British exploration over the prospecting tasks of the twentieth-century Canadians. This mapping metaphorically marks their enterprise – like that of Flora Shaw's men of the Klondike – as masculine, visual, imperial, and commercial, as a re-enactment of colonial voyages of exploration and exploitation.[1]

In this mapping all of the men of the crew, and the places they come from, are implicitly named as either European or archetypically male. Canada as a historic construction nearly vanishes, in that only that Canada north of Yellowknife survives here as visibly other-than-European, as 'separate' or 'barren.' The mapping of the men as synonymous with both European imperialism and culture in general makes even more urgent J.L.'s assertions of female difference, and of the priority of this difference. As a construction of men, of European patriarchal history and its male explorer-heroes (whose descendants now live out that history in summer quests for the power metals, uranium and gold), and as a concept implicitly designed to privilege men over women, the culture/nature dichotomy has no place for woman. She cannot be a bear; although she has more 'connection to the earth' (121) than the men of the crew and can anticipate a landslide, she can also not be merely the earth that the men's claim-stakes are driven into. Seeking ostensibly to contest or at least blur this dichotomy, to use her 'natural' abilities to secure a role in culture, she will eventually hammer in the stakes for eight of the crew's gold claims, revealing herself, even in the mind of Mackenzie (227) not merely as J.L. but as the biblical Ja-el, who slew the Canaanite captain

---

1 One could perhaps read this mapping of the names of arctic explorers over the names of the male characters as an attempt to historically situate patriarchy – as an attempt to suggest that patriarchy is a specific development of Renaissance Europe, and that women outside the influence of European culture may be free of oppression by males. However, the novel's frequent generalizations about 'men' and its general employment of these explorer-names as typology rather than history work against such a reading.

Sisera with a tent-peg (Judges 4). Like Ja-el she will become a power-woman, who will outfight Jerome for his Magnum revolver and gain the right to her own geological stakes. But whether her various appropriations of symbols of male power actually contest the dichotomy remains ambiguous. Do the stakes she drives pierce male flesh, as did the peg of Ja-el, or at least penetrate an earth no longer coded as male or female? Or do they merely penetrate earth that continues to be woman's body, and provides the 'ground' for J.L.'s forays into phallic culture? The novel's emphatic construction of her stakes as 'peace'-bringing (in contrast to the lethal peg of Ja-el) offers at least some support for the latter reading.

The Tent Peg is narrated in brief first-person chapters by J.L. and the various male characters in turn. Twenty-two chapters are narrated by Mackenzie, seventeen by J.L., fifteen by Thompson, nine by Milton, eight by Ivan the helicopter pilot, six each by Hudson and Cap Kane, and five or less by each of the others. This fragmentation of the narrative act has the potential to create conflict and dissent, not only in terms of the interpretation of specific incidents but also in terms of what is considered narratable and what focuses the narrative should have. However, although it does produce some differentiation among the characters – Milton's concern with sexual morality, Ivan's zest for flying, Jerome's sadistic desire for power, Mackenzie's struggle to understand his wife's leaving him some fifteen years earlier – it produces very little narrative conflict. The characters agree that the central element in their collective lives is J.L.'s presence and tend to discuss this in terms of the same incidents. The main effect of the novel's distribution of narrative authority, oddly enough, is convergence rather than divergence, and a strengthening of the text's narrative authority. Comments by one character are frequently confirmed by others or by the character commented upon; incidents are related from a variety of perspectives, and details known only to particular individuals are joined together. The focus of the male characters on J.L. constructs her as the central character, even though Mackenzie makes more appearances as narrator, and Thompson nearly as many. It also constructs among them a nearly homogenous masculinity; despite individual differences all the men are preoccupied with enacting or understanding their yearnings for power over actual or symbolic females.

The various chapters are also similar stylistically and structurally, and give firm signals thereby of the presence of the text's constructor.

Most are narrated in the present tense, focus on immediate events, and report conversation as direct speech. Almost all attempt to conclude on a witticism, a dramatic moment, or a terse insight. There is again implication of uniformity among the male characters, of a shared desire not only to understand or control women but also to direct and control narrative. Not only does Milton want a docile Mennonite bride, Cap Kane a camp cook who will respond sympathetically whenever he says, 'I'm horny' (108), Hearne a 'perfect photograph' of J.L. (210), Thompson a woman he can be certain will wait for him every summer, and Mackenzie a wife who will appreciate his predictability, but all seem also to prefer stories that take a masculine narrative line towards a quick, terse climax. Beyond these characters, and their similar concerns and ways of articulating these concerns, one becomes aware of another constructing consciousness with its own verbal habits and its own tendency to map the world into North versus non-North and male hunters versus female prey. This consciousness also causes J.L. to end her narrative reports in terse verbal climaxes, giving further homogeneity to what superficially, at least, seems to be a dispersed or heterogeneous text. It is this constructing consciousness that has de-individualized the leading male characters by giving them the names of early European explorers of Canada, and has superimposed the J.L.-Deborah, 'tent-peg' narrative on the biblical Ja-el story related in Deborah's song (223), de-individualizing them through the figure of the culturally transcendent female.

Throughout the novel J.L.'s insistence that there is some essential difference between men and women – that men's experience is primarily visual while women's is aural, that men seek power for its own sake while women seek power to save men and themselves from male desperation, that women have access to primeval knowledge that men need to bring calm to their frenetic lives – is supported by the actions and observations offered by the other characters' narrations. Implicit throughout the novel also is an argument, liberal feminist only in its claims, that any culture-versus-nature coding of the male/female binary is false – that women can perform traditionally 'male' tasks equally well as men, that their often not choosing to undertake these tasks is based on nothing more than their viewing such tasks as trivial. Belying this argument of female difference, however, is the lack of discursive difference between J.L. and the male characters: both construct narratives that are action-oriented and seek quick resolution.

The Tent Peg's struggle to articulate a feminism is marked by not a few difficulties, including its own discursive limitations and the near cliché quality of the elements – male guns, female dancers – on which it chooses to found its terms. The power it claims for women – an earth-power to be wielded in crises – often appears to replicate the nature/culture coding of gender which it would refuse. In addition, this claim of power abandons humanity's routine historical/political activities to men and implicitly views both these activities and the men who eagerly undertake them with a weary and patronizing cynicism. Men can be left with their silly games, the book suggests, as long as Deborah sings knowingly and Ja-el/J.L. is available to save them from their self-created disasters. The Yukon landscape the novel takes as its strongest, least obscured image of the female is also one in which not even a woman can survive without the social infrastructure and technology which the book condescendingly assigns to male management.

On first reading, *The Tent Peg*'s assumptions appear to be those of an essentialist feminism. A simple dichotomy encloses, on the one hand, questing, gazing, exploring men who variously struggle with a need for power over both women and landscape and, on the other, women whose songs and subversive actions rest on both ancient biblical precedents and timeless connections to earth. This dichotomy transcends time: Thompson, Mackenzie, Franklin, Hearne, and Cap Kane are typologically tied to their namesakes; J.L. is tied both to Ja-el and to the bear that comes to camp to advise her. Apart from the contradictory coding of patriarchy as European there is little implication in the narrative that this gender dichotomy is historically constructed and thus changeable. J.L.'s actions in the camp are to help the men live with the handicap of their will to power, to reconcile them to it rather than change it. The men one by one come to her with the 'burden' of their desire, expecting her to 'shape the bundle neat and tidy, so they can carry on with their predestined world' (172). At the end 'they're fed and they're confessed and they're redeemed,' J.L. reports, 'and I have done nothing more than what I had to do' (214).

It is the biblical story of Ja-el and the tent-peg, and J.L.'s claiming of it, her claiming to have given each of the men rest by symbolically driving a tent-peg through their temples into the earth, that problematizes this feminism. Essentialist feminism normally celebrates the specific powers of female sexuality and privileges those powers over those of the phallus. *The Tent Peg* finds power for its women both in variations of the patriarchal 'handmaiden' role and in appropriations of the phallus which implicitly acknowledge its primacy. The tent-peg itself is tied metaphorically to the authoritative phallus of the prospector's stake, the stake that gives the prospector 'rights to' the earth the stakes enclose. It is tied also to the phallus of the camp firearms, to the .303 rifle that J.L. quickly learns to shoot and the revolver that she seizes from Jerome, threatening to 'shoot his balls off.' In the concluding chapter of the novel Mackenzie imagines the tent-peg being hammered once again into his skull, nailing him lovingly 'to the earth.' The tent-peg that J.L. affirms can bring her men 'rest' and 'trust' appears in many respects to be simply the phallus linking the man to female earth. Although J.L. avoids sexual intercourse with her male companions, she remains their handmaid, assisting them by pounding in the climactic final stakes of their gold claim, and symbolically hammering *their* tent-pegs into the rest-giving Gaia.

Men. A paradox, a quandary, whole centuries of snakes and ladders. I wouldn't trade. And yet they've got it all, they've managed so sublimely to capture the better half of the world and put us to work for them. Nerve, they're born with it, they carry with them blind, unhesitating presumption. After all, it has been given.

'J.L,' in *The Tent Peg*, 172

The novel's preoccupation with sexual 'givens,' with issues outside of history and politics, leads it to construct 'north,' 'non-north,' and Canada itself outside of politics. Franklin, Mackenzie, Thompson, Hearne, and Kane, in their twentieth-century or earlier incarnations, are in this text ultimately conceived as men – restless, desirous, proprietary – rather than agents of European capitalism, British imperialism, or Enlightenment empiricism. Social conflict, together with the units and historical situations of that conflict, vanishes beneath gender generalization. Ja-el herself is de-historicized, ceases to be an eighth-century B.C. Hebrew woman in a tribal, nomadic society, and becomes simply a woman. The explorers of the Canadian northwest cease to be Christian members of expanding national capitalist economies, cease being British or (in Kane's case) American, and are merely men. The location and ownership of the resource company that employs J.L.'s prospecting crew is unspecified – its head office may be in Edmonton, Toronto, New York, or Tokyo.

The absence of regional, national, and historical signs in *The Tent Peg* has some similarity to the homogenization of such signs that occurs in novels like *Slash* and *Joshua Then and Now*. In each case another politics has been given priority over a national one. In *Slash*, however, this other politics is firmly situated in history; in *Joshua Then and Now* an individualist politics is affirmed against the demands of an international history which itself is viewed as trivializing national and regional concerns. *The Tent Peg*'s preoccupation with gender division invites comparison also to novels like *Heroine* and *Ana Historic*, in which national political conflicts also fade beneath feminist concerns. What distinguishes *The Tent Peg* from those novels, however, is the extent to which it typologizes history; history is pervasively present in *Heroine*, and is present in *Ana Historic* until politically rejected by its main character; it is subsumed within gender categories in *The Tent Peg*.

The Yukon here is not constructed as a Canadian region, or even as a society, but as an environment that simplifies and intensifies universal gender. The competitive phallic power drives of the men – 'controlled by hormones, excretions' (64) – become starkly apparent within the exposed politics of the arctic camp, their need to resolve these drives more powerful. J.L., who had previously guarded her femaleness beneath signs of ambiguous sexuality, finds herself coded as emphatically female, and in the final episode dances on the burning camp table in a gypsy skirt:

> I lift up my arms and I whirl, the skirt heavy around my thighs, dance for them until that table shivers. Whirl and kick in the ecstasy of the flames beneath me, devouring the summer under my feet. (225)

The northern land beneath the table could be the land of any country where there are men to dance for, tables to dance on, and women who see themselves doomed to difficulty in negotiating the burden of their heavy skirts and 'the ecstasy of the flames beneath.'

Marrying the Hangman
The Biggest Modern Woman of the World

... five hundred miles of heavy timber covered the south shore of Lake Superior and the north shores of Lake Huron and Lake Michigan; and in these woodlands were rivers, mountains, creeks, springs, lakes and waterfalls in great variety.

It's a fine healthy country – a made-to-order breeding place for a king among men like Paul Bunyan. This land has given millions of feet of logs and millions of tons of iron and copper ores to the world. Best of all it gave Paul Bunyan to mankind – Michigan's and Russia's bounty to the Universe.

Stan Newton, *Paul Bunyan of the Great Lakes* (1946), 21

Canada's great strength among trading nations has historically been in producing natural-resource products. If we want to seize the opportunities of the emerging global economy, our best strategy is to build on this special strength.

Peter H. Pearse, 'Building on Our Strengths,' *Globe and Mail*, 10 Jan. 1992, A13

The biggest modern woman of the world comes from New Annan, Nova Scotia, a small place in what, in 1846, is a small British colony, but finds her fortune in the large and self-magnifying world of New York City, Broadway, and P.T. Barnum's American Museum. Building on her strengths, as Peter Pearse advises above, she refuses the pastoral life offered her by another Nova Scotia giant, Angus McAskill, only to marry the 'Kentucky Giant' Martin Bates, and with him erect an oversize farmhouse in Seville, Ohio. At least six major oppositions mark the life of Anna Haining Swan, the title character of Susan

Swan's 1983 novel *The Biggest Modern Woman of the World*: pastoral versus industrial, large versus small, women versus men, 'freakish' versus 'normal,' the United States versus Canada, and Confederate South versus Yankee North. But none of these oppositions can serve as a metaphor for another: their terms conflict; the affiliations they engender divide and redivide the individual, much as the Kentucky giant himself is divided, born in a state which took both sides in the U.S. Civil War, claiming at various times to be both a pacifist and a war hero, consistently desiring the signs of 'normal' life – a uniform, a home and family – yet also intent on siring a new race of physical and spiritual giants.

In its narrative structure *The Biggest Modern Woman of the World* resembles both the fairy tale and the *Künstlerroman*. Anna Swan is the ugly duckling in the swan's nest, the ungainly child who cannot stand upright in her parent's immigrant cottage, who can't work in the fields like her younger brothers and sisters but, weakened by her continuing growth, must stay indoors, peering through the crescent window her father has cut especially for her above the cottage door. She is the magical child, an unexplainable prodigy who, convinced she has special powers, vainly sings a 'growing song' to encourage the growth of both her father's crops and her hard-working siblings. Ultimately she becomes the family Cinderella, the girl with the unique shoe size, whose unmatchable qualities bring fame to her village, and wealth with which she can assist and enrich her family. Anna is also the reflective, creative child, who composes her 'growing song,' who hopes to study piano, and who, when she joins Barnum's museum, seeks not only to become a 'serious actress' but to write her own script. Anna moves from childhood failure to success as a showwoman, but this success supplements rather than replaces failure. Even in her moments of triumph Anna remains a freak, a woman unable to walk anonymously down a street, one whose regular bodily functions can have disastrous, irregular consequences.

These two generic signs, fairy tale and *Künstlerroman*, both involve conflict with social practice. In the former the magic child can often overcome an oppressive and bigoted society by being special, by proving to belong to a privileged class within that society (Cinderella) or by having access to special powers that enable her to overcome oppression within the privileged class itself (Sleeping Beauty). In the latter, creative ability can enable the child to locate an identity that allows her to distinguish herself from 'philistine' social practice (*Great*

Expectations) or to transcend society through the achievement of 'timeless' insight (*The Mountain and the Valley*). Anna Swan, however, remains oppressed by social responses to her size throughout her life. Her special mark, her size, enables her to escape her home town and enter Barnum's magic castle, but she does this only as a 'freak,' as someone who still cannot venture outside without attracting stares or inquiries about the 'weather up there.' Her creative abilities bring her mostly frustration and unhappiness. Her father's crops do not respond to her 'growing song'; her ironic 'etiquette' on 'how to behave in the company of giants' is rejected by Barnum; her theatrical ambitions are channelled into farcical roles as Glumdalclitch or as parodies of Shakespearean heroines. Far from transcending the commercialism of her society, she remains trapped within it, valued, like too many women, only for her power to attract the paying spectator's gaze.

This failure to achieve the transcending or distinguishing sense of identity of the *Künstlerroman* protagonist is signalled early and throughout the novel by its multiple narrative viewpoints. Like most such protagonists she relates her story in the first person but, unlike them, not in a single, achieved discourse. She speaks of her life first in a 'spiel,' the openly artificial discourse of the carnival, and later mostly in letters, each tied to the specific context of her motivation at the time of writing and her perception of her correspondent. The insufficiency of her narrative as a ground for identity is emphasized by the numerous other perspectives the text offers – those of her mother, her manager Ingalls, the dwarf Lavinia Warren, her husband's friend Virgil Shook, her childhood friend Hubert Belcourt, her doctors J.D. Robinson and A.P. Beach, her father, her husband, the dwarf George Washington Nutt. This fragmented narrative signals a fragmented rather than achieved self, a pastiche of royal, theological, theatrical, and mercantile images that Lavinia Warren's short, unlinked sentences are given the final chance to evoke:

> Their home was a showplace. Anna was a pope in taste. I slept in a crib she had had made for her baby. It had silk sheets. My room had velvet curtains and wallpaper right from London, England. Anna carried me up every night and tucked me in. She took care of me and then I took a troupe on the road and met Count Magri. We were married two years after the death of Tom Thumb. (340)

We are living in the middle of a turbulent revolution – the advent of the machine age – and you are gone fishin'. Angus there is a wind rustling my handbills whose name is PROGRESS. We are on a chasm. Enormous scientific changes are coming. We must prepare ourselves.

Anna to McAskill, in *The Biggest Modern Woman of the World*, 87

Scattered throughout *The Biggest Modern Woman of the World* are numerous reminders of the rapid and decisive social changes of the time in which Anna lived. The glamorous Victoria has become a shrunken, eccentric widow. Barnum's museum is three times destroyed by fire and is succeeded by the first of his itinerant circuses. Nova Scotia moves from being a quiet rural colony to a province in a hopeful new nation. The American conflict between an ambitious, industrializing North and a conservative, agrarian South culminates in civil war. The oversized Confederate captain's uniform the Kentucky giant Martin Bates is fond of wearing changes quickly from the sign of a rearguard army in the field – a waning giant – to one of nostalgia, marketing, and theatricality. Overall, the world is becoming increasingly homogeneous, its vistas larger, its spaces fewer.

Anna herself has been born into a family of crofters, displaced with thousands of others like them by the industrial revolution and the enclosure of Scottish pastures, to lives of poverty in rural Canada. The forces that displaced them continue to press upon them, particularly in the form of entrepreneurs like P.T. Barnum or Jacob Dunseith who seek to persuade them to exhibit Anna for profit in the United States. These are the forces of emergent capitalism, which in both Europe and America are rationalizing and segmenting commodity production and alienating labour into purchasable quantity. In America these forces are also creating mythologies of industrial gigantism, in which Canada is figured as raw material, and the entire globe as an industrial landscape, as in 'Paul Bunyan' stories like those of Stan Newton quoted above. Capitalism's claiming of the Scottish pastures as one of many components in a complex textile industry and of the Lake Superior forests as part of a 'world' lumber industry is echoed in Barnum's claiming of Anna as an additional component in his five-storey American Museum. The museum itself, with its floors dedicated to different genres of display, from the murky aquariums of the basement, the lecture hall of the third floor, to the 'Happy Family' triumph of the fifth, in its careful sequentiality and organization by category, resembles both capitalism's factory and department store. Even the symbolism of the 'Happy Family' exhibit, 'a vast cage in which one owl, two pigeons, some guinea pigs, a nest of rats, one basset hound, and two kittens' drowsily coexist because drugged by laudanum (43–4), evokes a capitalist dream of a monolithic, lethargic, consuming society.

In contrast, both of Anna's giant lovers are affiliated with the pre-industrial, with the pastoral dream of self-sufficient farms and quiet villages. Despite his reluctance to fight in the Civil War, Bates remains associated throughout the book with the Confederacy, its defence of plantation life and hostility to an industrializing North and, when he leaves show business, attempts the life of a gentleman farmer. Angus McAskill openly opposes the 'BIG CITY' and eulogizes 'the backwoods ... where we who work the land and the sea are the sustainers of life' (40). He gives up his job as one of the many salaried inmates of Barnum's museum in order to operate a general store in his Nova Scotia village. Anna describes him as keeping 'a vigil on the shore of St. Ann's Bay for the old ways. I believe he hoped to stop the migrating flow to the city with his powers of concentration and his fidelity to the land' (52). It is the 'big city,' however, which eventually kills Angus. Lured back to New York by Anna's presence there, he is drawn into a strong-man competition with Bates on the city water-front. Although he easily lifts and pitches a 2,700-pound anchor, one of its flukes catches his shoulder, inflicting the 'fluke' injury which will become fatally infected some five months later.

The Canadian dimension of this conflict between two ideals – the rural, self-employed individual and the urban worker, who makes a limited contribution to a production that synthesizes the labour of many – is Confederation. Its story lurks behind the narrative of Anna's life, coming momentarily forward only in chance comments in Anna's letters or in strongman Louis Cyr's brief appearance in one of Anna's travelling shows. Canadian Confederation, with its attempt to join small political units into a single larger and more efficient one, is here made parallel to the Industrial Revolution's alterations to business practice, the shift from handwork to mass production. Like Barnum, Confederation creates a larger stage for larger economic actions and grander ambitions. In 1871 Barnum asks Anna how she has enjoyed her recent visit to her birthplace:

'I am too sophisticated for the backwoods,' I replied. 'I felt like a snob in

my own family. Like most well-travelled Victorians I've become opinion-
ated in matters of taste and I couldn't look at their plain ironstone china,
the crude hooked rugs, and hand-carved chairs without shuddering.'

Barnum nodded. 'My family in Bethel is the same. They have not yet
learned that the last manufactured pattern is the best.'

'I thought my family's home looked like one of your museum exhibits
– so rough and crude did the log house appear to me, nestling on a wooded
rise above a dirt track.'

'Of course, opportunities must be better now that your province is part
of a nation.'

'The atmosphere is charged with political hostility and suspicion. Already some leaders want the Blue-noses to separate because they think
the new situation is ruining trade with the Yankees.'

'The Canucks should join us and then there'd be no problem.' Barnum
grinned. (154)

Confederation in this passage is figured as a means of helping the
Canadian to 'progress' from the hand-made to the manufactured. It
disrupts local trade patterns, as between Nova Scotia and 'the Yankees,' in order to create a more efficient, integrated national trading
unit. (Unspoken is the decline in local manufacturing Confederation
brought to the Maritimes, in favour of centrally located large-scale
industry in Quebec and Ontario.) If this new trading unit does not
bring prosperity, the next step – as Barnum indicates – is the creation
of an even larger trading unit through union with the United States.

The fairy tale that Anna hopes will remove her from her too-small
home and home town and take her to wealth and acceptance in a
larger world is thus paradoxically mixed with both the capitalist enterprise and Canada's national aspirations. Anna's dreams of material
comfort are also industry's goals of 'manufactured' middle-class comfort for the consuming masses who come to Barnum's museum. Her
goal of being accepted as a person and a 'serious actress' is to be
achieved within an economic system that, like Barnum, configures
individuals as commodities with exchange value. As the poems Bates
recites with her in mid-Atlantic indicate (178–84), Anna is also to be
read as Canada the young giant, the bride of America, 'New World
Wahine ... [with] untapped vagina.' She goes to find her fortune in
America and in the American entertainment 'industry' much like the
new provinces of Canada attempt in 1867 to find theirs in an international corporate model.

> Americans have their faults but they possess the courage to be themselves while Blue-noses like you sit on your verandas, ridiculing the world beyond their doorstep. If you weren't so rule-bound and narrow-minded, you'd notice that Americans are a Goddamn lot more lovable than most peoples elsewhere. Yes Momma, I am blaspheming. I am tired of your provincial prejudices and your mean-spirited fault-finding. Don't you realize how boxed-in your critical ways make those around you feel?

> *The Biggest Modern Woman of the World*, 289

Many of Anna Swan's political comments in the novel constitute critiques of Confederation, particularly of the 'provincialism' which makes individual regions of Canada suspicious and resentful of both other Canadian regions and the United States. These comments rest in part on Anna's conception of herself, given by Barnum, as a 'woman of the world,' for whom local space will always be insufficient but for whom the 'larger world' may offer companionship and community. Anna ventures into the world, to New York, to London, into the American Midwest, with hope that on these larger stages she will at last find a welcome as large and generous as her own body. She sails to Europe anticipating a continent 'where centuries of culture have taught its citizens a civilized approach' (158) and an opportunity to follow Tom Thumb in 'winning the heart of Queen Victoria' (74). Her critiques of Confederation rest also on Barnum's conception of the world as a single homogeneous field, one which he can represent through exhibits such as 'THE PALESTINIAN GIANT,' 'Commodore Nutt, THE SHORTEST OF MEN' (3), 'the Biggest Modern Woman,' 'the BLUE WHALE, LARGEST IN THE SEA,' and 'the AFRICAN BUSH ELEPHANT, LARGEST ON LAND' (1).

Her ideal for Canada is a country that is both economically progressive and internationally responsible – both qualities she sees in herself. When her husband begins quarrelling with their new fellow villagers in Seville, Ohio, she comments,

> I feel I am acting out America's relationship to the Canadas. Martin is the imperial ogre while I play the role of genteel mate who believes that if everyone is well-mannered, we can inhabit a peaceable kingdom. That is the national dream of the Canadas, isn't it? A civilized garden where lions lie down with doves. I did not see the difference until I married Martin. We possess no fantasies of conquest and domination. Indeed, to be from

the Canadas is to feel as women feel – cut off from the very base of power. (273–4)

This ideal requires an outer world as civilized as the one Anna herself anticipated on travelling to New York and London. It views 'the Canadas' as becoming a single garden, free of contention, conflict, and provincial assertion. She experiences this Canada as 'cut off' from 'power,' unaware that the maintenance of such a 'civilized garden' would require some considerable peacekeeping force.

When confronted by the anti-English declarations of Louis Cyr, Anna attempts to contain him by invoking this genteel, civilized model, 'two nations' that mysteriously function as one country, and implying that this politics has a different relationship to power than does U.S. 'empire':

> 'We are a country of two nations,' I said. 'And we are not part of the American empire.'
>
> The ability to function without a national consensus in the Canadas is a mystery to the Yankees who cannot fathom a system that isn't modelled on theirs. The Buck-eyes stared in puzzlement. Suddenly, Louis flung up his arms in a dramatic gesture of exasperation. He took my hand and tucked it under his arm and I felt for the first time the fabulous muscled breast which had grown strong under his mother's bag of oats. Louis smiled. 'The Americans, Annie. They'll never understand.' (265)

The constructor of the novel makes a similar move here, making Louis take Anna's arm in a gesture of kinship and solidarity that confirms the non-coercive national unity Anna has asserted.

Although the various binary tensions on which the novel is constructed (big/small, male/female, United States / Canada, Yankee/ Confederate, freakish/normal, pastoral/industrial) do not fit easily on one another (and in fact tend to deconstruct one another – a big person can be female or come from a small or pastoral country), several of them are mapped closely around the Canada / United States opposition. Canada, in Anna's experience, is rural, politically small, and culturally too small for a big woman. In the political mythology of the novel Anna Swan becomes Canada, the young giantess, female to the male United States, country girl in its biggest city, a freak in relation to its strongly nationalist norms, and eventually a bride to its ambiguously Confederate/Yankee 'Kentucky Giant.' The love songs

which make up part of her troupe's performance text while sailing
to Europe on the *City of Brussels* portray Anna in these terms and
also interpret the meaning of the marriage she will shortly undertake.
These songs begin with Ingalls's 'Verse Warm-up,' in which he characterizes Martin Bates as representing America's transformation from
a rural to an industrial culture:

> Anna, your bridegroom
> is looking up from his cities
> smiling through his smoke-stacks
> ...
> a hill-billy gone citified
> ...
> his eyes are like machines
> whirring at the stars (178)

The second song, 'The Kentucky Giant's Hymneal,' even more explicitly names Anna as Canada – a Canada that is about to become
America's mate. It begins by identifying her as 'the giantess next door'
and forecasting that her name soon shall be the Kentucky giant's 'all-
American girl.' She is America's 'future,' 'vast' with 'legends of min-
eral wealth,' 'gas / and oil,' 'the American Dream.' Characterizing
her through participles that suggest passivity and immobility – 'untapped,' 'promised,' 'gazing,' 'waiting' – the song invites her to abandon her 'diversity' and open herself to various metaphoric penetrations:

> Your lips are the north-west
> passage waiting
> for underglacial submarines
>
> Beloved – I will rise up
> in your empty heights
> and plunge through your
> regions of softwood
> to the end of your Atlantic
> depth ...
> ...
> My will shall grow in your void. (180–2)

Although in the third song, 'Anna's Answer True,' Anna emphatically
declines the political and sexual parts of the Kentucky Giant's pro-
posal, she does not contest either his equation of her with the young

Canada or his assertion that Canada is America's bride-to-be. It is only the price that America must pay for its bride that is in question:

> The world knows
> we have an eternal engagement –
> but I'm not the sort of giantess
> who gets laid
> for one or two silly visions.
> Such is the heart of your fresh-water virgin,
> Sons of America. (183)

The language of these songs follows that of other passages in the novel in conflating major binary oppositions – active/passive, male/female, hot/cold, dominant/submissive, old/young – onto both Anna's relationship with Bates and Canada's with the United States. Their genre, the operetta, gives them a light-hearted, parodic tone, but although Anna may comment that they are merely 'political conceit, put on for showbiz reasons,' the serious use of their images and dichotomies elsewhere in the novel, and the actual marriage of Anna and Bates that soon occurs, contextualize them as parodies that confirm rather than contest their target. *The Biggest Modern Woman of the World* is a story of the marriage of Canada and the United States. Young giantess Canada, her aspirations unaccommodated by her rudimentary civilization, her sexual appetites unsatisfied by her languid national lover Angus McAskill, looks to the United States for learning, personal legitimation, international recognition, and love. In marrying Martin Bates, she chooses not only a 'darkly handsome' husband but the various signs with which he marks himself – especially the military of his Confederate uniform, and the *homo 'Americanus'* (119) of which he claims to be the outstanding giant example.

As a possible scenario for a Canada-U.S. union the marriage of Anna Swan and Martin Bates is not especially propitious. Martin is not only unable to fill Anna's seventeen-inch vagina but is impotent – his undeveloped 'organ ... no longer than a baby's' (209) – and incapable of relations with even normal women. His impotence so depresses him that he refuses to masturbate her and declares that he is 'renouncing carnal activity' (298). Eager nevertheless to 'father' a child, he subtly encourages her to resume an affair with the Australian-born non-giant Ingalls. Anna bears Ingalls a second child (one from their brief earlier affair was stillborn), but it dies shortly after birth.

A blustering, rhetorically masculine United States conceals its sexual immaturity and creative impotence beneath its rhetoric. A progressive, impressionable female Canada hopes for a union that is satisfying both materially and physically but discovers her husband's sexuality ends with rhetoric and with legal possession of her body and its offspring. Outside of marriage she also fails to find an appropriate mate: McAskill yearns for Europe's rural past, and his 'organ' is 'a mere foot' long, only 'the diameter of a doorknob' (58); Ingalls, despite his ardour, is inappropriately short and impregnates her only with dying children. Anna Canada dies young and childless, all but $8,500 of her estate going to her American husband. This conclusion in a sense resolves nothing. None of the pastoralism of McAskill, the wily individualism of 'Apollo' Ingalls, nor the progressive industrial modernity claimed by Barnum and Bates has been sufficient to assure Anna's happiness. Her mates have been unequal to her expansive vision. Her modernity has been premature, has resulted more in crisis and disillusionment than in freedom and wealth; her bigness has been exploited and wasted by individuals and societies that have yet to become 'big,' that value their own parochial rhetoric more than the vast generosities of the 'modern' Anna. In the last words the text gives to Anna she despairs of human society but still hopes for the large spaces for which she left Canada: 'I was born to be measured and I do not fit in anywhere. Perhaps heaven will have more room' (332).

———————————

Th[e] coincidence of similar problems of self-definition in nationalist and feminist ideology would go some way to explain why so much attention is being paid to women writers in Canada at the present time, for their stories seem the natural expression of the insecurity of their society and in many ways they provide models for stories of Canadian national identity.

Coral Ann Howells, *Private and Fictional Worlds* (1987), 26

Discourses which conflate nationalist and feminist causes, like Anna's suggestion that 'to be from the Canadas is to feel as women feel' (274), and which represent a 'colonized' Canadian nation in the figure of the patriarchally colonized Canadian woman have been a small but significant part of Canadian fiction and criticism since the 'ice maidens' of Margaret Atwood's *Survival* and the nationally troubled heroines of her *Surfacing* and *The Journals of Susanna Moodie*. The popular representation of Canada in the figure of the woman threatened or wooed by international men has an even longer history in figures like Laura Secord, Mary Pickford, and Barbara Ann Scott and textual figures like Clara de Haldimar in *Wacousta*, Advena Murchison in *The Imperialist*, Rosemarie in *Rosemarie*, and Morag Gunn in *The Diviners*, although in general male representations of Canada as the 'growing lad' (Ranald Macdonald of *The Man from Glengarry*, Neil Macrae of *Barometer Rising*, Brian O'Connal of *Who Has Seen the Wind*, Johnnie Backstrom of *The Words of My Roaring*) have tended to be more common. In contrast to the latter, which usually construct Canada as about to take its place in a world of manly commerce, recent theorizations of Canada as a colonized woman have tended to regard commerce itself as patriarchal and oppressive, and the Canadian woman as doubly colonized when her body that is exploited by patriarchy must dwell in a country whose wilderness is similarly exploited by international capitalism.

Although *The Biggest Modern Woman of the World* contains the materials for such a nationalist/feminist construction – Anna's 'natural' Canadian body is indeed both conflated by the text with the Canadian landscape and appropriated by the industry of American entertainment – the novel directs very little indignation at the terms of this transaction. Anna's failure to obtain the brass ring of happiness is depicted, not as inherent in the economic or gender relations in which she is obliged to seek success, but rather as caused by the individual failings of characters like Barnum, Ingalls, and Bates. Despite the conflicting signs it has offered in Anna's story, the novel remains sympathetic to the global stage for which she left Canada. It views the bargain she has agreed to – to exchange her body for 'world-class' success – as both a worthy one and one she deserved to have fulfilled. When Anna dies, it does not have her condemn capitalism or patriarchy, even though it has given her the means to do so, but instead has her affirm the goals within these that she failed to reach: 'Yes. I have made my bed and I have to lie in it, as the Blue-noses put it – that nation of scoffers who don't understand the need to dance up to the aurora borealis. Yet I am content' (332). By implication Canada too, young 'giant' of nations, and Susan Swan, 'tallest woman freelance writer in Canada,'[1] are also constructed as free to parlay their assets into success on a global stage.

---

1 From the publisher's biographical note on the back cover of *The Biggest Modern Woman of the World*

While *The Biggest Modern Woman of the World* departs sharply from *The Tent Peg* through its clear marking of Canada and association of its protagonist with the Canadian national text, it also, like *The Tent Peg*, firmly refuses nationalism. This refusal is not founded on a transcendent feminism, however, but on a new, 'modern,' and historicized world economy that is already displacing the national state. Rather than the ground of a new nation, Canadian Confederation is merely an early 'free trade' agreement, an anticipatory model for the transnational economic order that is about to develop. Anna, hoping to be a gigantic Moll Flanders of this order, perhaps was born too soon, but for a post-national Canada Peter H. Pearse's 'emerging global economy' may still await.

The Country of Her Own Body
Ana Historic

Prehistoric and early historic mankind knew very well that women's menstruation was a central fact of existence, and that at the period of menstrual flow woman was at her most magically powerful, shamanistic and mysterious. Since the parallel between the Moon's phases and women's was obvious, the dark of the Moon was equally obviously the Goddess's menstrual peak. Then she, too, was at her most powerful and mysterious, and humans were very careful about what they did, or refrained from doing, at that awesome time.

Janet and Stewart Farrar, *The Witches' Goddess* (1987), 24

Daphne Marlatt's 1988 novel *Ana Historic* is an Oedipal story narrated in both personal and national contexts. It is a novel about immigrants in which the usual triad of old culture, new land, and immigrant subject are variously recast as Culture, Land, and Subject, as Father, Mother, Child, and as the Lacanian Law-of- the-Father, Phallic Mother, child Subject. The external narrative in which Annie, the focalizing character and first-person narrator, comes to Vancouver in the 1950s as a colonial British adolescent, with her father, Harald, her mother, Ina, and her sisters, Jan and Marta, contains a second narrative in which one of pioneer Vancouver's first schoolteachers, a Mrs Richards, arrives from England in 1873 with strong memories of paternal injunctions and of a mother who died in childbirth. Through the symbol of the logging industry, which both pays Mrs Richards's salary in the 1870s and employs Annie's father as an administrator in the 1950s, these narratives are not only linked but also become a story of Canadian exploitation: a land marked as female is exploited for material profit by a male population – to the exclusion and alienation of women who are required to abet and celebrate the exploitation as well as identify with its victim.

This equating of woman and land is more similar to the figuration of woman offered by *The Tent Peg* than to that by *The Biggest Modern Woman of the World*. In both *Ana Historic* and *The Tent Peg* the landscape that is constructed as female is primeval and pre-national. In *The Biggest Modern Woman* it is a national, culturally marked landscape that is merged by the text with Anna Swan; this landscape/nation is not so much a symbol of woman, as the land tends to be in *The Tent Peg*, as Anna herself is a symbol of the nation's 'giant' potential and difficulty. In *Ana Historic*, however, there is no symbolic relationship at all between land and woman; instead the land and woman's body are conceived as mythically contiguous, and the oppression of one as contiguous with that of the other. The land's male oppressors – again different than in *The Tent Peg* – are specifically historicized as Canadian; numerous quotations from histories of Vancouver and the B.C. logging industry not only specify this oppression but link it metaphorically to the activities of later male characters, particularly Annie's father and husband. *Ana Historic* creates thereby a powerful binary opposition between nature – female, corporeal, primeval – and culture – male, conceptual, technological, and 'Canadian.'

However, although 'Canada' is named and given visible historic detail in *Ana Historic*, by the end of the text it has become a peculiarly homogeneous concept – undifferentiated in its parts, undifferentiated from the rest of North America, and ultimately undifferentiated in the world at large. As culture rather than land, 'Canada' – whatever the particularities of its history – is for *Ana Historic* ultimately no more than an extension of a ubiquitous patriarchal symbolic order.

———————

The novel has all three of its immigrating women – Mrs Richards in 1873 and Annie and her mother in the 1950s – mistake Canada initially as an 'other' to the countries they have left. Mrs Richards first sees its social signs as 'foreign,' 'outlandish,' 'odd':

> She gazed at the piles of lumber, the heavy smoke, the low sprawling sheds. So many men, so foreign looking, dressed in such an outlandish assortment of clothes. They were shouting to those on board in a great bustle of hawsers and fenders – the oddest English she had ever heard. (15)

Annie perceives especially strongly a linguistic difference that sepa-
rates her from her new school mates: 'my difference i was trying to
erase. my English shoes and woolly vests. my very words' (23). Mrs
Richards and Annie's mother both generalize on the basis of their
Vancouver experiences the rawness and newness of a North American
Canada. Mrs Richards does this in positive terms: 'I am orphaned
here at the end of the world – Yet I feel no grief, for I am made new
here' (30). Ina generalizes in negative terms: 'a cold country, Canada
... people don't care' (9); 'Canadians don't know how to speak proper
English' (17); 'Canadian women have no pride' (57).

Yet what the novel has all three eventually come to feel is that,
for women, this new country is no different than their old one: Lacan's
'Law-of-the-Father,' the rigorous 'law' of language which names and
enforces male and female roles, applies as strongly here as elsewhere.
Mrs Richards's perception of newness (which she reported in a letter
to her 'Father') has been an illusion; the social proprieties and conventions which grant authority to men and exclude women from both
administrative decision-making and official history govern her life
here as much as they did in her father's English rectory. In Ina's case
the illusion is her conviction that the colloquial British English she
has brought with her can safeguard her genteel femininity. Her struggle to maintain this English against what she perceives to be a vulgar,
masculine, and utilitarian North American slang is misguided because
both are merely different faces of a general patriarchal discourse oppressive to women. The 'true' language of her British dictionary understands women as 'conforming to a rule, standard or pattern' (17);
the North American language of *Readers Digest*, for which she am-
ateurishly aspires to write, merely proposes other patterns in which
she is to 'shape' herself:

> how it hurts to think of your 'scribblings' under the bed (the bed!) in a
> language which was not yours. 'laughter is the best medicine.' 'grin and
> bear it.' those bannerheads you tried to muster up to: woman's valiancy.
> trying to shape up. (133)

Annie, like Mrs Richards, is constructed as initially seeing North
American language as capable of liberating her from the genteel assumptions through which British discourse limits women – as choosing its 'sexy' and 'cute' over her mother's vocabulary of 'decent,'
'unladylike,' and 'nice': 'it wasn't that i wanted to be a "lady," i

wanted to be like the other girls, sexy but not too much, just enough to be liked, just enough to be cute' (33). Only when she reaches middle-age does she realize that both vocabularies belong to a patriarchal language that limits women by fitting them to male definitions; both require women to seek a 'look' – 'decent' or 'sexy' – that will satisfy a male gaze.

At the time of her stream-of-consciousness narration Annie is married to her former college history professor, for whom she now does research, has two teenage children, and is secretly working on a fictional retelling of the story of Mrs Richards into which her own life story keeps intruding. Her narration – which may in fact be the book she is secretly writing – focuses on the hidden part of her life, both on her obsession with Mrs Richards and on her haunting and confusing recollections of her mother, who has recently died. This narration is often fragmentary in its sentence structure, shifts rapidly among discourses of recollection, imaginary interview, and citation, and moves among three narrative chains – Annie's re-imagination of her childhood with her family, her hypothesizing of Mrs Richards's life as a schoolteacher, and the framing first-person narrative of Annie's life as a researcher, unhappy wife, and would-be writer in the present. However, despite numerous abrupt shifts in time and place, the novel has Annie unfold each of these narratives coherently and significantly – the childhood narrative towards her mother's nervous breakdown and death, the present one towards leaving her family for a lesbian lover, and the Mrs Richards narrative towards Mrs Richards's leaving teaching for either a husband or her own lesbian lover. Each narrative structure implies climax and resolution, with the conclusion of the framing narrative of Annie's present life marked by utopian signs – a return to the pre-Oedipal mother, and a lyrical 'luxury of being' passage suggesting lesbian orgasm on its final (and significantly unnumbered) page.

An ostensible intensity and directness in Annie's narration challenges the reader to locate any narrative space around it, particularly any divergence between the signator, 'Daphne Marlatt,' whom the book says has constructed this narrator and the narrator herself. Annie is purported to write the entire text of the novel. She is committed to writing it in a fragmentary, disorganized manner – as 'a book of interruptions' (37) – and to sharing her narrative role with the voices of many characters and authors – with her mother, lover, and husband, with Mrs Richards, and with various historians, journalists, and psychologists. She is represented as believing that she is discovering, rather than constructing, the symmetries of the three stories she narrates, the three women's experiences of oppression by patriarchal cultural codes and their parallel searches for a repressed primal mother.

Her dialogical text, however, is itself firmly contained within signs of a constructing signator. This signator has provided Annie with the initial resemblances between her life and those of her mother and Mrs Richards, enabling her thereby to seize upon the latter as her research focus. It has given her and her mother the names 'Annie' and 'Ina,' thus enabling her to signify further similarity by imagining Mrs Richards's first name to have been 'Ana.' It has supported her perceptions of patriarchal power with further namings: the name it has given her daughter, 'Ange,' links her both with 'Annie,' 'Ana,' and 'Ina' and with male idealization of the female – the 'Teen Angel' (82) of boyhood fantasy; the ones it has given her husband, 'Richard,' and her father, 'Harald,' recall English kings; the one it has given her lover, 'Zoe,' argues her relationship with Annie as the alpha-omega or mystic unity of women's experience. The signator has also given the text's characters economic and vocational roles consistent with the thesis Annie will come to argue. It is the signator that has associated both Mrs Richards's employers and Annie's father with the 'masculine' logging industry and constructed Annie's husband as a history professor and thus as deeply complicit in the patriarchal depiction of events. It is the signator that has constructed Annie as Richard's homebound wife and that had the power to construct her otherwise; and that has cast most of the novel's women as either interlopers in textual production – Mrs Richards's nocturnal diary, the notebook Ina hides under her bed, the novel manuscript Annie conceals beneath the research notes she compiles for Richard – or as involved in disruptive, non-textual activity – Birdie Stewart's brothel, Zoe's visual art. But most importantly, this signator has also written Annie's narrative in a discourse that is positivist and incorporating. Bracketing the desire it gives her to admit many voices, it has allowed Annie's overall quest for certainty about the causes of her mother's mental collapse to dominate her citation and organization of these voices; all the voices she cites are framed so as to contribute to her concluding conviction that she, Mrs Richards, and Ina were all victims of discursive alienation from their own and their mothers' bodies. On the final non-numbered page, Annie's multivocal text offers *Ana Historic*'s unequivocal meaning.

Ana Historic foregrounds its political and psychological concerns through the numerous quotations it has Annie incorporate from texts on clinical psychiatry, Vancouver history, and logging practices in British Columbia, and through the bibliography of these texts, and others, which it offers at the end. It specially foregrounds its Freudian and Lacanian understandings of child-parent relationships through its emphatic depiction of Annie as having been invited by her father to displace her mother. Annie constructs and accepts her mother's accusation, '– yes, you were the Perfect Little Mother ... you could have replaced me. you tried hard enough ...':

> trying. a trying child. trying it on for size. the role. all that she had been told would make her a woman ...
>
> ...
>
> yes I tried to efface you, trace myself over you, wanting to be the one looked at, approved by male eyes. (49–50)

To this Freudian Oedipal situation the novel adds Luce Irigaray's theory of the significance of the male 'gaze' in patriarchal constitutions of the female subject (1985 [1974], 53), showing a pubescent Annie soliciting 'the look' (50) from her father, playing 'the intricate game of the look' (51) at school, sunbathing 'to be seen, be certified' (82) by teenage boys. It has Annie offer an overdetermined paraphrase of Irigaray when conducting an imaginary argument with her mother:

> the truth is (your truth, my truth, if you would admit it) incest is always present, it's there in the way we're trained to solicit the look, and first of all the father's, Our Father's. framed by a phrase that judges (virgin/tramp), sized up in a glance, objectified. (56)

The effect of such passages is to construct Annie as an enthusiastic and uncritical consumer of psychological and feminist theory, one who distorts and reduces in her eagerness to have an understanding of her past. In paraphrasing an Irigaray who counsels against 'truth' and clarity ('No clear or univocal statement can ... dissolve this mortgage' [178]), Annie replaces the theorist's nuanced, teasing, and equivocatory style with the positive and univocal one she sought to avoid. Annie's eagerness for certain knowledge leads her to imagine her own story and that of Mrs Richards virtually as case studies for the most influential feminist concepts of the 1970s and 1980s: the housewife as lost and imprisoned until her children return from school

(24); the glamorous woman as a construction of the cosmetics industry (58); 'history' as a displacement of 'her story' (28); the Virgin Mary as an oppressive ideal of motherhood (101); the woman's genitals as a 'split' that alienates a potentially whole self; Cixous's *'ecriture feminine'* concept of the menstrual flow as a model for women's writing (49, 90, 125–6, 135–6). Because the text does not historicize Annie's encounters with these concepts, but instead has her embrace them as if they were always already available, her enthusiasm for them is marked as belated as well as ingenuous and reductive.

↳ but liberating

The quarrel which *Ana Historic* constructs for Annie is with the positivism of official history ('the real story the city fathers tell' [28]) and the relentless and unitary pragmatism of a male-dominated culture. It is the insidious 'reasonableness' of this culture which her father has brought from his office to his marital quarrels:

> ... we heard you slam out of the room where you'd been 'discussing,' his voice flat, trying to be calm, 'be sensible, Ina,' and yours on a rising note, 'there you go, sitting on the fence again so you can be above reproach and it's easy enough for you to say when i'm the one tormented by enemies – oh yes, you can afford to be sensible, can't you?' bitch, we'd think, witch. how can he be so patient? (93–4)

His pragmatism finds its ultimate expression in the electric-shock therapy he and Ina's male doctors eventually employ as a cure for her unhappiness.

The attack which the novel has Annie make on the monological power of this pragmatism involves both the location of a multiple, dialogical alternative and the deconstruction of some of the binary 'male-female' oppositions on which much of the pragmatism's power rests. Abandoning the univocal patriarchal historical narratives of her husband, whose books merely note 'to my wife without whose patient assistance this book would never have been completed' (79), Annie sets out to write a narrative that includes many voices – fragments from the disputed journal of Mrs Richards, passages from published celebrations of the masculine energies of pioneer logging and settlement, the advice she intermittently receives from Zoe, and her own imagining of both conversations with her dead mother and of more revealing journal material by Mrs Richards. She claims to be writing without plan, 'tapping like someone blind along the wall of her solitude' (45), to be 'just scribbling,' to be compiling 'bits and pieces thrown in,' to be writing a text 'cut loose from history and its relentless progress toward some end' (81). But Annie's text of fragments becomes, despite its bits and pieces, as unitary as the one it opposed. Her imagining of her mother's and Mrs Richards's words becomes an appropriation and occupation of their names; in her imagination the views and fears of the two women become increasingly congruent with her own. Her various citations and quotations are framed within her own insistently interpretative discourse. The syntactic 'tick' through which the text betrays Annie's monologism is the conjunction 'as if,' which occurs more than twenty times in the 154 pages:

> ... don't be silly, darling, i'm here, you see how silly you are – as if *saying* it makes it so. (11)

> ... tomboy, her mother said. tom, the male of the species, plus boy. double masculine, as if the girl were completely erased. (13)

> ... Ina, how you used to enter the North Van library as if entering a medieval cloister ... (16)

> ... they crowded past her as if she were a bush, a fern shaking in their way. (42)

> ... the sort of grace i was meant to have as a body marked *woman's*, as if it were a brand name. as if there were a standard shape ... (52)

> ... 'so touching' ... as if the male touch ... required its polar opposite to right the world ... (63)

> ... lighting up when he saw her as if she were a grouse flushed out of the bush ... (102)

This 'as if' operates as the sign of transformation and reduction through which Annie converts various perceptions and memories into component certainties of a new interpretation.

Annie assembles the 'bits and pieces' which she gathers into a discourse of knowledge that grows in confidence and certainty as it continues. Towards the end the semantic marks of certainty – 'i know,' 'never,' 'no one,' 'always,' 'none of,' 'no rightful' – become overwhelming:

> now i know the pressure that drove you against the balance of his approach, sagacious, carefully reasoned ...

for it was the walls that closed in on you, picture windows that never opened, doors that stayed shut against the cold. none of the openness of that stone house in the tropics ... where we had no rightful place.

you never lived alone. you went from your parents' colonial house to boarding school, then back to your parents and into marriage with your own servants. always you lived surrounded by voices ... you never lived alone until you came here ... you were always home where your place was, with the sawdust furnace ... always the question: 'how you gonna git yo' day's work done?' when it is never done, never over with, and there is no one there to witness your accomplishment. (136–7)

These marks of certainty are reiterated in Annie's portrayal of Zoe, who stands in metonymical relationship to the growing knowledge Annie asserts, and whose choice by Annie as a lover parallels her rejection of masculinist interpretation. Zoe is presented as chthonic and oracular, 'brown eyes, brown, challenging me. perched behind her coffee cup, an air of ruffled insistence, persistent' (90). Her characteristic speech of terse questions, riddles, and admonitions – 'so write it that way then' (90), 'it's *your* novel' (140), 'and you, do you really exist' (141) – marks her as superbly confident, as commanding knowledge Annie can only dimly imagine. She is portrayed as both possessing the 'answers' Annie seeks, and as withholding them so that she will discover them on her own. Even when Annie recognizes her erotic attraction to Zoe, her description of Zoe's response – 'she isn't surprised' (152) – indicates she had known about this for some time.

The simple structure of the replacement of one monological authority by another is repeated in Annie's attempts to dismantle the binary oppositions on which the masculinist assumptions of her father, husband, and Mrs Richards's male acquaintances rest. Such oppositions, as Derrida first theorized in *Of Grammatology*, implicitly privilege one term within a pair and, as Cixous has elaborated, usually mask an underlying male/female, strong/weak, positive/negative paradigm (1975, 115–18). Against such assumptions as those which interpret man as 'Spirit' and woman as 'Soul' ('Soul has "positively no wishes of its own, no preferences"') Annie adopts the deconstructive strategy of positing an overlapping of the terms – 'what does Soul, what does a woman do with her unexpressed preferences, her own desires?' (35). Against masculinist constructions of woman as 'lady' or 'tramp,' 'nice girl' or 'slut' (34), Annie undertakes a second deconstructive strategy of positing a third possibility – the 'monstrous,' that which lies outside of civilized (binary) conceptions, a 'monstrous' which is finally revealed to her as lesbianism.

However, at the same time Annie constructs a new set of binary oppositions which come to subsume her deconstructions. These new binaries grow out of her critique of the utilitarianism of male work patterns and of the 'Big Book' to which their historicizing discourses aspire. Early in the novel the text has Annie assert the secret woods ('the Old Wood'), in which she and her sisters play behind her home, against the larger woods ('the Green Wood'), in which the neighbourhood boys play. The 'Old Wood' is marked by semantically 'feminine' attributes:

> ... the Old Wood, moulted and softened with years of needle drift, tea brown, and the cedar stump hollow in the middle where they nestled in a womb, exchanging what if's, digging further with their fingers, sniffing the odour of tree matter become a stain upon their hands like dried blood.

The Green Wood is associated with boys and male instrumentality and pragmatism:

> what if the boys came down from their fort in the Green Wood with slingshots and air gun? would their own string bows and crookedly peeled arrows hold them off? standing on the rockery for practice, shooting at the bull's eye in the field (a stone in an empty lot), she despaired of herself, her sister-archers, her camarades – their arrows fell off the string, plopped on the dirt like so many cowpies ... but what if the men tried to bulldoze their woods? so what could *we* do? her little sister shrugged. (12)

Lurking behind this contrast are much older dichotomies involving 'sister-archers,' the Amazons and the Greeks, and Artemis and Actaeon; in each, the women are constructed as representing an older, more 'natural' culture, one eventually displaced by masculine authority, while the men are associated with hunting and conquest.

Annie's association of women with soft, moist, mossy, fern-clad spaces and men with rationalizing, conquering, bulldozing, and land-clearing projects continues throughout the novel until in the final pages Annie and Zoe's lesbian romance leads them into a bedroom that is variously 'a dark river,' 'trees ... a moon,' a room 'bleeding and soft' (152) and that is located within a house whose sounds make Annie want 'to listen, as i used to listen in the woods to the quiet

interplay of wind, trees, rain, creeping things under the leaves ...'
(151). This 'green world' of female bodies, with its promise of female
authenticity, points to a number of related binaries which the text
also has Annie maintain: the man's official 'Big Book' versus the
woman's 'own story' (79); the woman constructed by male-inspired
cosmetics versus 'the you that was you' (58); 'roman/ce (heroes)'
versus 'stories out of a life' (67); the masculine manipulations of a
pen versus the Cixousian menstrual 'writing the period that arrives
at no full stop':

> writing the period that arrives at no full stop. not the hand manipulating
> the pen. not the language of definition, of epoch and document, language
> explaining and justifying, but the words that flow out from within, running
> too quick to catch sometimes, at other times just an agonizingly slow
> trickle. (90)

The 'not ... but' syntax here firmly encloses Annie's potentially dialogical 'flow' within a dichotomous paradigm.

---

the silence of trees
the silence of women

if they could speak
an unconditioned language
what would they say?

   Ana Historic, 75

The notion of dialogic flow, linked in the novel semantically to the
liquidities of the green wood, to menstruation, to 'torrents' of women's
speech, is asserted more and more throughout the novel as an alternative to the women-excluding, hierarchy-creating, and historicizing
discourses of men. Such a flow of speech would be 'unconditioned'
in being outside of all social determination and construction. It would
also be outside of politics and hence outside of national cultural constructions. A key moment in Annie's movement towards accepting
such a possibility is her imagining of Mrs Richards's assisting in an
1874 childbirth, the first 'white' birth in the Vancouver townsite of
Gastown. She sees the child arriving as a linguistic event, 'a massive
syllable of slippery flesh slide out the open mouth' (126). The mother's vagina is 'a mouth working its own inarticulate urge, opening

deep' (125): 'mouth speaking flesh. she touches it to make it tell her present in this other language so difficult to translate. the difference' (126). The text has Annie experience these images as if they constituted her own rebirth, a birth not into culture and nation but Venus-like out of the waves of a woman's labour into 'the country of her own body':

> to be born in, enter from birth that place (that shoreline place of scarlet maples, since cut down) with no known name – see it, risen in waves, these scarlet leaves, lips all bleeding into the air, given (birth), given in greeting, the given surrounds him now. surrounds her, her country she has come into, the country of her body. (127)

Here the lost 'nameless' primordial trees, the 'scarlet maples' cut down by woodsmen, become the scarlet labia of the birthing mother; the landscape merges with both 'country' and women's body. It is these trees and scarlet lips that Annie will literally regain when in the final pages she enters Zoe's room with its signs of 'trees,' 'moon,' 'bleeding and soft.' The discourse here moves decisively towards both the ecstatic rhythms of theorists like Cixous and the imagery of more popular feminists like Janet and Stewart Farrar (see epigraph, above) or Mary Daly, with their emphasis on source, birth, divinity, and liquidity:

> Radical feminism is not reconciliation with the father. Rather it is affirming our original birth, our original source, movement, surge of living. The finding of our original integrity is re-membering our Selves. Athena re-members her mother and consequently re-members her Self. Radical feminism releases the inherent dynamic in the mother-daughter relationship toward friendship, which is strangled in the male-mastered system. (Daly, Gyn/Ecology, [1978] 39)

The lyrical conclusion of Ana Historic, however, with its merging of lovers and its return to birth, represents a moment impossible in both Lacanian psychology and any but its most naïve feminist elaborations: a regaining of the Oedipal mother and leap back to a time before the mirror stage. The pronouns of this lyric – 'she and me. you.' – telescope Zoe, Annie, and Ina (the referent of 'you' throughout the novel) into a single, undifferentiated utopian body:

> we give place, giving words, giving birth, to each other – she and me.

you. hot skin writing skin. fluid edge, wick wick. she draws me out. you she breathes, is where we meet. breeze from the window reaching you now, trees out there, streets you might walk down, will, soon. ([153])

Even the text of the novel seems to leap here out of time – the page numbering ends on the previous page; the lyric moment occurs outside of time and numbering.

In the theories of Lacan, Irigaray, and Cixous on which *Ana Historic* rests the central life-event is the simultaneous recognition and acceptance by the child of its fundamental and irreducible separateness from its mother and its entry into the symbolic order of language. This event brings both profound loss – the loss of the illusion of unity with mother and environment, the possible loss of the mother – and the always inadequate substitute of language – language for Lacan can at best 'stand in' for things lost. Every use of language, with its recalling of that initial moment of rupture, evokes both loss and desire. The event is forced upon the child by the presence of the Father (not the biological father but that which is outside or other to the mother-child dyad), the Lacanian outside, who both is desired by the mother and forbids the child's desire 'to be the exclusive desire of the mother.' Many of the feminist elaborations by Kristeva, Irigaray, Cixous, and others to Lacan's theories of the child's entry into language have focused on his threefold distinction among the order of language, *the symbolic*, its unpossessable referents, *the imaginary*, and that ever-returning Oedipal moment of impossibility and rupture on which they rest, *the real*; on his linking of the Symbolic with the Father; and on his conviction that there can be no reality outside the Symbolic order ('How return, other than by means of a special discourse, to a pre-discursive reality?' [1975, 33]) and thus no feminine outside of language. Irigaray, for example, has argued that women have special access to the *imaginary*, an access demonstrated in the past through their deployment of such discourses as mysticism and hysteria. Cixous has theorized that the speaking woman has privileged access to pre-Oedipal realities, to 'the lost mother. Eternity: ... the voice mixed with milk' (1975, 173). Kristeva has re-configured Lacan's forever separated *symbolic* and *imaginary* as a *symbolic* and a partially accessible pre-Oedipal *semiotic*, with the latter disrupting the former through silence, contradiction, nonsense, and rhythm, and thus equally available to women and men; here women's position in culture is produced within its discourses rather than produced by the gender of language.

Marlatt's text implies a theorization of language and childhood that borrows heavily from both Lacan and Cixous, but moves unlike either

to make the pre-Oedipal moment totally available to the female subject. Both the male and female child in *Ana Historic* are born into a
'natural' pre-Oedipal condition; unlike in Lacan, however, they are
alienated from this condition, not by the acquisition of language, but
by the socializing processes of a masculine symbolic order: 'we give
birth to boy babies and men make men of them as fast as they can.
they try to make us think they make women of us too but it's not
true. it's women imagining all that women could be that brings us
into the world' (131). Whereas in Lacan the necessity of language,
his 'Law-of-the-Father,' requires both sexes to give up the illusion of
pre-Oedipal unity for the inadequate significations of the symbolic,
here women's imaginings defeat male socializing strategies and re-
store that original unity. The inescapable burden of lack and desire
that for Lacan was the lot of all humans becomes here only the lot
of men. Men enter into symbolic language, and into social and political life, construct and are constructed in language, but women,
through their imaginations, have access to primal being: 'to be there
from the first. indigene. *ingenuus* (born in), native, natural, free(born)
– at home from the beginning' (127). In Annie's own case, through
imagination she can recover the pre-Oedipal mother by constructing
Zoe as the new guarantor of unity, who can make good all previous
loss.

What may appear superficially to be a political novel, a novel that
challenges from a feminist perspective how society is structured, what
discourses and roles it allows to women, is in the end not a political
novel at all. For the pre-Oedipal space it both dreams of and realizes
as the 'home' of woman is yet another utopian plenitude, eternal,
natural, before (or at least aside from) the symbolic realm of language
and thus apart from the social and political clashes and negotiations
that the symbolic enables. Although Zoe and her housemates are
mailing a set of flyers when Annie arrives for the final scene, that is,
ostensibly engaged in a politics, these flyers and their names are left
earthbound by the action and imagery that follow – 'Annie / Ana –
arose by any other name, whole wardrobes of names guarding the
limitations – we rise above them' (152).

Yet the text's peculiar and sometimes contradictory relationship to
Annie – occasionally exposing her ingenuous positivism, at other times
appearing to celebrate her new happiness, and at still others over-
determining her discourse of certainty – also suggests that this claim
to have transcended politics may be itself a desperate and extreme

political gesture. In the extreme authority of the discourse it allows Annie, *Ana Historic* not only often signals uncritical solidarity with her, but also lets show its own extraordinary anxiety both that she find an explanation for her estrangement from her mother *and* that this explanation scapegoat her father. The cynical exclusions of women from power experienced by Ina and Annie – especially the abuse of Ina's body by positivist psychiatry – may in some sense 'explain' the extravagance within the text of Annie's similarly positivist counter-actions, but they do not explain the positivism of the text itself.

In the novel's final pages the narrative discourse of *Ana Historic* establishes no ironic distance from Annie, but instead continues to identify itself with both her utopian claims and her passionate homogenizing of Canada's social, economic, linguistic, and regional difference as 'patriarchal' oppression. The text's message in the final chapter title, 'Not a Bad End' (138), directly endorses Annie's concluding judgments. Not a bad end may be also not a good end, of course, and still be for Annie perhaps the best possible 'end' within extraordinary circumstances. But for the novel itself, is this end indeed a good end? For the patriarchal order still stands. Annie has reversed her place within it, usurped its discourse of certainty, and with it the male prerogative to 'love' a woman. And beyond Annie's narrow vision, beyond Zoe's room, within the various signs by which she has represented and dismissed that patriarchal order – 'history,' 'North America,' 'Canada,' 'worker' – other huge conflicts continue.

Totally Avant-garde Woman
Heroine

The Tent Peg, The Biggest Modern Woman of the World, and *Ana Historic* all glimpse the question of how women might achieve 'larger' lives as a political one but in various ways retreat from that perception. *The Tent Peg* and *Ana Historic* retreat by dehistoricizing both woman and the national and multinational social conditions which have limited her. Woman becomes a trans-historic being inseparable from the primeval tundra or forests of the novels' settings; patriarchal social forms, despite the novels' successes in linking these with eighteenth-century imperial European expansion, or with early twentieth-century industrial capitalism, are given a similarly archetypal figuration – made to resonate back to Sisera's attempt to sexually appropriate Ja-el and Actaeon's forced entry into Artemis's forest. This approach implies the unchangeability of most social forms, and results, if not in a total rejection of politics, as seems implicit in the archetypal appeals of *The Tent Peg*, at least in the parochial gender politics that is presented as the desperate goal of *Ana Historic*. Another and perhaps equally bold possibility for woman is to claim the land or state itself, to declare it female, as explored by Coral Ann Howells in *Private and Fictional Worlds*, and hyperbolically proposed in *The Biggest Modern Woman of the World*. While this approach is certainly political in its suggestion that the state or landscape to be administered is inherently more accessible to women's understanding than to men's, it also risks, in its underlying binary assumption, homogenizations which could exclude political process. In Margaret Atwood's *Surfacing*, for example, the narrator's decision that she cannot live in the bush with which she feels so viscerally and atavistically attuned, but must return to her male lover and the city, implies both a refusal of binary thinking and a decision to return to a kind of politics. In *The Biggest Modern*

Woman, where the female protagonist is more identified with the Canadian nation than with its land, this identification leads to a monological construction of Canada as a resource-rich trading nation, and to minimal consideration of how women might contribute to a Canadian polity. The 'great' woman, in fact, must leave Canada to find a stage large enough for the roles to which she aspires.

Oh Mama why'd you put this hole in me?

Heroine, 31

How can a woman be a 'heroine,' socially and/or politically, when she is recurrently haunted by her own desire, hunger, self-dissatisfaction, emptiness, lack? Or when her own society, her own 'Mama,' has constructed her to herself as hollow, as lacking? The lament to 'Mama,' which itself haunts Gail Scott's 1987 novel *Heroine*, raises an enormous and complex set of political questions and meanings – questions which perhaps go a long way to explaining the desperation of *Ana Historic*, or the extreme reluctance to engage political issues of *Ana Historic* and *The Tent Peg*. The lament insists on politics rather than biology or essence; the 'hole' is not natural to the woman, but it has been 'put' in her. It puns on the vagina as a negative signifier, a signifier through absence, and plays with various psychoanalytic reflections on the construction of female sexuality from Freud's castration complex to Irigaray's *This Sex Which Is Not One*. It plays also on a number of Lacan's theorizations – most notably that to become a separate human subject requires the losing of direct knowledge of the world and its replacement by language and its forever inadequate signifiers, and that the regulator of language and its meanings is the Phallus, which thus stands as a sign of its own inadequacy – a reminder of both the loss of metaphysical 'truth' and the mere systematicity of the symbolic code of language which has replaced it. Addressed to 'Mama,' who as a separate subject was herself complicit in the symbolic order of language which enabled her to be so constituted (the capital *M* reminds that 'Mama' is a word, a linguistic category), the question not only asks, Why did you let me be so constructed as female? but also, Why did you let me be human? – why did you let me come to exist in language, hungering and desiring, split from certainty and wholeness, compelled to experience a linguistically mediated world as unfilling and unsatisfying.

The site in which 'G.S.,' the protagonist of *Heroine*, asks her anguished questions and seeks the always inadequate phalluses – a man's love, a career as a writer – that might fill her 'hole' is Quebec, itself the site of both Canada's major 'split' from wholeness and French North America's split from its originating culture. Signs of both these splits also abound in the novel. Quebec nationalist graffiti – 'QUÉBEC LIBRE' (45), 'QUÉBECOISE DEBOUTTE' (28), 'SOS FLQ' (144) – glow on its walls. Its francophone characters repeatedly classify themselves and anglophone Canadians as 'français' or 'anglais' as if to reconstitute unity with the two founding nations. The RCMP spies on nationalist, socialist, and Marxist organizations alike as if any dissent could endanger a confederal imagination of unity. The 'hole' in the central character is thus also a national 'hole' – a 'hole' in a Quebec that can never be the French utopia which it can imagine, a 'hole' in a Canada in which a francophone can never trust 'une anglaise,' or in which to gain that trust the *anglaise* must 'stand up ... and shout "Vive le Québec libre"' (90).

———————•———————

The aspect which most distinguishes *Heroine* from a feminist novel like *Ana Historic* or a 'Montreal' novel like *Joshua Then and Now* is the rigorous way in which it insists that all personal and political identities are constructed in language. There is no Ur-woman to recover, goddess to reawaken, lost matriarchy to reconstitute, or spurned universals to reacknowledge. Throughout the novel various ideologies call out their constituting phrases to the narrator, 'G.S.,' offering her instructions and injunctions: 'the relaxed woman gets the man'; 'qui perd, gagne' (11); 'good wool lasts forever' (18); 'hysteria is not suitable in a revolutionary woman' (19); 'possessiveness reifies desire' (21);'under capitalism, you get it while you can' (26); 'a woman who loves herself doesn't put up with a man who deprives her of affection' (27); 'put the best foot forward' (39); 'androgyny is beautiful' (54); 'You have to live and let live' (54); 'a good political movie should bring out the fight in people' (67). Popular songs offer melancholy nostalgia ('I miss you most of all, / when autumn leaves start to fall' [56]; 'Nobody cares for me' [126]), or romantic defiance ('Je ne regrette rien,' sings Edith Piaf [39]; 'there's no tomorrow, baby' [12], 'freedom's just another word for nothing left to lose' [65], sings Janis Joplin). Banners, graffiti, T-shirts, advertisements, photos, TV images, and radio voices all add in various languages their own messages. Lacking any possibility of a 'real' self, G.S. wanders among their discourses and ideologies, attracted to many of them, trying to be 'québecoise' when she arrives in Montreal, to be a Marxist revolutionary when she falls in love with the leader of a Marxist cell, and to be a feminist activist when this relationship collapses. Finally she begins to try to write a novel in which she can reinvent herself as a 'heroine': '... could the heroine, in the whole picture, lean even more to darkness than to light?' (160); 'The heroine, to balance her particular brand of pain, must constantly strive to find other forms in life and art to express the diffuse and varied tone of poetry in her' (162). That is, G.S. begins to try to construct herself in discourse. By the end of the novel the 'heroine' who began as only a remote and idealized possibility to G.S., distinct from her, begins to become the person she, G.S., I, Gail, friend of Marie, can identify herself as:

> The heroine keeps walking. Wondering why a woman can't get what she wants without going into business on every front. Social, political, economic, domestic. Each requiring a different way of walking, a different way of talking. She looks instinctively for her own reflection in a store window. But it's as yet too dark to see clearly. What if Marie is in Bagels'? (181)

In the overall discourse of the Canadian nation, G.S.'s biography has unmistakeable meaning. She is a working-class Ontario girl who grows up beside the Trans-Canada Highway in the ironically named Sudbury suburb of Lively. Her father is a Sudbury miner who became mine foreman. Lively is a town where cows moo 'lazily in the cool grass' and where the accepted view of young women as rural Eves, quick to bloom and fade, is indicated by the general store calendar of 'a cute little red-cheeked girl biting on an apple' and by the advice the calendar's 'old maid' owner gives to G.S., 'Watch out, iris stems fade quickly, when uprooted' (43), when providing the address of her Westmount niece. G.S.'s choice of Montreal as the city to which she will flee from Lively constructs it, as so often in the English-Canadian imagination, as a place of glamour, romance, sophistication, and art:

> There's something about an island city built around a mountain that seems so different, alive, romantic. It has to do ... with the boats in the harbour, the street fairs on boul. St-Laurent, the sound of hooves on cobblestone in Vieux Montréal ... The wandering poets, the sidewalk artists, the ritual bus and métro strikes. Baseball and hot dogs; hockey and beer. The friendly bars, the snobby bars, the bars that are always changing names and faces in an endless search for the truly hip. And the food: health food, ethnic

food, fast food, specialty food, fattening food, diet food, take-out food, deli food, coffee and croissants and crêpes. Food and ambiance, food and dancing, food and drink, drink, and some of the best cuisine this side of paradise. (Macrea, *Montreal Magic* [1982], 13)

G.S. arrives at the niece's house at the moment in 1969 when the FLQ blows up the Westmount Armoury. The next day she walks east along downtown Sherbrooke Street:

Fancy rugs, glasses, lingerie in pink and black and purple. There's nothing like a woman with lace next to her skin. Very classy, very French. I passed the Ritz. The suitcase was growing heavy. Suddenly the buildings were lower, sagging even, so they seemed to lean together. On a wall in fresh white paint was written QUÉBEC LIBRE. AMOUR ET ANARCHIE.

I opened the next door. Its sign said La Hutte Suisse. In the semi-darkness waitresses carried huge trays of drafts with their solid arms. The guys in the booths were skinny with tinted glasses. Little beards on pale skin. I could see the titles of reading material spread on the tables, *Le Monde*, *Socialisme québecois*, *Liberté*. I could tell this was a hangout for radical French intellectuals. It felt so good. I sat as near them as I could, trying to make eye contact. (45)

When G.S. rewrites this arrival story for her 'heroine,' she excludes the initial visit to Westmount and gives even greater emphasis to the signs of culture and romance and to the indications that here female possibilities include not merely 'cute little girl' and 'old maid' but also 'beautiful woman':

... she climbed off the bus from Sudbury. The smoke hung stiff in the cold sky. At Place Ville Marie she found the French women so beautiful with their fur coats and fur hats under which peep their powdered noses. If anybody asked, she'd say she wanted a job, love, money. The necessary *accoutrements* to be an artist. She immediately rented a bed-sitter. Stepping off the Métro that night and turning a corner, she saw the letters FLQ screaming on an old stone wall. Dripping in fresh white paint. Climbing the stairs to her room she knew she'd come to the right place. (22)

What is fascinating about the signs of art and culture which *Heroine* attaches to Montreal is the extent to which these are European as well as Québécois. The bar G.S. first visits is La Hutte *Suisse*. On its tables are not only *Liberté* and *Socialisme québecois* but the Parisian

Le Monde. Her first Montreal lover is a man who has raced formula-1 cars. Her second is Jon, a young Pole and Marxist leader. She first meets him in the Cracow Cafe amid numerous signs of Europe and European political theory:

> You were sitting under a Polish poster drinking coffee from a thick cup. Lennon glasses on your pretty nose.
>
> ...
>
> ... some hookers came in. They had snowflakes on their hair and eyebrows. To keep warm one of them was dancing wildly. Left foot over right. Until she saw you had your eye on me. She stopped and stared angrily from under her wide pale brow. Very French. And I noticed she had middle-class skin. Therefore no hooker, just one of your socialist-revolutionary comrades dressed up to help organize the oppressed and exploited women of The Main. (23)

G.S.'s relationship with Jon takes her very soon on a vacation to Morocco, and to Hamburg, Gdansk, and Marienbad. 'Walking white streets eating almond-cream buns. The falling snow giving an air of harmony' (18). The harmony here is the harmony of the cosmopolitan, which for G.S. is what Montreal signifies – not Quebec culture but Marienbad.

Although G.S. and Jon also travel with their cell, the 'F-group,' by train to Vancouver, and although hints of other parts of Canada occasionally enter the text, Montreal remains the only Canadian gateway to the exotic, and itself remains predominantly French/European. And despite G.S.'s unhappiness with her relationship with Jon, her feeling of being less beautiful than Quebec women because *une anglaise*, and her gradual disillusionment with the politics of the F-group, Montreal continues in the novel to be exotic and idealized. In a sense it is the lover G.S. has left Ontario for – much like Quebec itself was cast as male English Canada's love-object in *Caprice*.

> Recalling the thing She loved, a wedding, and the thing She hated, marriage.
>
> *Heroine*, 47

As well as mapping Canada as a stolid anglophone nation that contains a vibrant, exotic and Europeanized Quebec, *Heroine* also maps it as severely fractured by various conflicts concerning gender, wealth, language, and sexuality. Here, rather than being 'different' from English Canada, Quebec serves as a metonymy for it. In fact, running against both the novel's idealization of Quebec and the Quebec nationalist ideologies proclaimed by many of its revolutionaries is the narrator's involvement with causes that cut across nationalism: particularly causes of economic justice and sexual equality. Although the F-group's individual members are mostly sympathetic with the ideal of an independent Quebec, the F-group's work is, in theory, directed to ending the exploitation of female prostitutes, to unionizing waitresses, and to fighting the Pinochet dictatorship of Chile and, in practice, focused largely on the sexual conquests and intrigues hinted at by its name. G.S. indeed experiences herself as marked as 'different' in the F-group – but less by her cultural and linguistic background than by her gender. Francophone nationalism is virtually taken for granted by her and by most of the novel's other characters; at no point do they subject it to critical interrogation. When the Parti Québécois wins the 1976 election, 'everybody's happy, although, of course, we'd spoiled our ballots. For revolutionaries cannot support bourgeois-nationalism in any form' (89). But they devote endless intellectual debate to formulating social and political principles about human relations in general, and sexual relations specifically. As a result, Heroine's extensive portrayal of the 1970s cultural ferment in Quebec characterizes that ferment not as peculiarly Québécois but rather as North American and international. Its intuitions and banners may be nationalist, but its social preoccupations are transnational.

The faint but implicit criticism in Heroine of Quebec nationalism as poorly considered, and potentially in conflict with the transnational ideals of many of those that espouse it, is echoed in G.S.'s own attraction to Quebec and its national romance. The Quebec she is drawn towards is one marked in her mind, not specifically as 'French' or 'Québécois,' but as a place that offers 'experience,' creativity, and love. On her second day she looks 'for a cafe where [she] could sit and write' (45). She takes an undemonstrative Québécois lover for 'the experience': 'I didn't have much choice if I wanted the experience. Because in that particular period québécoise was beautiful, leaving a low premium on English women' (46). After two years she becomes involved with the F-group because she experiences an immediate sexual attraction to its leader. 'You had the sweetest smile I'd ever seen on a man. My first thought was that this was exactly what I wanted' (23). She self-consciously endorses the group's reflexive declarations of support for Quebec independence more to retain her social status in the group and Jon's affection than to express political belief.

'Slightly embarrassed, I stand up, raising my glass, and shout "Vive le Québec libre"' (90). As her unhappiness with her relationship with Jon grows, her fascination with Quebec nationalist politics increasingly yields to interest in individual women and feminist issues. Although one of these women is the ex-revolutionary, lesbian, and now independent film-maker Marie, who continues, she says, to be 'profondément indépendantiste' (89), another is the Manchester-born Anne, in whose shelter for battered women (itself a transnational sign) the narrator does volunteer work. Much as she experienced Jon and the F-group as a field of ideological conflict, here too she experiences these women as discursive possibilities, as conflicting pressures upon her from outside. By the end of the novel when she is struggling at last to become her own 'heroine,' she walks a Montreal street everywhere assailed by assertions of what 'must be,' what is 'trendy,' or what one 'should' do:

Eating, she thinks that in the 80s a story must be all smooth and shiny. ...

But walking back down The Main ... she thinks: Yet I feel this terrible violence in me. In any story, it will break the smoothness of the surface. ...

She thinks: Maybe I should talk to someone.
Startled by a sudden glimpse of her reflection in a window, she thinks: Maybe I should get a job. Then I could buy one of those second-hand men's coats trendy women wear this year ... Or else one of those beautiful expresso pots I saw in the window up the street. (182–3)

By this point in the novel both the glamour of Montreal and Quebec nationalism have implicitly become merely two of numerous discursive claims, two of many 'trendy' demands like literary style or 'beautiful' expresso pots.

From the mountaintop, the Black tourist turns his telescope. The grey woman sloshes through a yellow puddle and climbs some outside stairs. Her sister died there. Twas the novocaine before Christmas. She was allergic but failed to tell the welfare dentist.

Heroine, 38–9

From the opening paragraph *Heroine* is framed by two figures, ostensibly created by the narrating G.S. – a male black American tourist who inspects the city by telescope from the top of Mount Royal and a 'grey' indigent woman who wanders the streets below oblivious to the telescope's gaze. These two figures further problematize any unitary resolution of the novel's politics by introducing even more discourses and their claims of value – discourses of race, power, wealth, and poverty. Both figures represent categories that the F-group has little concern for and that play no part in the narrator's erotic and romantic ambitions.

The black tourist, as an American, as one enabled to travel, as one standing on top of a mountain, is associated with wealth and power. The only entry his blackness makes into the category of racism comes through the narrator's self-consciousness about having specified his colour, and her move throughout the next few references to him towards naming him only as 'the tourist.' Nevertheless, his colour operates to qualify his position of power, to serve notice that it is a winnable position, one only recently won. The telescope he holds operates in another direction, however, associating him with a long history of male dominance. It marks him, like the camera that Jon carries, as the specular man, the one whose gaze, like that of Annie's father in *Ana Historic*, legitimizes female beauty, frames and defines reality, and extends the effective range of control and power.

Contrastingly, without access to telescope, mountain, or power, is the grey woman, who is constituted by the telescope's reach but powerless to look through it. She is the 'grey' woman, without colour, without even the controversial blackness of the tourist. More marginal than he, more marginal than the anglophone narrator, 'the grey woman stands, her filthy skirt falling about her stained legs' (57). 'Her shoulders shake and shake from coughing' (166). She is the ultimate version of *Heroine*'s excluded women – the revolutionary women who serve mainly as bedmates for the revolutionary men, the exploited waitresses, the young hookers, Polly the Mafia wife, whose estranged husband's well-paid lawyers legally take her children from her, or the elderly steno who was exposed to so many alien forms of language throughout her career that now 'everything that goes in her ears goes out her mouth' (43):

> *Political situation prostituting fascist referendum wife of Frank's girl's legs mufflers getting expensive four-to-one the Expos under conditions for selling stocks on St James' the church over the bridge at skis in the oracle ...* (42)

The grey woman, like her sister who forgot to speak to her dentist, exists even further outside of discourse, living alone on streets where no one may ever speak to her.

—————————•—————————

'You'll never be anything but a fellow traveller.'

'Why?' I asked in a small voice (my lip twisting like Hers on the verandah) ...

'Because you're an artist. The way you mother that little Chilean kid makes us also think you have parenting ambitions. Tandis qu'un vrai révolutionnaire appartient 100 pour cent au groupe.'

Heroine, 98

G.S.'s concerns about what what she 'should' do as she, like the grey woman, wanders the streets of Montreal and her recurrent preoccupation elsewhere about whether she is loved sufficiently by Jon, or whether she should have accepted Marie's lesbian advances, might very well strike her F-group comrades as signs of bourgeois individualism, and possibly even lead a 'bourgeois nationalist' to accuse her of granting inappropriate priority to the personal over the collective. This emphasis on the personal over the collective, however, is as much a property of the novel itself as of G.S. the character. Despite the concern it shows in its 'black' and 'grey' frame characters about systemic exploitations and exclusions, *Heroine* gives by far most of its attention firstly to G.S.'s individual relationship to Marxism, lesbianism, feminism, and romantic idealism and secondly to how the individual self is constituted and to the relative instability of this constitution. Even its portrayal of 1970s Quebec is overshadowed by its concern with the way in which G.S.'s hungry, desiring self is constructed, reconstructed, but never satisfied by the various discursive assertions she encounters. The only note of consistency the novel gives its first-person narrator is the anguish of her cry to Mama: 'why'd you put this hole in me.' Otherwise it presents her as a mélange of names, lacks, phrases, and ideologies. It shows her desperately needing the romantic exclusionary image she and Jon project as a 'beautiful couple' (18) or 'the perfect revolutionary couple' (16) while also feeling she must visibly reject monogamy in order to 'improve [her] revolutionary image' (98). It shows her wanting also some distinct legitimacy among the F-group women as a radical feminist, and so writing and presenting the paper 'The Issue of Equal Access to Sexuality for Women in Non-Monogamous Heterosexual Couples'

(65) in a vain attempt to bridge both male and female interests. It has her name herself variously 'G.S,' 'I,' 'Gail,' 'widow,' and 'heroine.' It has her seek advice from conflicting sources – from Jon, from the lesbian Marie, even from an anglophone psychiatrist at McGill University. Throughout most of her narration the novel shows her lying in a bathtub, masturbating beneath the faucet, and both sorting her conflicting identities, desires, and memories, and making various literary efforts to frame these for the novel she hopes to write. The flowing water from the faucet emphasizes the fluidity and mutability of her memories and viewpoints, while the enclosing tub emphasizes the paralysis of indecision that her life has reached.

The novel also works to discredit notions of unified subjectivity through G.S.'s changing views of other characters. On her arrival in Montreal G.S.'s desperation to possess a unified self-image is paralleled by her projection of unity onto the people she meets. She perceives the 'green-eyed girl' who is her main rival for Jon's affections as an archetypally jealous schemer who will deploy Marxist doctrine to discredit her or pose as a lesbian to conceal her own heterosexual designs. She sees Marie as the strong, decisive 'new woman' and overlooks the ambivalent desire Marie's repeated visits to her suggest. She sees Jon as a hero, a teacher who will enable her to 'learn of politics and culture' (18). His professional work as a photographer – he works as a wedding photographer by day and a revolutionary creator of social documents by night – increases his aura of authority: 'Later, my love, taking pictures, when it seemed to me we saw it all the same, I began to think of you as an extra window on the world. Helping me figure out what real is' (40). She is consequently distressed when any of these characters behave inconsistently or in ways that imply disapproval of her. But, of course, within the novel itself they too are discursively constructed characters, who also experience the various discursive conflicts the various chapter titles encode: between romantic love and pragmatic reality ('Car Wrecks and Bleeding Hearts'), between self-sufficiency and social responsibility ('Free Woman and the Shadow in the Bank'), and between creative independence and immersion in another ('I Was a Poet before I Was You').

Initially the heroine that G.S. would construct of herself as the protagonist of the novel she hopes to write is a woman who would meet all discursive expectations and transcend their contradictions. 'Her goal is to maintain a certain (modern) equilibrium. To be on every front a totally avant-garde woman. ... Detachment is part of the image she's working on' (62). To some extent this heroine is a parody of the demands G.S. makes of herself in aspiring to be an emotionally fulfilled lover, a Marxist revolutionary, and a radical feminist: 'Strong and passionate, her own person. Any pain she feels, she keeps hidden ... So that the external image with the black leather jacket, handrolled cigarette and heavy eye makeup is impeccably courageous' (58). Later, even though the narrator allows her more latitude – 'a heroine can be sad, distressed, it just has to be in a social context' (84) – she appears to be an idealization of the narrator:

> I have to admit my mind also turned to my own slight lack [of a sex life]. And I said: 'I'll never write a word untouched like this.' But twas only a passing moment. The heroine wouldn't have this problem, having learned a certain flair (example: the way she combs her hair or wears a sweater) by coming up to Montréal. Yes, she views the savoir-vivre as a part of her struggle against whatever she hated back in Lively. This vision of a future where everyone is beautiful buoys her determination to live each day as the perfect revolutionary. Striving constantly to combine the political with the personal. (102)

Only when the narrator leaves her bathtub do she and the heroine-persona begin to converge. 'The heroine stands up. Drawing her blanket close, she takes the blue sheets and puts them on a violin stand beside the television. She steps back' (180). 'Heroinism' at this point, however, no longer has political content; it has become merely an individual's 'brave' attempt to continue to live – to leave a bathtub, or take a mundane walk outside one's home. 'The heroine keeps walking' (181).

Heroine's emphasis on feminism and on a woman's subjective well-being is evident even in its narrative structure. As Marcia Blumberg has pointed out, *Heroine* consists of a sixty-one-page section entitled 'Beginning,' an eight-page Section II, untitled, and a hundred-page section III titled 'Ending.' Blumberg identifies this structure of substantial outer sections surrounding a slight centre as similar to the structure Toril Moi has noted in Luce Irigaray's *Speculum of the Other Woman* – 'a hollow surface on the model of the speculum/vagina,' 'the centre ... framed by the two massive sections' (Blumberg, 58; Moi, 130). The overall text of *Heroine* would appear to be a gynaecological rejoinder to the Phallus and patriarchy, and an assertion of the priority of gender politics over both national and other transnational ones. The phallus itself, together with Jon's powerful camera, is reduced by *Heroine* to a 'single eye' (9): a sadly specular water faucet that G.S. controls, not to penetrate her vagina, but to spurt 'warmly over [her] uh small point' (36), to 'stay warm as [a] sperm river' (126).

Neither Canada nor Quebec has a large role in the imagination of *Heroine*. English Canada is a place of banishment when the F-group is warned by the police to go there during the Olympic Games; Quebec, at first glance, is an exotic foretaste of international culture and avant-garde politics – a place that becomes, however, much less exotic once the condition of women within it becomes evident. The official politics of both Canada and Quebec are dismissed by *Heroine* as regressive – as protecting bourgeois materialism by exploiting the weak, especially women like the 'grey' lady or the elderly stenographer. As in *The Tent Peg* and *Ana Historic*, what engages the novel's imagination is not a feminism within national politics but a transnational feminism. However, *Heroine*'s transnational feminism has few hints of the assumptions of transcendent gender that inform those two novels. This feminism seeks action rather than essence, envisions socially situated expansions of women's fields of action: greater choice of discourses, larger spaces in which to write one's own script, or construct one's own heroine; enlarged space for this heroine to walk out into any city's 'grey light ... standing on the sidewalk ... her pale red curls her one sign of beauty' (183).

Individualist Nationalism
Cat's Eye

While many women in Margaret Atwood's fiction have been as isolated and alone as *Heroine*'s G.S., almost none has displayed her intense political desires or the wish to connect with other women that brings her out of her apartment in that novel's final pages. Atwood's female characters have extreme difficulty with relations with other women, particularly with women – like Lora in *Bodily Harm* or Moira or Ofglen in *The Handmaid's Tale* – who construct themselves through political action. Characters who attempt to act politically or socially, in fact, are often parodically portrayed in Atwood novels as clown figures, trendy, superficial, or naïve – from Clara in *The Edible Woman* and David in *Surfacing* to Offred's mother in *The Handmaid's Tale* – much as they are in Robertson Davies's fiction.

Most of the action of *Cat's Eye*, Margaret Atwood's seventh novel, takes place in Toronto, either around downtown Queen Street West or in the midtown Yonge–St Clair middle-class neighbourhoods. Other large portions of the novel take place in northern Ontario and Vancouver. Yet despite the unmistakable marking of these settings, it is not always easy to find Canada or Canadianness within this text. Although Elaine Risley, its first-person narrator, has considerable awareness of the differences that she has possessed at various times in her life through being a girl, a woman, a stranger to urban life, and an artist, she is constructed as having almost none of how she may have been different through being born Canadian. Through her eyes the Canadian places she inhabits often appear to be indistinguishable from places elsewhere, and to have become so because of the eagerness of most Canadians to embrace the fashionably foreign.

Every morning, after Miss Lumley blows a thin metallic note on her pitch-pipe, we stand up to sing 'God Save the King.' We also sing,

Rule Britannia, Britannia rules the waves;
Britons never, never, never shall be slaves!

Because we're Britons, we will never be slaves. But we aren't real Britons, because we are also Canadians. This isn't quite as good, although it has its own song:

In days of yore, from Britain's shore,
Wolfe, the dauntless hero, came

Cat's Eye, 80

Almost all the Canadian institutions visible in *Cat's Eye* – public school, high school, university, department stores, public broadcasting – are heavily overlaid with foreign signs and images. During the 1940s classrooms are festooned with Union Jacks and photos of British princesses; small girls collect colouring books of Hollywood actresses; while their families listen to the Jack Benny show 'punctuated by singing commercials for Lucky Strike cigarettes' (213). One high school that appears in the text has been transformed into a miniature Scotland by an overzealous Scottish principal:

Burnham High has a school plaid, a school crest with a thistle and a couple of those Scottish knives they stick in their socks, and a Gaelic motto. The plaid, the crest, the motto, and the school colours all belong to Mr. MacLeod's personal clan.

In the front hall, alongside the Queen, hangs a portrait of Dame Flora MacLeod with her two bagpipe-playing grandsons, posed outside Dunvegan Castle. We are encouraged to think of this castle as our ancestral home, and of Dame Flora as our spiritual leader. In choir we learn 'The Skye Boat Song,' about Bonnie Prince Charlie escaping the genocidal English ... I think all this Scottishness is normal for high schools, never having gone to one before; and even the several Armenians, Greeks, and Chinese in our school lose the edges of their differences, immersed as we all are in a mist of plaid. (206)

In Toronto, twenty years later, young would-be painters sit 'in the dark, listening to folksongs about women being stabbed with daggers, and smoking marijuana cigarettes, which is what people do in New York' (324). U.S. draft-dodgers arrive and become 'depressed because

Toronto isn't the United States without a war on, as they thought it would be, but some limbo they have strayed into by accident' (335). The narrator's Hungarian-born art teacher aspires to direct movies in the United States because 'Toronto has no gaiety or soul' (305). Forty years later the narrator suggests Torontonians have found yet another way to betray their colonial feelings – through eager cosmopolitanism: '*World-Class City* is a phrase they use in magazines these days, a great deal too much. All those ethnic restaurants, and the theatre and the boutiques. New York without the garbage and muggings, it's supposed to be' (14).

Simultaneously another genuine transnational set of signs broods over the action in the scientific research of the narrator's father, an entomologist, and brother, an astrophysicist. Throughout the novel the father makes wry predictions of planetary disaster and human extinction; the 'we' of each of these predictions is not local or national, but global. During the early years of the Cold War he mutters that 'we'll probably blow ourselves sky-high before the end of the century, given the atom bomb and the way things are going. The future belongs to the insects' (66–7). When insulin is discovered, he 'cheerfully' forecasts that because diabetics are now living long enough to pass on their genes to their children, soon

> we'll all be diabetics, and since insulin is made from cows' stomachs the whole world will be covered with insulin-producing cows ... The cows burp methane gas. Far too much methane gas is entering the atmosphere already, it will choke out the oxygen and perhaps cause the entire earth to become a giant greenhouse. The polar seas will melt and New York will be under six feet of water ... Also we have to worry about deserts, and erosion. If we don't get burped to death by the cows we'll end up like the Sahara Desert ... (216)

In the 1960s he more gloomily warns his family 'that nitrogen fertilizers are destroying fish life by fostering an overgrowth of algae,' that 'a new disease ... will turn us all into deformed cretins unless the paper companies are forced to stop dumping mercury into the rivers' (288). He leaves his job at the university to return to research at Sault Ste Marie, saying that 'the lower Great Lakes are the world's largest sewer and that if we knew what was going into the drinking water we would all become alcoholics,' that Toronto's air 'is so full of chemicals we should be wearing gas masks' (329–30).

The narrator's brother, Stephen, is initially fascinated by biological science also but grows rapidly towards an abstract, cosmic perspective of life that leaves his father feeling small and earth-bound (217). His attention leaves the social and political contexts his father's had remained attached to and, usually without employing personal pronouns of any sort, focuses on questions about the nature of time and the structure of the universe: 'is the universe more like a giant ever-enlarging blimp, or does it pulsate, does it expand and contract?' (290). The planet that his father experienced as so fragile is, for him, a mere 'fossil, a leftover from the first picoseconds of creation, when the universe crystallized out from the primal homogeneous plasma' (332). He becomes lost in his own scientific detachment, dangerously unconcerned and ignorant about social codes or political passions.

Because both these characters are positively marked within the novel as well-meaning, even if socially naïve, the transnational systems of scientific law which they announce operate strongly against both the forces of international fashion and those of national distinction. The collapse of the universe or the collapse of species will be delayed by neither international boundaries nor the sudden return to popularity of the Peter Pan collar or mini-skirt. Both international fashion and cosmic science, however, operate against specificity, and thus against 'authentic' human relations. Stephen loses his life because of the intrusion into it of Islamic fundamentalist passions of a kind his rational mind has long ago dismissed as trivial and boring in the larger context of the explosive creation of stars and the sundering of planets. At another extreme the families of Elaine's childhood friends lose the ability to know and care for one another in their fascination with 'twin set' sweaters, theological strictness, or with sophistication that consists of wearing 'cashmere sweaters and pearl button earrings,' smoking cigarettes and speaking of them as 'ciggie-poos' (209).

Until we moved to Toronto I was happy.

Cat's Eye, 21

As Elaine narrates her life story, *Cat's Eye* constructs an ever-widening circle of loss around her. A Wordsworthian structure of lost primal innocence not only underlies the overall narrative but is frequently reinvoked by specific narrative incidents. Elaine's decisive journey from innocence to experience occurs in her eighth year, when her father decides to give up his nomadic life as a forestry field researcher, who houses his wife and two children in tents in the summer and unwinterized cabins in the winter, to take a teaching position at the University of Toronto and purchase a house in one of the city's post-war subdivisions. The novel presents Elaine as having thus far grown up in ignorance of most social practices, particularly those practices that define girlhood and womanhood. It portrays her parents as social eccentrics, as 'authentic' idiosyncratic individuals who have led their lives careless of most conventions of socially endorsed behaviour. In Elaine's memory the parents have no friends, only casual interactions with motel-owners and gas-station operators. Their closest contact with social structures outside the family seems to be through the radio, through which 'the war filters in ... remote and crackly, the voices from London fading through the static' (24). The Second World War provides one set of codes that transparently intrudes into Elaine's life, in the form of the infantry games that she is enlisted into by her older brother: ' "You're dead," he says.' ' "Yes you are. They got you. Lie down" ' (24). Another set is offered by the images in the school read-ers which her parents give her: 'two children who live in a white house with ruffled curtains, a front lawn, and a picket fence. The father goes to work, the mother wears a dress and an apron, and the children play ball on the lawn with their dog and cat' (29). Elaine preserves her sense of innocence by rendering both these intrusions 'exotic.' War becomes a game for her that has meaning only in terms of the social dynamic between herself and her brother. The school-book images occupy a world, she says, in which 'nothing is anything like my life.' When she and her brother 'draw with coloured pencils,' they each enter into these distant semiotic systems as if they were fantasy worlds, parallel to, rather than extensions of, their own ex-istence:

> ... he draws wars, ordinary wars and wars in space. His red and yellow and orange are worn to stubs, from the explosions, and his gold and silver are used up too, on the shining metal carapaces of the tanks and spaceships and on the helmets and the complicated guns. But I draw girls. I draw them in old-fashioned clothing, with long skirts, pinafores and puffed sleeves, or in dresses like Jane's, with big hairbows on their heads. This is the elegant, delicate picture I have in my mind, about other little girls. I don't think about what I might say to them if I actually met some. I haven't got that far. (29)

Elaine's family's move from northern Ontario to suburban Toronto propels her abruptly into this 'parallel' system of her Dick and Jane reader. The other girls she meets here – Grace, from a religious, thrifty lower-middle-class family, Carol, from a trendy middle-class family, and Cordelia, from an apparently affluent, upper-middle-class family that disdains the department-store tastes of the other two – all possess complex, widely operating, and partially overlapping codes of speech, dress, and behaviour. Their possession of these codes, plus the codes' institutional confirmation on playground, in church, on the radio, in catalogues, or on store shelves, give the girls enormous power over her and allow them – Cordelia, in particular – to persecute her for more than four years as if she were 'stupid' (165), or 'nothing' (199).

This initial grand loss, and fall into social practice, occasions a series of further losses. Her mother and father, despite their innocent non-conformance, are made by the text to appear increasingly irrelevant and marginal to Elaine the more culturally embedded her own life becomes. When her brother leaves for college in the United States, she begins to sense that he, too, whose boys' world had always seemed impervious to the torments of her own fall into culture, is vulnerable to social danger. Even the various scenes of her childhood torment – her elementary school, the wooden bridge from which her school-mates dropped her hat – decay or are replaced, and become ironically precious to her because they have joined the lost. Lost as well is the possibility of 'sisterhood' (345), or even of friendship with individual women. All women except her mother appear to Elaine to have been socialized into codes of rivalry. They seem to her secretive, disingenuous, untrustworthy – like herself, 'vengeful, greedy, secretive and sly' (153).

These expanding circles of loss give *Cat's Eye* a decided tone of nostalgia. Everything captured in its words is impermanent and fading. The vast northern woods with empty highways, occasional settlements, and widely spaced motels are now crowded with cottages. The 1980s Queen Street fashions that greet Elaine as she wanders Toronto haunted by her childhood in the 1940s will soon themselves be ghosts of someone's past life. Elaine spends more than two-thirds of the novel lovingly recreating the textures, tastes, and smells of a postwar Toronto she claims to detest – details of its home appliances, slang, and fashion, sketches of its lost streetscapes, interiors of its vanished schools and stores. Although she claims that in her life this attraction is the fascination of death, that these details evoke the extreme unhappiness and failure of self-worth she experienced as a child, within the text of the novel these details form a shining, erotic, voluptuous surface:

> There's a little shop on a side street halfway home where we stop and spend our allowances on penny gumballs, red licorice whips, orange popsicles, sharing everything out equally. There are horse chestnuts in the gutters, wet-looking and glossy; we fill the pockets of our cardigans with them, uncertain what to use them for ...
>
> The dirt path going down to the wooden footbridge is dry, dusty; the leaves of the trees which hang over it are dull green and worn out from the summer. Along the edge of the path is a thicket of weeds: goldenrod, ragweed, asters, burdocks, deadly nightshade, its berries red as valentine candies. (74)

Love as well as danger lurks on these lost pathways. These 'lost' images also become the principal elements in Elaine's paintings.

———————————

> Cordelia's mother arranges the flowers herself, wearing gardening gloves. My own mother doesn't arrange flowers. Sometimes she sticks a few into a pot and puts them on the dinner table, but these are flowers she picks herself, during her exercise walks, in her slacks, along the road or in the ravine. Really they are weeds. She would never think of spending money on flowers.
>
> *Cat's Eye*, 71

Partly through the hypersensitivity to language and social coding which *Cat's Eye* gives Elaine, the novel constructs an implicit argument that discursive and social conventions deform and limit the individual human subject. This argument rests both on the 'innocence' of Elaine's life in northern Ontario, in which she is mostly uninscribed by playground, schoolyard, and commercial convention, and on the 'innocence' and independence of her parents as unmediated subjects. The text allows neither of her parents to develop a close friendship after the move to the city. It shows them uninfluenced by common social norms – furnishing their home pragmatically with odds and ends of functional furniture, rather than 'decorating' it, refusing to accept certain mass media enactments of social practice by refusing to buy a television set. It gives her father a 'bleak' view of human nature (288), which he increasingly extends to the scientific and academic communities; it has him ultimately reject the latter community when he withdraws from teaching and returns to research. It sends her mother on solitary walks, dresses her in comfortable, out-of-fashion clothes:

> My mother is not like the other mothers, she doesn't fit in with the idea of them. She does not inhabit the house, the way the other mothers do; she's airy and hard to pin down. The others don't go skating on the neighbourhood rink, or walk in the ravine by themselves. They seem to me grown up in a way that my own mother is not ... My mother will turn up on their doorsteps, wearing slacks, carrying a bouquet of weeds, incongruous. They won't believe her. (156)

The mother in particular is associated by the text with semes of inappropriateness, with not fitting into sets or patterns. Several times it associates her with weeds, plants that fall outside the organized system of garden vegetation. She not only carries weeds, as in the quotation above, but evades classification ('hard to pin down') and seems not 'grown up' as if she had not yet been processed through the socializing codes of childhood. While the other mothers exhibit their placement within social codes through their 'twin sets' or 'aprons' or (Cordelia's mother) 'painting smock' (117), Elaine's mother becomes 'even more indifferent to fashion, and strides around in improvised get-ups, a ski-jacket, an old scarf, mitts that don't match. She says she doesn't care what it looks like as long as it keeps out the wind' (213). She is placed by the text in a particularly problematic relationship to feminine, heterosexual conventions. She is shown often neglecting to wear make-up, and displaying in her dress neither the flirtatious signs that Carol's mother displays nor the fear of sexuality that Grace's mother signals. She 'takes up ice-dancing,' learning the romantic dance-steps of 'tangoes and waltzs in time to music' but practising these 'holding hands with other women.' She is often made to appear oblivious to the conventions she flaunts: 'She never says *What will people think?* the way other mothers do, or are supposed to. She says she doesn't give a hoot' (214).

Against the parents' example of subjecthood ostensibly unmediated by fashion or social convention (there are echoes here of *Ana Historic*'s search for women who might be 'indigene,' who might speak an 'unconditioned language'), the text constructs a general population that defines and models itself through numerous competing and overlapping sets of codes, foremost among which are commercially driven codes of dress, furnishing, and entertainment. Elaine's first major indications that there are standards of behaviour beyond her parents' eccentricities come when her first Toronto friends, Carol and Grace, introduce her to Eaton's mail-order catalogue:

> ... we treat these catalogues with reverence. We cut the small coloured figures out of them and paste them into scrapbooks. Then we cut out other things – cookware, furniture – and paste them around the figures. The figures themselves are always women. We call them 'My lady.' 'My lady's going to have this refrigerator,' we say. 'My lady's getting this rug.' 'This is my lady's umbrella.'

Here Elaine learns that an individual can gain status not only by possession of objects that carry socially assigned value, but also by acquiring these possessions within socially approved discursive frames – through 'the thing you have to say':

> Grace and Carol look at each other's scrapbook pages and say, 'Oh, yours is so good. Mine's no good. Mine's *awful*.' They say this every time we play the scrapbook game. Their voices are wheedling and false; I can tell they don't mean it, each one thinks her own lady on her own page is good. But it's the thing you have to say, so I begin to say it too. (53)

She repeats this learning process at dinner with Grace's parents, with whom she learns not to eat before saying grace, at Grace's church, where she discovers she is obliged to wear a hat, and at Grace's Sunday school, where she finds she must memorize psalms, the names of the biblical books, 'the Ten Commandments and the Lord's Prayer, and most of the Beatitudes' (124). At school she must learn the rituals of classroom behaviour, the conventions, rules, and verbal codes of skipping games and marbles, the 'etiquette of play-going' (127).

Everywhere outside her family Elaine finds a heavily scripted and coded social world in which those who do not possess the appropriate words, gestures, or objects risk being ridiculed, punished, or ignored by others. In the three years that follow her family's move to Toronto she is driven nearly to suicide by the mockery and harrassment of her first 'friends.' Her teen years are somewhat better, mostly because of her quicker mastery of convention; she learns in school home economics classes enough sewing technique to sew fashionable clothes from patterns, learns to cook from the *Betty Crocker Picture Cookbook* (217), learns 'rules for necking ... approach, push away, approach, push away. Garter-belts are going too far and so are brassieres. No zippers' (239). As an art student she learns that the black clothing necessary to signal her 'allegiance' to her fellow students at the art school makes her suspect and 'arty' at the university (276). She marries Jon, a young painter who goes through a series of fashionable artistic styles – 'pure painting' ('a moment of process, trapped on the canvas' [317]), hard edge ('blocks of flat colour,' 'straight lines or perfect circles' [325]), pop art ('pictures that look like commercial illustrations: huge popsicles, giant salt and pepper shakers, peach halves in syrup, paper dishes overflowing with French fries' [335]), construction ('a motorized furry bedroom slipper that runs around on the floor by itself, and a family of diaphragms fitted with monster-movie eyes and mouths and jumping legs underneath that hop around on the table like radiation-damaged oysters' [342]).

> I keep my cat's eye in my pocket, where I can hold on to it. It rests in my hand, valuable as a jewel, looking out through bone and cloth with its impartial gaze. With the help of its power I retreat back into my eyes.

> *Cat's Eye*, 155

The one effective defence the text allows Elaine against being overwhelmed and overwritten by the various styles, fads, conventions, and fashions that society calls her to observe is to withdraw into herself. Her initial defence against her persecuting childhood friends is to faint; her second and more effective defence is to refuse even to 'need them': 'Nothing binds me to them. I am free'; 'I stop going to Sunday School. I refuse to play with Grace or Cordelia or even Carol after school' (193). As an art student Elaine makes a similar strategic withdrawal when she recognizes that the egg tempera technique she has chosen and the 'gingerale bottles, wineglasses, ice cubes from the refrigerator, the glazed teapot, [her] mother's fake pearl earrings' she wants to paint 'are not fashionable' and so decides to work 'in secret' (327). She gradually finds herself painting objects that seem to emerge unbidden from her past, things that come from within her but without conscious will:

> I know these things must be memories, but they do not have the quality of memories. They are not hazy around the edges, but sharp and clear.

They arrive detached from any context; they are simply there, in isolation, as an object glimpsed on the street is there.

I have no image of myself in relation to them. They are suffused with anxiety, but it's not my own anxiety. The anxiety is in the things themselves. (337)

Elaine's locating of the source of these images within herself, together with her refusal to acknowledge power over them, constructs her artistic process as the opposite of Jon's. While her images 'float up without warning' (338), he consciously chooses both his style and images according to current aesthetic theory – the avoidance of 'sentimentality' (325) or the use of 'common cultural sign systems to reflect the iconic banality of our times' (335). While his is a social art that works selectively within available public and artistic codes, hers is a private, intuitional art that works through mystery and through belief in a self that operates beyond consciousness. Like the novel's construction of her parents her art refuses Althusserian understandings of the subject as 'hailed' by ideology and convention – in fact, refuses to be hailed, asserting instead some essential identity within: 'There's something hard in me, crystalline, a kernel of glass.' This 'kernel' that keeps Elaine distinct amid modernist fashion is, of course, the 'cat's eye' of the novel's title – the special marble, 'pure ... like something frozen in the ice,' that can both 'protect' her and give her, even at age ten, the transcendent convention-piercing vision of her adult paintings:

Sometimes when I have it with me I can see the way it sees. I can see people moving like bright animated dolls, their mouths opening and closing but no real words coming out. I can look at their shapes and sizes, their colours, without feeling anything else about them. I am alive in my eyes only. (141)

The novel's emphasis on a 'cat's eye' kernel of inner being, together with its satire of social conventions of all kinds, leaves very little room in it for any sort of social affiliation. People who group together here are invariably suspected of doing so out of enthusiasm for trendy projects or causes:

Carolyn and Jody and Zillah ... all seem to have more friends than I do, more close women friends. I've never really considered it before, this absence; I've assumed that other women were like me. They were, once. And now they are not. (350–1)

Grouping together into close friendships, whether by children like Grace, Cordelia, and Carol or adults like Carolyn, Jody, and Zillah, is, in *Cat's Eye*, presented as a signal of the sacrifice of personal integrity to conformity and mass values. Among the novel's various couples only Elaine's parents appear to have managed a relationship that combines intimacy with individual eccentricity. Elaine's first marriage, to Jon, is a tempestuous union of two self-absorbed people, with Jon in particular unable to reconcile his need to live the public stereotypes of the artist – careless with money, sexually profligate – with his need for a stable, shared life with Elaine. Her second marriage, to Ben, who offers 'mundane enjoyments,' 'nothing dramatic,' and help with her income tax (381), is portrayed as an affectionate business relationship. Particularly problematic for Elaine, and for the novel overall, is collective action by women. Women are perceived by Elaine, and to a large extent by the novel that constructs her perceptions, as so deeply socialized in codes of rivalry, fashion, and consumerism that they tend either to subvert each other in the name of a code or to band together in its service. Elaine is uneasy at having been given a retrospective show by 'an alternative gallery run by a bunch of women.' She is made uneasy in part by the gallery's name, 'Sub-Versions,' which she calls 'one of those puns that used to delight me before they became so fashionable' (15).[1] When she meets the women who run the gallery, she finds their 'take-out gourmet sprout and avocado sandwiches,' their 'hair arrangements' and 'abstract art earrings' so resolutely 'artistic' and 'fashionable' that they seem 'a species of which [she] is not a member' (87).

Earlier Elaine had, on two occasions, sought out groups of women. When newly married to Jon she had joined a women's artist discussion group and felt shocked and excited by the anger expressed there. But she had also felt there were rules not 'actually said' but agreed upon by the group – that it is 'worthier to be a woman with a child but no man,' that 'if you stay with the man, whatever problems you are having are your own fault,' that some things she might say 'might

---

1 The gallery's name is nearly the same as the title of Lorna Irvine's 1986 book *Sub/Version* (Downsview, Ont.: ECW Press), a study that argued that the narrative strategies of various Canadian women writers (Atwood, Munro, Engel, Gallant, Rule, and Thomas) constituted feminist subversions of linear 'patriarchal' narratives.

be the wrong thing.' As at the gallery, she feels excluded: 'as if I'm standing outside a closed door while decisions are being made, disapproving judgments are being pronounced, about me' (344–5). When three of these artists invite Elaine to participate in a group show with them, she feels excluded by what she perceives as the didactic feminism of their work:

> ... in this context my pictures are too highly finished, too decorative, too merely pretty.
>
> I have strayed off course, I have failed to make a statement. I am peripheral. (350)

The text here leaves in play two contrary interpretations of Elaine's response to the group. One is that Elaine is transferring her traumatic memory of her childhood treatment by Cordelia, Grace, and Carol onto a new and mostly benign situation. The other is that this group's beliefs are indeed programmatic; they embody a feminism that is every bit as fashionable and narrowly 'politically correct' as was Jon's series of painting styles.

In its portrayal of the second group which Elaine joins, a group of women artists in Vancouver, the text is less ambiguous. Again the women are characterized as holding implicit assumptions:

> Confession is popular, not of your flaws but of your suffering, at the hands of men. Pain is important, but only certain kinds of it: the pain of women, but not the pain of men. Telling about your pain is called sharing.
> ...
> A number of these women are lesbians, newly declared or changing over. This is at the same time courageous and demanded. According to some, it's the only equal relationship possible, for women. You are not genuine otherwise. (378)

And again Elaine feels excluded by these assumptions, much as she did by the expectations of her girlhood friends:

> I don't want to share in this way; also I am insufficient in scars. I have lived a privileged life, I've never been beaten up, raped, gone hungry.
> ...
> I know I am unorthodox, hopelessly heterosexual, a mother, quisling and secret wimp. My heart is a dubious object at best, blotchy and treacherous. I still shave my legs.

> I avoid gatherings of these women, walking as I do in fear of being sanctified, or else burned at the stake. I think they are talking about me, behind my back. (378–9)

But the tone of protest the novel gives Elaine is stronger here, more satiric, and the proscriptions it associates with the women are openly uttered rather than merely suspected or inferred by Elaine. When Elaine remarks, 'Women know too much, they can neither be deceived nor trusted' (379), it is a statement largely supported by the evidence of the text. Elaine may admire her new friends' 'conviction, their optimism, their carelessness, their fearlessness about men, their camaraderie,' but it is a heavily qualified admiration. For her, the women have sacrificed individuality to achieve these things, have entered a group discourse 'like troops [who] go boyishly off to war, singing brave songs' (379). The simile evokes naïvety, self-deception, and lethal sacrifice.

Readers familiar with Atwood's other novels will read *Cat's Eye* with awareness of how much its narrative and symbolic structures resemble those of her earlier fiction. Like all of Atwood's novels, with the exception of *Life before Man*, it is a doubly plotted first-person narrative. A crisis in the narrator's present – here Elaine's return to Toronto – motivates her to review the critical events in her life which have brought her to the current situation. The text has the narrator alternate regularly[2] between presenting the present and the retrospective action; her understanding of the dynamics of the present action is implicitly to be found in her sorting of the past. This essentially Freudian narrative model has been that of many recent Canadian feminist novels, Laurence's *The Stone Angel* and *The Diviners*, Scott's *Heroine*, and Marlatt's *Ana Historic* among them.

In at least three of Atwood's novels – *The Edible Woman, Surfacing, Lady Oracle* – the narrator is a woman artist who frames her life as a movement from childhood innocence into codes of discourse and

---

2 The novel's short episodes are structured through two interwoven number systems, an arabic one from 1 to 75 that enumerates separate episodes, and a roman one, from I to XV, in which each number groups several episodes under a thematic title. The initial episodes in each group move chronologically through the 1980s events of Elaine's Sub-Versions show; the remainder move chronologically through her past, from her childhood to her escape from her first marriage. The regularity of this narrative arrangement gives special emphasis to the text's Freudian understanding of Elaine's situation.

genre. The mid-Toronto neighbourhoods and ravines of *Cat's Eye* appear in Joan's childhood in *Lady Oracle*; its northern Ontario land-scapes, and the contrast between these and urban Toronto, appear not only in *Surfacing* but in several of the short stories of *Dancing Girls* and *Bluebeard's Egg*. The contrast between a nomadic northern Ontario childhood and a Toronto adolescence appears also in At-wood's occasional autobiographical essays.[3]

By invoking these and other signs of the author's literary and bi-ographical past – Atwood's father was like Elaine's an entomologist who did research in northern Ontario, and Atwood, like Elaine, at-tended mid-town Toronto schools and studied at the University of Toronto – Atwood's writing, like Elaine's painting, has offered itself as a kind of feminist 'life writing'[4], and invited appropriation by individualist feminism as an exemplary 'woman's story.' In the case of *Cat's Eye* the text openly deploys the sign of autobiography. This sign plays a particularly important role in the struggle the book en-codes between the integral self ('innocent,' 'northern,' 'eccentric,' 'un-fashionable') and the mass self. *Cat's Eye* is overall an 'eccentric,' individual, local discourse: it is Elaine's autobiography, just as the paintings the Sub-Versions Gallery is about to show are also her autobiography: 'Chronology won out after all: the early things are on the east wall, what Charna calls the middle period on the end wall, and on the west wall are five recent pictures which I've never shown before' (404).

In its insistence on the specifics both of the author's past and of Elaine's life – the affectionately detailed refrigerators, skirts, bedroom suites, and school buildings that contribute both to the novel's text and Elaine's paintings – *Cat's Eye* asserts the particular life against the amnesia of mass fashion. There is repeated emphasis on memory as an antidote to current fashion – on remembering the actual 1940s diner while eating in an 1980s reconstruction (363–4), on remembering the ambiguities of a failed marriage while listening to feminist condem-nations of men (378). At the same time, the text implies that the past is never totally recoverable – that perception is selective and partial, that the remembered perceptions are never 'fair' but, like Elaine's art, recalled in 'vengeance' and 'blindness' (405). The history they pre-serve is as much of the creating subject as of the object remembered.

3 For example, 'Travels Back,' *Macleans*, Jan. 1973, 28–31, 48
4 For an exploration of various feminist views of 'life writing' see *Tessera* 7 (Fall 1989), an issue titled 'Auto-graph(e).' See also Ruth Latta, *Life Writing: Autobiog-raphers and Their Craft* (Burnstown, Ont.: General Store Publishing Co. 1988).

The emphasis on individual life, private perception, home ground, and home city – the Ontario settings of the novel are Atwood's 'home' territory as well as Elaine's – is also made against invasive internationalism. The fashionable ideologies that threaten to take over individual lives in *Cat's Eye* – multinational consumerism, international feminism, modernist aesthetics – all come from outside of Canada. They threaten to destroy all lives equally, whether corrupting Grace's mother with religious bigotry, Grace with department-store materialism, or the planet with the environmental death that Elaine's father fears. Standing in for the latent evil in all of these, for their utter lack of interest in the individual, are the anonymously hooded Islamic terrorists who hijack Stephen's airplane and, against a background of 'saccharine, soporific' (391) taped music, randomly select him for execution.

The human Canada that *Cat's Eye* asserts as valuable is thus narrowly individual and almost totally lacking in social codes and discourses. It is an individual space, or a space that permits individuals, rather than a public space. This individual space is not based on a choice of discourses, as in *Heroine*, but on resistance to them – resistance to 'world-class' cities, feminist proscriptions, Hollywood images, New York art, and MacLeod tartans. The national is present in the book mainly as a kind of freedom from the power of transnational 'fashion,' and as a composite of particular, local images. The concerns of *Cat's Eye* are thus similar to those of *Joshua Then and Now* – the relationship between the individual and international politics, between the local and transnational – but the perspective on them is very different. The individual of *Cat's Eye* is to be local rather than universal; his or her individual past is to be valued and preserved rather than mocked as trivial or parochial. Although both novels must finally return their narrators into the narrow shelter of surviving family, these are very different families: for Richler the family is a garden, a nourishing, salving universal family; for Atwood the family seems merely a social improvisation, a minor comfort that helps to sustain the private individual in a cosmos where the only affirmable value is a light which is 'old' and of which 'there's not much.' 'But it's enough to see by' (421).

For behind this human Canada of free-standing individuals, half-hidden amid the numerous threatening international urban images, remains that primeval Canada of Elaine's early childhood, a transcendent 'cat's eye' land beyond politics, beyond social discourse. This is an impossible Canada, but an enormously powerful one nevertheless. It resonates through the nation's culture in the canonical paintings of the Group of Seven, whose work began in the same Algonquin and Lake Superior forests as Elaine's memories, and culminated in Lawren Harris's visionary images of a crystalline arctic. This pure northern Canada, in which social codes of all kinds are intrusions on identity, is one Elaine can only have had an illusion of inhabiting, yet it underlies even her and the book's final image – 'night, clear, moonless and filled with stars ... echoes, of something that happened millions of years ago: a word made of numbers. Echoes of light, shining out of the midst of nothing' (421). As by so many of the novels of this study, the reader is left by *Cat's Eye* not with people working out, tragically or otherwise, their collective meanings, but with yet one more large compensatory image of plenitude.

yet is plenitude woman not nature.

Polis Is Difficult Here
Badlands

The sight of Anna Yellowbird's tipi, below them in the valley, her house of bones, made Dawe remember his own: and he told himself, this first expedition, this season in the field must be my last. He would stay at home with his wife, have children, raise a family. He said it to himself, in the rain, the season half over and he with only one skeleton to his credit: he would stay at home with his wife and family and work in the museums there in Toronto, in Ottawa, the careful scientist, the new Cope or Marsh or Lambe, identifying the specimens, restoring, categorizing, writing learned articles.

Badlands, 170–1

The various signs of history, home, family, community and individual ambition that run through Robert Kroetsch's 1975 novel *Badlands* are complex, diverse, and confusing in their range and ambiguity. Here, more than half-way into a somewhat ruthless and obsessive quest to unearth unprecedented specimens of dinosaur fossils from the Alberta badlands, and to thereby become *'famous'* (210), to gain 'immortality' (127), William Dawe, the central male character of the novel, is moved by the sight of an Indian girl's makeshift tipi to desire that which his narrow quest is obliging him to abandon: home, family, and the larger civilizing structures of institutions and professional disciplines. The movement of the signs in this passage is intriguing: from *bone*, sign of the organic, biological, and communal base of zoological creatures, Anna Yellowbird has built a *tipi*, sign of western North American Indian family and communal life. This tipi is then associated not only with Dawe's own wife and possible family, but also with large eastern Canadian clusters of domestic shelters, Toronto and Ottawa, and with the shared institutional codes on which such communities are based. In those communities Dawe knows he could work within the shared codes of his own discipline, working in 'museums,' being a 'careful scientist,' 'categorizing,' and 'writing learned articles.'

Conflicts similar to Dawe's, between individual ambition and the attractions of home, family, and society, occur in nearly every Kroetsch novel and represent a very different configuring of the individual-versus-social-codes conflict from the one evident in Atwood's fiction. In a Kroetsch novel these conflicts have no simple outline or easy resolution; eccentric individual quests are most often self-indulgent and narrowly anti-social, but they are also often creative, flamboyant, and life-affirming; community may offer utopian promises of friendship, social harmony, and sexual freedom, but most often it also delivers restriction and repetition. Rather than opening into a community, the house may merely be constructed – as Dawe's daughter Anna perceives her home to have been – as *'fortress'* and *'prison'* (45).

Nearly all the major male characters of Kroetsch's novels have been, like bone-salesman William Dawe, eccentric entrepreneurs – unorthodox businessmen who seek the triumph of success much more than they seek material reward. Whether struggling to establish a line of stud horses, like Hazard Lepage in *The Studhorse Man*, win an election like Johnny Backstrom in *The Words of My Roaring*, follow in the steps of Grey Owl like Jeremy Sadness in *Gone Indian*, operate as a 'completely free' (7) agent for a millionaire collector like William 'Dorf' Dorfen in *Alibi*, or unearth and sell dinosaur skeletons like William Dawe, these men share a dislike of restriction on their freedom of action, as well as a view of sexual achievement as metonymic of larger success. If they participate in a surrounding community, they do so ironically, like Backstrom, or through the amusingly specific terms of their own interests, like Lepage or Dorf. By the conclusion of the novels they often have become reclusive – William Dorfen, Demeter Proudfoot of *The Studhorse Man* – or through focus on their own obsessions have died or are about to die – Lepage, Dawe, Jeremy Sadness, Peter Guy of *But We Are Exiles*. Visible behind all of them is the image of Odysseus, solitary archer and voyager, himself torn between the pull of the family and community that waits and the life of wily independence that the voyage continually promises. Betrayals, desertions, secret unexpected departures – Lepage sneaking away from the sleeping Miss Cockburn, Dorf flying without notice to Europe in the midst of a romantic week with Karen Strike – occur repeatedly in the plot lines of their lives.

Concurrently with these structures of fixation, betrayal, and isolation, however, most of these novels also offer intense and somewhat sentimentalized images of community. Johnny Backstrom addresses his potential supporters:

> 'I've been trying to *earn* a living, like the rest of you. And I haven't done any great shakes of a job. Just ask my wife.'
>
> The chuckles were intimate and warm, like those of old companions forgiving a foible. They understood about wives and foibles. Maybe that's what worked on me – that touch of intimacy. That little touch of genuine mercy.
>
> 'So I'll add something else,' I said. 'And a penniless man hates to say this. You'd be bigger clowns yourselves for voting for me – unless it rains by election day.
>
> I choked up in my throat. I've never been quite sure I intended to say that. I got carried away. Everybody kind of choked up. (*The Words of My Roaring*, 112–13)

Backstrom's entrepreneurial emphasis on *earn*ing a living leads quickly and ironically into the 'intimacy' of shared experience, to his being 'choked up' by his sudden acceptance into common humanity, and then to his sentimental impulse to tell his listeners what these drought-plagued farmers most wish to hear – that it may rain. The pull of community may be psychodramatic, as here, rudimentary, like the domestic comforts of Martha Proudfoot's farm that draw Lepage, or Dionysian, like the Greek mud-bath that Dorf enters in *Alibi*:

> There were, I would guess, nearly eighty women in the mud at the time.
> ...
> Twenty hands at least, quite possibly more, found and touched my vulnerable body in that deepest mud. The hands of those women. Twenty and then more. Some in secretive delight, some in mere curiosity. Some in surest abandon.
>
> Women with arthritis who were still, nevertheless, able to reach out. Women with back pains from lives of lifting and chopping and digging and carrying children and feeding men. Women who couldn't get pregnant. Women who feared they might have cancerous lumps or nodes or sores. Women with migraines. Women who didn't want to grow old. Women who were dying and didn't know why. Women with rashes and bruises.

Women with swollen feet and stiff knees and tumors and lesions, with aching teeth and falling hair and crooked spines.

...

... I, there in the Lapsi mud, was caressed with passion, and I, with passion, came. I came indeed. The stroking and rubbing hands, in their friendly need, turned me over ... I was covered in mud, not an inch of me showed. But the touching and the fondling hands, the hands in the mud, in their loving, found all ... (177–9)

Regardless, the emphasis in these extended images of community falls on signs that transcend individual subjectivities – here on the affliction and pain that inscribe all the bathers as representative woman. Rather than marking individual success, sexual climax in these images marks social acceptance, entrance to community. Dorf's momentous orgasm here, in fact, marks a union not only with womanhood but, through the sign of the mud as the clay of creation, with humanity itself.

Badlands, like so many of the novels examined here – *Cat's Eye, Heroine, Ana Historic, Obasan, Fifth Business,* and *Joshua Then and Now* – is a double narrative, one in which a narrator recounts an inquiry into, or recollection of, a past story while concurrently narrating that past story. Here, however, Anna Dawe's past story focuses not on herself but on her palaeontologist father, and on his crucial first field trip, into the valley of the Red Deer River in 1916. The two narratives are formally separated, with the larger one of the 1916 events printed in roman type, recounted in the third person, and naming the central character as 'Dawe.' The smaller one is printed in italic, recounted in the first person, names the central character 'my father,' and invites reading as a commentary on the larger. Bridging the two are Dawe's field notes, which the narrator possesses and eventually destroys in the first-person narrative but which are quoted in the third-person one. This bridge, together with the fact that the action of the first-person narrative is Anna's research into the story that constitutes the action of the third-person one, suggests strongly that Anna narrates both. So too do the flashes of intense, exaggerated rhetoric that punctuate both narratives ('the single preposterous unnatural white butte of Web's impossible and uncontradictable and total victory' [209]), the numerous noun and verb phrases that both employ as emphatic independent sentences, and the stress both narratives give to what they present as characteristically 'male' actions and obsessions. However, such a relationship between the two narratives is never made explicit, nor is the authorship of the third-person 'Chronology' with which the novel begins.

In their narrative structures the two actions both resemble and dis-resemble one another. Anna appears to see her narrative as an in-version of her father's, in part because he drifted down the river by raft, into the concavities of the badlands, whereas she drives upstream by car into the convexities of the mountains: *'We got out of the car, we stretched and shouted; and God we had turned the Badlands upside down, we were in the Rockies ...'* (265). He focuses obsessively back-wards to the Cretaceous fossils which will bring him fame, both re-jecting and sexually exploiting Anna Yellowbird and allowing his youngest crew-member to die, while his daughter embraces Anna Yellowbird as a companion, throws away the past of his photos and field notes, and marches forward claiming (in her narrative's final words) to *'not once look back, not once, ever'* (270).

Yet both narratives very much concern a search for source. William Dawe is said by Anna to have laboured *'as if he must one happy morning get back to the source itself, the root moment when the glory of reptiles ... was focussed in one bony creature, one Adam-seed burrowing in the green slime'* (139). Anna's own search has been for the source of her own unhappiness, for that critical moment in the badlands when *'his success began'* and *'he ceased to love.'* Dawe's search has been for the primal phallic saurian 'bone'; the forty-three-year-old Anna's for the originating phallic moment of her spinsterhood and virginity. Although Dawe hired a three-man crew, and he and Anna were both joined by Anna Yellowbird, both end their narratives alone. Dawe suicides forty-six years after the expedition, from a canoe on Georgian Bay; Anna ends the events of her narrative staying day after day in a hotel *'in the mountains, where I can look to the east, and downward, to where it is all behind me'* (264). Despite the claims of her last words, her last actions appear as retrospective and solitary as any of her father's.

For in his summer of 1916, in the Badlands of the Red Deer River, discovering the Mesozoic era, with all of Europe filling its earth with the bones of its own young – he removed himself from time.

Badlands, 139

Although both Anna and her father appear overwhelmingly concerned with personal salvation – he with acquiring 'eternal' fame and patriarchal standing, and she with rescuing her life from the passivity and inadequacy into which his active and goal-oriented life had appeared to cast it – their two quests take place in a wide social and institutional context. At the time of Dawe's expedition the First World War is in full fury. The text gives the war several direct effects on the action. It makes it the cause of Dawe's wife's decision to marry him and thus ultimately of Anna's conception: women of Elizabeth Kilbourne's Great War generation expected to marry men who were about to depart into danger: '... it was the fashion and rage to marry a man who was going away to die, the deep and secret courtship becoming not only the dreamed courtship of death but the death itself' (191). The war had previously taken away her lover, a soldier who had 'believed he was going overseas to die and therefore would marry no one' (258).

The text also makes the war the cause of Anna Yellowbird's presence in the story, and of Tune's being recruited for Dawe's crew. Dawe hires Tune only because the wartime manpower shortage in Drumheller has made no other experienced miner available. Anna Yellowbird encounters Dawe's expedition in the course of her own journey eastward in search of her dead husband, who has vanished '*in an iron ship bound for something called England, for something called the World War.*' She mistakes the land of dead bones for which Dawe searches for '*the place of the dead*' (148) that holds her husband. The First World War frame metaphorically defines Dawe and his expeditionary companions as soldiers, and their journey into the badlands as an epic descent into the underworld. With its emphasis on Europe – Anna Yellowbird's husband seems to have gone directly from reservation to England – and its conspicuous lack of Canadian references, such as Canadian training camps or military units, the frame names the stage on which they act as both international and archetypal, as both an extension of Europe's battlefields and a re-enactment of classical story.

The institutional frame within which Dawe conducts his fieldwork similarly acts to name the stage of his work as international rather than Albertan or Canadian. He has been inspired by the great turn-of-the-century international palaeontologists, Barnum Brown and Charles Sternberg. He plans his own expedition with 'the reports of the most recent and final expedition of the American Museum of Natural History spread out on his desk, Barnum Brown back in New York from the Red Deer River of Alberta with the finest collection of

Cretaceous dinosaur skeletons ever collected anywhere in the world'
(223). His aim is to find 'skeletons to grace the museums of the civilized world' (37). After his fame has been established by his badlands
discoveries, he continues his fieldwork around the world; in his field
notes Anna reads *of his ventures into deserts and jungles, into Africa
and Texas and Patagonia, into the Arctic islands. I read of his brave and
absurd and (needless to say) successful expeditions into Mongolia – in
search of dinosaur eggs'* (138–9).

Against this surrounding context of armed conflict, conquest, and
transcendent personal ambition Kroetsch's novel offers only small
local habitations and their divergent and limited comforts – Anna
Yellowbird's tipi, Elizabeth Dawe's Georgian Bay house, McBride's
farmhouse, a Drumheller whorehouse. All are associated with women,
with the conflict between men's and women's narratives that is encoded in the novel's double narrative structure, and with the mo-
mentary sentimentalizing or utopianizing of community that occurs
so frequently in Kroetsch novels:

> McBride ... dreamed his sleeping children, his quartersection of rich black
> dirt, his greening wheat, his stabled horses, his Saturday drive to town,
> his Sunday rest, his garden behind his house, his peas in blossom in the
> morning sun, his potatoes swelling in the dark earth, his set table, his
> blessed food; he dreamed his wife's surprise at the figure returned from
> the water's edge, her cry of joy and her quick embrace. (51)

McBride's desertion from the expedition to return home echoes William Dawe's annual returns (*'plead[ing] deprivation and repentence and
lust'* [3]) to his wife in Georgian Bay and the temporary idealizations
of home they embody.

At the same time the signs of family, home, and community are
given associations of female oppression and emprisonment that they
rarely receive in other Kroetsch novels. The Georgian Bay house that
Dawe returns to is above all a woman's structure, a house Anna Dawe
says *'I ... inherited from my mother, who inherited it from her mother'*
(3). In Dawe's mind it is a 'mansion' that offers 'splendid comfort'
but is also dominated by his wife's visiting friends, men and women
'not driven to go out into obscurity to seek fame' (58) but instead
'polite, successful, polished, secure,' carrying *'into the mock-wilderness
of the lake for a weekend the mock-drama of their mock lives'* (94). To
his daughter it is both her mother's house and her father's prison,
the *'fortress and prison'* where he kept and protected her *'honour from
human decency'* (45).

The duplicity of the house as a sign – its signalling both female rejection of male adventure and male confinement of women – informs the entire novel. Women both choose the house and are confined to it. It is part of their inheritance as women and from women, but a part they are also obliged by social convention to inherit. Anna struggles repeatedly with this ambiguity: her father *'locked me up in the house I had inherited. Or was inheriting ... He locked me up in an education I might as well have inherited, it was so much mine before I realized it was given me; he locked me up in the money I did not know until years later, too late, was not even his to give'* (110).

Possibilities for community in *Badlands* are closely tied to women and their houses. However much Dawe may scorn them, his wife's vacationing visitors comprise a community of shared values. Anna Yellowbird's tipi, with the well-worn trail that connects it with Dawe's camp, suggests a sexual community, a group constituted by the common link of her body. Dawe and his questing companions, however, are characterized as avoiding community through male competition and violence, and as refusing specifically to enter the 'community' that Anna offers. Anna Dawe reflects at length on this refusal:

> ... *the curious thing about all those men on our frontiers is the sexual lives they lead. Where the two most obvious answers to their presumed needs are to love each other or to share a woman, they will do neither. They avoid violent relations with each other by violence; the squaw wrestling of their pale bodies is meant to deny the wrestling of their spirits together. And the notion that a woman is not to be shared is one of their notions also.*
>
> *We have the instinct of community, will share or be shared ...* (162)

A close link is asserted here between the house that Dawe is reluctant to enter, or to share with his wife's visitors, and the woman's body he also will not share. The house that is made a prison can also be the body made a prison, like Anna Dawe's *'goddamned virgin'* (263) body that her father, *'shutting out instead of letting in'* (269), has protected from 'human decency.'

The doubleness of the house image as both prison and site of community and decency is especially evident in the section of the novel concerning Drumheller, the only 'community' Dawe's expedition visits. Dawe's own responses to the town tie it to his wife's Georgian Bay house. As they enter he thinks 'the last town we have to look at before we get there. And a good riddance. Damn civilization' (64). As they drift downriver away from it, he dreams of Georgian Bay, and when young Tune asks him 'how he liked Drumheller,' his 'ironic answer' is: '*It was like home*' (94). Dawe's main experience in Drumheller is his unsuccessful descent into the ABC Mine to hire an experienced explosives man; Grimlich, the man he wants to hire, chooses to stay working in the mine – 'The weather is fine here. I sleep right here. Wong Lee brings in some food. I eat right here. When something happens here, I make it happen' (81). His refusal is ambiguously a preference both of the mine community and of the kind of control – 'I make it happen' – that men tend to assert in the novel whenever in houses. It also appears to be a fear of using dynamite for personal gain: 'I killed my ... trying to dynamite ... a fishing hole ...,' he tells Dawe, as if such a use were different from its use with fellow miners beneath Drumheller.

The text has Dawe's crewman Web encounter similar ambiguity in his meeting in Drumheller with two women, one the dark-haired 'Woman in Green,' who leads a temperance demonstration, and the other the blonde 'America,' who reads fortunes in bars and works from cubicle seven in Mary Roper's brothel. In contrasting ways both speak for affiliation and community. The woman in green 'talks of lost families, lost homes' (67), and invites the 'gathered miners, hundreds of men from all the pits of Europe,' who dream of saving 'from the nightmare past their almost forgotten children, their dreamed women' (67–8), to join together in signing a pledge of abstinence. America, who counsels Dawe to 'hold back nothing' (71; cf. his daughter's accusation that he 'shuts out' rather than 'lets in'), as a whore joins men together in being shared by them, much as Anna Yellowbird would have conjoined Dawe's crew. The brothels she works in, like the house on Georgian Bay, are ambiguously constructed as both prisons and places of female safety and community. It is Anna Dawe who so constructs them, in describing the few married women of Drumheller as 'desperately alone.' They are as 'sadly alone,' she says, 'as the women who, as cloistered as nuns, ran the half-dozen whorehouses on the lower side of town: unless those women were happy.' Anna's own ambivalence about sexuality – can whores be happy? – joins here with the novel's ambivalence about community: are people alone there or together? are they cloistered forcibly or voluntarily?

Anna will in a few pages be made to attempt to dissolve the virgin-whore opposition the woman in green and America have seemed to enact – an opposition the text has attributed to Web, 'total and absurd male.' She reports not only that the two women were sisters but also that they may not even have had archetypally contrasting hair: America only appeared to be blonde. The women *'lived together,'* and *'when the penitentiary was built in their town ... [they] established inside the penitentiary a library and a lounge'* (76). The text has Anna work here to remove distinction and affirm community. One sister may preach against 'the sickness of the bawdihouse' (68) while the other works within one, but they can reside 'together' and share a social project. Against the punitive and divisive 'penitentiary' Anna has them assert the communal terms of 'library' and 'lounge.'

Badlands presents itself primarily as a feminist critique of male discourse. Anna Dawe's woman's story overtakes and retells William Dawe's man's story. His field notes are literally destroyed within her tale. The *'formal telling,' 'the curious little narrative tricks of a male adventure: the lies that enable the lovers to meet, the mystery of who did the killing, the suspense before victory,'* are displaced by Anna Yellowbird's simple declaration *'I will go with you'* (27). The male desire to memorialize through museums, mythology, or photography, to transcend time by acquiring fame and accomplishment, is replaced by what the text proposes to be a woman's acceptance of death, time, and annihilation; the museum itself replaced by the fragmentary specimens of Anna Yellowbird's house of bone: *'They have their open spaces, and translate them into a fabled hunting. We have only time to survive in, time, without either lies or mystery or suspense; we live and then die in time'* (27).

Beneath this foreground of gender politics, however, the text grapples with issues of social organization that cut across gender. Solitary entrepreneurship – the man as head and protector of family guarding his stone house with a shotgun, or selfishly leading an expedition to gather materials that will memorialize his own name – leads to bitterness, boredom, and isolation. Like the photographer Sinnott, the entrepreneur carries 'a pocket of darkness ... carefully locked up, captured, preserved' (113), darkness that will not let him *'say one word, give ... one glance, that confessed he was sorry'* (233–4). Yet beyond such individualism the text can offer few alternatives. In the far distance the massed armies of the First World War rage, almost without comment. The Georgian Bay holidayers arrive for their mock-dramatic weekends. In Drumheller the dark-haired woman, supported by six men and 'a straggling group of women and children,' leads an ostensibly communal temperance campaign that endorses family and group values, but the campaign is covertly supported by *'bosses sweetly advocating order, work, taxes tradition, family, possession of house and wife'* (63): sophisticated entrepreneurs prefer a stable community. The two Annas, one white and wealthy, one Indian, profligate, and poor, join briefly for their badlands romp, and then appear to separate. Between individual acts of greed and exuberance in the Red Deer Valley and the apparently enclosing world-wide network of museums, armies, and wars there are only isolated pockets of human contact – Anna attempting to talk to her father on her mother's rug, Grizzly and Web trysting with Anna Yellowbird, Mary Roper welcoming guests to her whorehouse. There is little politics of any kind in the novel because there are so few instances of social affiliation, and so few occasions when individuals experience the presence of social or institutional structures except, like Dawe, as opportunities for personal legitimation. The few institutional structures that are present – the armies and museums, for instance – appear to have come into being without the participation of the characters. Overall, the novel offers no way for any of the characters to take action except as individuals or within, at best, local groups.

Although the novel contains both a Chinese character, Grizzly, and the Indian Anna, neither these characters nor the others experience themselves as anything other than individual humans. Grizzly's refusal to cook after Dawe has permitted the death of Tune inscribes him, not as special because of his age or cultural difference, but only as more openly 'human.' His success among Anna Yellowbird's lovers was because of his not being able to talk *'about it.' 'Couldn't talk. Just did it'* (264). Anna's companionship with Anna Dawe transcends their cultural specificities through their gender; *'hand in hand, arm in arm'* (270), they are merely *'two middle-aged women,' 'two* drunk *women'* (265). None of the characters experiences herself or himself as culturally or politically inscribed – as Albertan, Cree, Ontarion, Canadian, or North American.

The national political implications of *Badlands* are in a sense not a great deal different from those of Margaret Atwood's *Cat's Eye*. Both texts place their characters within an international field of events that dwarfs all but the immediately local and individual. Both envision their characters groping for personal happiness outside or despite institutional structures. But although both assert humanist doctrines of the individual, these doctrines diverge considerably. *Badlands* locates the individual within a potentially universal humanity and 'decency' that can transcend racial, cultural, and gender specificities. *Cat's Eye* envisions an individual that is integral and irreducible, but endangered by culture. Both locate the major threat to human happiness within discourse but vary enormously in what discourses they see as dangerous and in how they theorize their operations. *Cat's Eye* locates its prime threat to happiness within politics itself, which it defines as various fashionable, socially constructed cultural discourses that seduce the individual to learn and embrace them in exchange for temporary social popularity; *Badlands* locates its within a discourse of time-transcending masculinity so powerful that it seems at times not something learned but an essentialized constituent of maleness.

The internationalism of *Badlands*, much like that of *Alibi*, rests on signs that transcend the national – male, female, Triassic, photography, death – on social relations in which close friendship is difficult and group affiliation virtually absent, and on a pattern of geographic signs that connects the individual and local directly to the international without passing through the national. William Dawe of Red Deer River and Georgian Bay belongs to the set *palaeontologist*, along with Barnum Brown of New York and India, and Charles Hazelius Sternberg of Kansas. Elizabeth Dawe and Anna Yellowbird belong to the set *women abandoned by men bound for war in Europe, the badlands, and Mongolia*. Red Deer River is indeed a significant spot on *Badlands's* global map – Sternberg entitled his second book *Hunting Dinosaurs in the Bad Lands of the Red Deer River, of Alberta, Canada* – but between the very local and the global, national constructions, even of the United States, England, or China, are scarcer than dinosaur eggs.

Post-National Arguments

Gaining the walk in front of Deighton House, she heard the hubbub inside, the clatter of glass, cigar smoke snaking out toward her as the doors opened to release three men deep in argument – 'they'll never bring 'er this far,' 'more sense to go with California, a damn sight closer.'

Ana Historic, 102

Thus *Ana Historic* constructs Annie's imagination of Ana Richards's overhearing of a political debate in nineteenth-century Gastown. Despite the passage's feminist signs – its association of politics with men and with the simultaneously phallic and satanic 'cigar smoke snaking' towards its secondary protagonist – the passage assumes Canadian readers equipped to identify its faint Canadian indicators. The "er' that may not be brought 'this far' is the Canadian Pacific Railroad; 'California' signals the debate that continued in British Columbia from Confederation to the 1885 completion of the CPR over whether to seek political affiliation with the United States or with newly constituted Canada.

Like *Ana Historic* all the novels considered in this book assume Canada in their assuming of the recognizability of a body of Canadian signs – geographical, historical, cultural – from Eaton's catalogue to the Hudson's Bay Company, from Ypres, Anne Wilkinson, Billy Bishop, the kidnapping of James Cross to the names of arctic explorers. Yet the novels overall also suggest many different and often internally conflicting understandings of the importance of this nation relative to other conceptions. In many, the Canadian reading community encoded in the vocabulary and references is vastly different from the community which the novels' characters inhabit or imagine, and different also from the communities the texts themselves appear to endorse. There is usually little faith or interest offered, even in the social and political processes by which communities are constituted or modern states constituted and maintained. As well, in the imaginary geographies the novels construct for their characters to inhabit, the Canadian home-ground is more often part of a global field than of any inter-regional Canadian one.

Only a few of the novels openly acknowledge the processes by which national decisions are made and socially consequential actions undertaken. The majority of these cast but a wistful eye at the possibility of a participatory politics, choosing ultimately to have their protagonists seek the shelter of individual salvation. *Joshua Then and Now* has its protagonist, who once idealistically attempted to avenge and redress the wrongs of the Holocaust, withdraw to the much narrower field of wife, father, and children. *Heroine* finds for its protagonist so much personal and gender exploitation in both left-wing politics and the bourgeois society this politics opposes that by the end of the text she is alone and able only with extreme difficulty to piece together a sufficient identity to venture outside her apartment. *In the Skin of a Lion* offers, in Alice Gull, a more sympathetic portrayal of the politically active and responsible citizen but, through her violent death and through the text's persistent preference for the aesthetic over all other social possibilities, finally rejects politics for art, implying that a society which values a 'beautiful' pre-dawn streetscape (244) may be more 'just' and 'human' than one which seeks justice through challenge and conflict. Like *Joshua Then and Now* it too has its protagonist affirm a small nuclear family structure in its concluding pages. *Badlands* looks wistfully on community – on the family William Dawe might have had, on the male community Anna Yellowbird might have centred, on the female camaraderie of Mary Roper's brothel – but can find no way into community even for Dawe's daughter, who, despite her brief companionship with Anna Yellowbird, ends the novel alone, looking eastward from a Rocky Mountain hotel.

Two of the novels that construct their characters as members of active communities, communities that are part of ongoing Canadian life, severely qualify this construction by basing it on 'natural' or 'organic' metaphors. Both *The Temptations of Big Bear* and *The Diviners* thereby place the source and responsibility for social interaction outside the social arena. The source of Big Bear's political wisdom – his ability to read through the obscurities of Euro-Canadian political rhetoric and the braggadocio of young warriors – is the 'Green Grass World' and the 'Only One' who has given him the totemic bear's claw. The model for Morag Gunn's non-directive relationship with her daughter, Jules Tonnerre, and her McConnell's Landing neighbours is the ebb and flow of the river that 'runs both ways' and 'keeps its life from sight.' Both novels thereby mystify politics, place its success beyond human action, and imply a utopian Canada that can be vaguely more 'spiritual,' less instrumental and directive, more 'natural' than other social possibilities, but only mysteriously attainable.

The two novels that assume a socially active and responsible citizenry, *Caprice* and *Slash*, both offer relatively restricted communities, although both also offer national constructions. In *Caprice* responsible citizenship and law and order prevail over both private revenge and entrepreneurial banditry. Québécoise Caprice joins with the BC Provincial Police in capturing U.S. outlaw Spencer, and is in turn embraced by a generous and multi-cultural Nicola citizenry. On a national level, however, the novel suggests that Quebec and British Columbia must, for the moment at least, follow separate, unhappy trails. The West may be getting smaller, as the narrator notes several times, but the journey from the Okanagan to Ste Foy is still extremely long; Caprice will return to her own people, and her lover, Roy Smith, team-player, will return to his school and baseball league, to his 'place' that, like that of Caprice, is 'already made.' 'Are you going to come back?' the anglophone Canadian asks his beloved (265). Only Mallarmé's shadows know.

In *Slash* the young narrator saves himself from jail, alcoholism, and drug abuse by increasingly affiliating himself with his people, his tribe, and with their surviving social institutions. It is by becoming a citizen, by participating in Indian meetings, protests, marches, retreats, and sweat lodge ceremonies, that Slash can cease to be a cultural derelict and acquire both a social role and a sense of personal value. Even his most personal affiliations rest on this assuming of citizenship; he becomes a husband and father only through the contacts he makes at political meetings. Although both here and in *Caprice* the texts leave their protagonists individually bereft – Caprice and Roy Smith part, and Slash's wife, Maeg, is killed – they do not leave them socially bereft. Roy and Caprice still have their communities; Slash still has his 'people,' his 'son and those like him' for whom he has decided to tell his story (253). His 'people' range nationally and continentally, with English their lingua franca, and with an anglophone Canada and United States constituted, through oppression, as the determining fields of their politics.

Although choosing radically different positions, at least ten of these novels appear to endorse protagonists who withdraw from politics – who give up on general society and either retreat into narrow individualism or embrace extra-social visions. A few of these ten offer ironic, backhanded endorsements of a functioning polity through the quantity of satire and vituperation they pour upon social failure, and through the disillusionment and bitterness these satiric passages signal. *Joshua Then and Now, The Wars,* and *Badlands* construct human society as male-dominated, selfish, materialistic, and violent, while also presenting protagonists who long for a companionable society. The model of Swift's *Gulliver's Travels* is directly invoked by *The Wars* and is vaguely perceivable within the structure of the other two. The protagonists – Joshua Shapiro, Robert Ross, William Dawe, and Anna Dawe – end their fictional lives in mistrust of society at large and in relative solitude – Joshua having withdrawn to his family, Robert having chosen horses over humans, William Dawe committing suicide, and Anna in reclusive retrospection. In each text it is not so much 'Canada' as a social unit that is under judgment as it is a male-dominated humanity which endows any social or political organization with treachery, betrayal, and actual or symbolic violence.

In another three of the ten novels the withdrawal from politics occurs because the text has constructed value, not as socially determined, but as resident in some extra-social dimension. The disdain which both the text and the narrator of *Fifth Business* show for social life – whether for small-town politics framed as narrow religious sectarianism or for a national politics framed as mere opportunism and cronyism – rests on a view which locates 'beauty and goodness' in the actions of saints, fool-saints, miracles, and devils, and in the partial and often misunderstanding gestures towards beauty and goodness of those who, like Ramsay, Liesl, and Ignatius Blazon, happen to believe in them. While the emphasis in *Fifth Business* falls on a powerful transcendent realm that renders human efforts towards social order absurd, in *Nights below Station Street* the emphasis falls on an intrinsic absurdity in human effort itself. Here too the achievement of good is constructed as external to human power, but as residing in bleak chance rather than in any joyous and capricious Liesl-like oversoul.

Although *Ana Historic*, with its emphasis on histories that can be rewritten and lives that can be radically altered, might seem to differ vastly from the determinism of *Nights below Station Street* or the Christian mysticism of *Fifth Business*, in its locating of the power for change outside of language and outside the social order – in the 'inarticulate' mouth of the vagina (125) and in the plenitude signalled by the 'fluid,' 'trees,' and 'breeze' of the concluding passage – it joins them in affirming the transcendent over the political. Like them too it constructs the secular order as corrupt and irredeemable. City government, official history, mainstream psychiatry, major industrial employers all unconsciously or cynically sacrifice workers, women, and the environment to the preservation of their patriarchal privileges. In dissenting from and opposing this corruption, *Ana Historic* moves out of the secular order itself, choosing instead mystery and the 'leafy tunnel' (107) of an organicized lesbianism: 'unconditioned language' (75), 'pure venting' (135–6), 'wind, trees, rain, creeping things under the leaves – this world of connection' (151).

The hope, in most of these novels which imply a rejection of politics, falls on a solitary individual, often solitary because of the failure of politics – *Heroine, In the Skin of a Lion* – or because of the intrinsic viciousness and untrustworthiness of social groupings – *Cat's Eye, The Wars, The Tent Peg, Joshua Then and Now.* Many of these characters are renegades, outcasts, self-styled 'heroes,' or in their own terms 'heroic' survivors. Anna Dawe sits for thirty years in her mother's Georgian Bay house 'alone,' buying 'gin by the case,' reading 'books by the parcel,' before setting out alone to retrace her father's first expedition. Robert Ross rejects his fellow officers to spend long hours in the troopship's hold with the battalion horses, and later becomes the leader of a group of horses in a futile battlefield rebellion against military practice. J.L. sets out, through trickery, to be the lone woman on an arctic prospecting crew. Joshua of *Joshua Then and Now* and Caravaggio of *In the Skin of a Lion* are lone artist-burglars; Patrick and Hazen Lewis of *In the Skin of the Lion* are solitary dynamiters. A few of the texts celebrate the lone, often socially disruptive, artistry of their protagonists – Caravaggio's subtle interactions with sound and texture, J.L.'s quick acquisition of skill with a gun, Elaine's idiosyncratic, anti-fashionable paintings, the clever tricks of social disengagement she learns while extricating herself from cruel childhood friends, a self-absorbed lover, an angry marriage. Most of these texts imply continuing estrangement between their protagonists and almost all other humans; the most any of them can expect is a close family that shields them from surrounding barbarism – *Cat's Eye, In the Skin of a Lion, Joshua Then and Now;* the least is solitary survival – *Heroine's* G.S. walking indecisively up The Main, *Badlands's* Anna 'staying living' (264) in her resort hotel. Very few of these novels, however – *Heroine,* and to some extent *Cat's Eye* – locate the strength of the individual within; most place it outside the individual in fragile shards of transcendence – in the mist of Rowena's breath captured in the final photograph of *The Wars,* in the biblical guarantees of *The Tent Peg's* Ja-el and Deborah, in the mythically resonant family garden in which *Joshua Then and Now* closes, even in the irreducible individuality symbolized in Elaine's 'cat's eye' marble.

Exactly half of the sixteen novels devise their stories as a double narrative, one in which a narrative of inquiry or research frames an earlier narrative which is the target of the inquiry. More than half are narrated under the sign of research, from scholarly research in *Fifth Business* and *The Wars* to personal review and reassessment in *Heroine* and *Cat's Eye.* Although the novel as a genre usually operates as a search for coherence and meaning, here both the sign of research and the construction of characters as questers into their own pasts operate to give the concept of coherence unusual emphasis. For most of the protagonists of the eight double narratives meaning resides not in the future but in crucial moments of their own pasts – in a thrown snowball, a family's scapegoating of the mother and consigning her to shock treatment, a rash or cowardly moment on Ibiza, a sexual molestation within sight of the family peach tree. Elaine Risley of *Cat's Eye* creates almost all of her paintings out of events and images she encountered in childhood and adolescence. Dunstan Ramsay's lifelong obsession with saints is launched by a woman he knew when he was a youth. Anna Dawe's spinsterhood begins eleven years before her birth at the moment her father allows Tune to die, so that a Daweosaurus may emerge from the badlands.

Of the other eight novels five are themselves based on research, offering historiographic re-imaginings of actual events of the North-west Rebellion (*The Temptations of Big Bear*), nineteenth-century Nova Scotia (*The Biggest Modern Woman*), late-nineteenth-century British Columbia (*Caprice*), the First World War (*The Wars*), and Depression Toronto (*In the Skin of a Lion*). Overall, the sixteen signal a profound uneasiness about the past, a fear that people have been crippled by it, a conviction that new interpretations of it, personal or cultural, may have to be established before the present can be re-engaged. The figure of psychoanalysis hovers throughout, both cultural psychoanalysis in the revisiting of sites of national trauma – Batoche, Ypres, Passchendaele, the Depression, the Japanese-Canadian internment camps – and personal psychoanalysis in the revisiting of private trauma – Naomi's loss of her mother, Robert Ross's implication in the death of his sister, Ramsay's assumption of guilt for the misfortunes of Mary Dempster, Annie's complicity in the betrayal of her mother, Elaine's nearly fatal persecution by her schoolmates. And the counter-figures of psychoanalysis, neurosis and psychosis, hover also in Naomi's and Anna's solitary spinsterhoods, Elaine's deep mistrust of women, G.S.'s self-confinement to her bathtub, Ramsay's obsession with saints, Robert's preference of animals to people, Patrick Lewis's obsessions with surface, form, light, and shadow. Emotionally crippled protagonists, incapable of complex networks of friendships and relationships, survive in solitude, exclusionary pairs, or minimal family units. These signs appear to echo metaphorically not only ongoing Canadian constitutional arguments over historical grievances and injustices, but also other signs of disruption that have been at play in the general anglophone-Canadian social text of the 1970s, 1980s, and 1990s – provincial rivalry, illegal 'cross-border' shopping, and profound disagreements on official bilingualism, multiculturalism, on the 'equality' of provinces, the 'distinctiveness' of Quebec, and aboriginal 'self-government.'

In days of yore
From Britain's shore
Wolfe the donkless hero CAME
(titters; but what means *Donkless?*)

    The Diviners, 56–7

The new national flag ... two red bands and a red maple leaf rampant on white, looking like a trademark for margarine of the cheaper variety, or an owl-kill in snow.

    Cat's Eye, 311–12

One surprise in these sixteen novels is their lack of nationalist discourses and signs, unless ironically deployed. What they offer instead, repeatedly and paradoxically, are various discourses of intimacy, home, and neighbourhood, together with others of global distance and multinational community. Between the local and the global, where one might expect to find constructions of region, province, and nation, one finds instead voyages, air flights, and international hotels. Home and family reside not within a nation but as nodes of international travel. *Ana Historic* sends both Annie and Mrs Richards directly from Britain to a Vancouver that thereby becomes a metonymy for North America. *Joshua Then and Now* maps Montreal as part of a world in which the major sites are Montreal, London, Ibiza, and Hollywood, and in which other parts of Quebec or Canada are rarely mentioned and never visited. *Heroine*, despite offering a view of family and politics vastly different from those in *Joshua*, offers a very similar map, in which Montreal is located alongside Morocco, Paris, Cracow, and Marienbad, in which Quebec settlements other than Montreal and Quebec City do not exist, and in which Lively, Ontario, and Vancouver, BC, are sites of naïvety or exile.

The general model for this map is provided by the travels of Elaine Risley's brother in *Cat's Eye*, whose interest as a physicist is unified field theory but whose life and discursive efforts are represented as anything but unified. His travels move him with apparent randomness among Germany, Nevada, Bolivia, San Francisco, New York, and the Middle East. His only communications are cryptic notes on postcards: 'great particle accelerator,' 'interesting life forms,' 'got married, Annette sends regards,' 'excellent butterflies. Hope you are well' (330–1). In many of the novels neither the text nor its protagonists inhabit any social geography that can be called 'Canada.' They inhabit a post-national space, in which sites are as interchangeable as postcards, in which discourses are transnational, and in which political issues are constructed on non-national (and often ahistorical) ideological grounds: fascism and materialism, aestheticism, liberal humanism, Christian mysticism, feminism, industrial capitalism. For some, like *The Tent Peg*, *In the Skin of a Lion*, or *Nights below Station Street*, Canada is an undifferentiable site in the human condition; the local is finely detailed but situated in a homogeneous human situation – mystic woman, the redemptive power of beauty, fallen humanity – that in turn homogenizes other Canadian regions and constituencies and trivializes political argument. For others, Canada is a 'world-class' site, part of a global commercial network in which William Dawe can sell his dinosaurs, William Dorfen find his collectibles, Joshua market his writing, Ramsay pursue his saints, Anna Swan market her height. Here all Canadian difference except the home-base of the protagonist falls from sight; however, at another extreme, should this global network fail the protagonist, all that can remain is that local base: Dawe

floating in Georgian Bay, Joshua in his garden, Anna Swan's mourn-
ing family in Nova Scotia. For still others, Canada is merely part of
an overwhelmingly powerful patriarchal order, with virtually no re-
deemable difference – regional, ethnic, linguistic, or class – within it,
and with only extra-social ideologies – mystic feminism, animal com-
munalism – as alternatives. In nearly all of the novels set outside of
Quebec the transnational mapping appears to eliminate or severely
reduce the significance of Quebec as a Canadian sign, as if on a world
stage of transnational issues and global significations the presence or
absence of Quebec in the Canadian federation were of minor consequence. Even the two novels set in Quebec oblige this sign, in
different ways, to defer to both transnational causes and the protagonist's individual welfare.

There are really only five novels here which openly resist the transnational. Against the post-national assumptions of Stephen Risley's
travels, *Cats' Eye* repeatedly asserts the signs of the local – the details
of Elaine's northern Ontario and mid-town Toronto childhood, the
specificities of her paintings, and her bridging of Far West and Central
Canada through her Ontario past and Vancouver present. It makes
Elaine, who stubbornly works in personal and Canadian images, the
marginally 'successful' Risley; it kills Stephen for his bland wanderings and lack of attention to detail. But the Canada it portrays is itself
following Stephen's model, seeking 'world-class' status, buying 'world-
class' twin sets, seeking to create 'world-class' New York art. Elaine's
resistance to the transnational is itself portrayed as individual rather
than social; she is constructed as incapable of profound affiliations,
incapable even of causing one friend or family member to empathize
with her art. The only symbol of resistance to the transnational the
novel can offer is the cat's eye itself – the shining, 'crystalline,' mysteriously essential self.

In contrast to *Cat's Eye*'s localisms the models offered by both *The
Diviners* and *The Temptations of Big Bear* are to a large extent national,
inclusive, and incorporating. Both assemble an extensive range of
Canadian signs from a variety of classes, regions, ethnicities, and
interests. *The Diviners*, in particular, repudiates the transnational in
Morag's decision not to visit Sutherland, but instead to locate her
ancestors 'where I was born' (391). In their narrative structures – *Big
Bear*'s omniscient narrator that oversees its action and orchestrates its
numerous voices, *The Diviner*'s I-narrator who reports the other characters' stories – both suggest a nation brought together by the generous imagination that can affiliate itself with minority perspectives

and environmental process. It is to the sign of harmonizing nature that both novels repeatedly appeal – a nature that, like the generous narrator, can reconcile contraries and accommodate difference. This is a sign, like the sign of the aesthetic or the mystical, that attempts to limit social conflict by positing an ultimate and common power external to society itself; paradoxically, of course, such a sign can have profound social power, particularly in redirecting and re-legitimating certain powerful groups – here white, university-educated, liberal nationalists, Margaret Laurence's 'tribe' – who may be able to appropriate it. But within these particular texts, it is unlikely that the sign offers any advantage to such marginalized figures as Jules or Piquette Tonnerre, Sits Green On The Earth, Bridie McRaith, Kitty McLean, Eva Winkler, 'A Canadian Volunteer,' Horsechild, or Christie Logan.

Caprice and *Slash* construct a heterodox and potentially populist Canada, one in which institutions can respond to and perhaps even belong to the citizenry, as the BC Provincial Police appears to in *Caprice*, and in which direct social action – town meetings, marches, demonstrations – can effect social change. In *Slash* this is both a crude though slowly developing actuality on a tribal and inter-tribal level, and an ideal on the national one. It is the possibility of citizenship as an Indian that draws Slash Kelasket out of his arrogant and narcissistic despair, that enables him to be a father and, as the book implicitly constructs him, a storyteller. On a national level it is the idealistic expectation of First Nation people that they may eventually be able to participate in the writing of constitutional and legislative documents which enables them to envision Canada as a field for their caravans, sit-ins, and demonstrations. In *Caprice*, although the transnational signs that mark so many of the novels abound – France, Spain, Germany, the United States, Austria, and Italy constitute the world of Caprice's travels and the first homes of many of Nicola's citizens – it is the Nicola social community and its various institutions that the novel endorses. The village's hospital, Indian tribe, newspaper, brothel, resident capitalist, and police force all make generous gestures of support for their Québécoise visitor, and thereby for each other. The transnational signs the novel layers onto this community – Chinese restauranteur, Irish tavern-keeper, Italian labourer, Indian language-teachers, Austrian newspaperman, English horse-breeder, Québécoise visitor – rather than effacing the national posit Nicola as a metonymy for a cooperating national community of ethnic difference.

The free trade debate of the 1988 Canadian federal election, as argued by the artists and writers whose advertisements appeared in the *Globe and Mail* of 19 November 1988, was between two models of anglophone Canada: one a monolithic Ontario-centred 'caring' society; the other a part of an open post-national arena of unrestrained economic opportunity and worldwide thought. In the sixteen novels only the second model makes itself powerfully present, although often as something as much to be feared as celebrated, and sometimes, as in *Badlands* and *The Biggest Modern Woman*, feared and celebrated in the same text. In addition, implicitly sympathetic with this post-national model are texts that take various humanist positions: *Obasan*, with its yearnings for an undifferentiated humanity; *In the Skin of a Lion*, with its repeated attraction to the aestheticist reductions of light and shadow; *The Wars*, with its humanist treasuring of Robert and Rowena's breath. Adding what may be unwitting support to it also are those texts which construct social evil as transnational and good as extra-social: *Nights below Station Street, Ana Historic, The Tent Peg*.

Most of the novels construct ambiguous binary models of the post-national culture and its alternatives – models in which the alternative term is often not nation, as both groups of free trade intervenors suggested, but the individual. Such a model should perhaps not be surprising, since the reduction of the significance of national boundaries, the reduction of regulations over travel, trade, and the transmission of information, tends both to increase the range and opportunities of the individual and to strip the individual of state protections. Anna Swan may be able to become the biggest modern woman *of the world*, but she is also vulnerable to being alone in that world, unsupported by family, communal, or national networks. Stephen Risley may be able to become a world-class physicist and diffidently travel the five continents, but when his life is threatened he is without friends, institutional support, or the effective assistance of his national government. What the conclusions of so many of these novels provide is not a 'caring' society but an isolated protagonist, obliged in the classical liberal model to pull herself up The Main by her own bootstraps, or to console herself with visions of transcendence.

Interestingly, in the Canadian public debates of the 1990s the power of the federal state as a mediating term between the individual and the transnational economic order has also been constructed as diminishing. These debates have portrayed the federal government as powerless to prevent the sale of illegally imported cigarettes, to alter the continuing control of Canadian film distribution by Hollywood interests, to protect Canadian truckers from the tax advantages enjoyed by U.S. trucking, to maintain national programs of arts subsidy, to deter mass 'cross-border shopping' and apparent smuggling by its citizens, or to prevent the moving of factories from Canada to U.S. border cities. Unlike most of the novelists, the editor of the *Globe and Mail*, William Thorsell, has constructed this new powerlessness, not as the product of multinational enterprises and discourses that dwarf even middle-sized states, but as the result of 'the historic struggle for individual political freedom [having grown] to include individual economic freedom.' The power of multinational corporations, according to Thorsell, is given them by the newly freed individual: 'Consumer sovereignty is challenging national sovereignty in the contest for global power, making business corporations a major medium of international relations and competition':

> The whole tendency of our liberal age undermines the independence of states from each other because it undermines the authority of states over their own citizens.
>
> This is what prevents a Canadian government from jamming foreign radio and television signals in defence of Canadian control of the airwaves. Individual Canadians would not accept government interference at that level in their consumption of foreign cultural fare. Liberal values make a mockery of a sovereign state's claim to control over culture. (*Globe and Mail*, 7 Sept. 1991, D6)

Thorsell's ingenuous selection of the jamming of radio and TV signals as his example of the kind of state prerogative the new individualism obliges a Canadian state to forego, and his omission of actual prerogatives it has surrendered through international agreement, suggests his uneasiness with his argument. The Canadian state has never jammed TV and radio signals, although at the time of Thorsell's writing it was indeed being assailed for undertaking trilateral trade talks with the United States and Mexico, and for having concluded the bilateral 'free trade' agreement with the United States and thus precipitating crises in Canadian trucking and manufacturing, and in the retail sectors affected by the cross-border shopping phenomenon. Individual shoppers in television and newspaper interviews have repeatedly invoked individual-rights arguments similar to Thorsell's in defence of their actions.

Thorsell's attempt to conflate the individualism and the post-national state echoes the election-eve call of the writers and artists in support of free trade for the removal of 'protectionism,' so that they might 'be seen and read by the whole world.' It echoes also the excitement and anticipation of opportunity many of the novels give to their characters when they first venture beyond Canada's borders: 'Oh Angus,' writes Anna Swan from New York. 'The view is staggering! The endless facades of rugged stone as high as four and five storeys! The spires and smoking chimneys! And the parade of life winding through in all directions, carrying along horses and carriages! That is my public, Angus' (82–3). Here the transnational world constitutes individual opportunity, unrestrained by local custom or national tariff. But Thorsell's argument contradicts the structural relation the majority of the novels – even *Joshua Then and Now* by free-trade supporter Richler – eventually give to the transnational and the individual. However they may flirt with Thorsell's notion that the global field is the individual's dream landscape, the novels eventually bring a wearied protagonist to solitary or near solitary refuge. And none of the novels suggests that individualism has created the transnational; they present it rather as already constituted and offering apparent opportunities for individual growth and creativity, in contrast to the various sites – Montreal, Georgian Bay, New Annan, Lively, Deptford, or Toronto – which they constitute as parochial.

The model of anglophone-Canadian interaction with the world offered by these sixteen novels is in only a very few cases a social one. Though the global stage invites, it offers, not community, but a rough-and-tumble field of competing political and economic interests. 'We are not fragile,' the thirty-nine supporters of free trade announced, but in these novels the characters who venture the furthest into the 'whole world' – Robert Ross, Joshua Shapiro, Anna Swan, William Dawe, Caprice, Stephen Risley – are fragile indeed. Of these, only Caprice is able to locate a supportive community to mitigate that fragility. For the rest, between the global field and their own immediate resources there is neither state nor polis; not even the small sites of Seville, Ohio, or Lake Memphremagog, Quebec, can offer a functioning polity. Meaning here is constructed transnationally – world economics, universal beauty, humanism, Marxism – or else it collapses on the disillusioned individual, who is left to build a personal retreat – a bathtub or a garden – for his or her own functioning.

Even in the novels which do not offer extensive maps of international signs, transnational meanings tend to be granted priority over local and national ones. Despite the specific Canadian historical circumstances of the Japanese-Canadian diaspora *Obasan* appeals throughout to concepts of universal nature and humanity. *Ana Historic* declines to engage the particular British Columbia social field it has defined as patriarchal, capitalistic, monolithic, and exploitive, and chooses instead a version of the universal feminine. *In the Skin of a Lion* develops an extended analysis of the social injustices of capitalist and state capitalist practices in Ontario, only to excuse these and deny social contestation in favour of attention to the intrinsic beauty of all objects and actions. *The Diviners* brings a huge cast of classes and ethnicities together only to erase their differences and potential for social dialogue in a river that transforms conflicting currents into 'undulating lines of gold' (453). Each text proposes its own notion of what should replace active contribution to community – delight in the lesbian body, search for numinous meaning, assertion that Canada is 'like every land,' delight in the luminous surface.

Every one of the sixteen novels communicates mistrust, usually profound mistrust, of social and political process, and often a narrow focus on a particular constituency. Their repeated portrayals of individuals left to their own resources, dying unloved and unattended, or subsisting on memory, appear to reflect not so much a preference for individualism as a despair about polity. Similarly, their frequent endorsement of benevolent powers beyond the social order – of some essential humanity, divine power, archetypal femininity, healing natural order, indemnifying will to beauty, or benevolent fortuity – signals a decided lack of faith that human cooperation can address injustice and accommodate difference.

This inability in all but a few instances to imagine a polity reaches out into the novels' construction of the nation and the world. Neither are constructed, except in *Slash, The Temptations of Big Bear*, and *Caprice*, as fields for social and political action. The continuities of action are mostly individual and evolve within a network of discontinous, interchangeable signs – international cities, famous explorers, chauvinist men, tall prairie grass, phallic guns. Despite the extensive travels of many of the characters in these novels they rarely encounter any sign of international order; none ever applies for a passport, passes through a customs check, or has significant official contacts in the countries visited. The state signs these characters do encounter tend to be arbitrary and obstructive, like the police Joshua encounters in Falangist Spain, or absurd, like the Queen Victoria who receives Anna Swan. Within Canada the characters similarly tend to encounter few if any signs of a supportive social structure, or even of Canadian societies beyond their immediate location. In *Ana Historic* the boundaries of British Columbia open onto Britain; in *The Biggest Modern Woman of the World* those of Nova Scotia open onto New York and London; in *Fifth Business* those of Ontario open onto continental Europe.

———————————•———————————

What this array of post-centennial Canadian fiction appears most strongly to announce is the arrival of the post-national state – a state invisible to its own citizens, indistinguishable from its fellows, maintained by invisible political forces, and significant mainly through its position within the grid of world-class postcard cities Stephen Risley flies inattentively among. Specific novels may argue for a humanist Canada, a more feminist Canada, a more sophisticated and worldly Canada, an individualist Canada, a Canada more responsive to the values of its aboriginal citizens, but collectively they suggest a world and a nation in which social structures no longer link regions or communities, political process is doubted, and individual alienation has become normal. The strongest will towards community in these novels is expressed in their construction of First Nations peoples – of Big Bear in his efforts to protect a community of his own tribe, its white prisoners, its land, and its animals, of the two Indians of *Caprice* who labour to understand white social practice, of the numerous Indians of *Slash* who work towards a pan-Canadian nation of Indian peoples. But for the novels' Euro-Canadians, even for the good citizens of Nicola, 'the world [has] started to shrink.' *Caprice*'s twentieth-century narrator laments a community of difference that has vanished: 'We are all Europeans now' (110).

Bibliography

Althusser, Louis. *For Marx*. Trans. Ben Brewster. New York: Pantheon 1969
- *Lenin and Philosophy*. Trans. Ben Brewster. London: NLB 1971
Armstrong, Jeannette. *Slash*. Penticton: Theytus 1985
Atwood, Margaret. *Survival*. Toronto: Anansi 1972
- *Second Words*. Toronto: Anansi 1982
- *The Handmaid's Tale*. Toronto: McClelland and Stewart 1985
- *Cat's Eye*. Toronto: McClelland and Stewart 1988
Bal, Mieke. *Narratology*. Toronto: U of Toronto P 1985
Barthes, Roland. *Mythologies*. Trans. Annette Lavers. London: Cape 1972
Berton, Pierre. *Vimy*. Toronto: McClelland and Stewart 1986
Bishop, William Arthur. *The Courage of the Early Morning*. Toronto: McClelland and Stewart 1965
Blumberg, Marcia. 'Rereading Gail Scott's *Heroine*: A Triple Lens of Sighting/Citing/Siting.' *Open Letter* 8, no. 2 (Winter 1992), 57–69
Bonnycastle, Stephen. 'Robertson Davies and the Ethics of Monologue.' *Journal of Canadian Studies* 12, no. 1 (Feb. 1977), 20–40
Bowering, George. *Caprice*. Toronto: Penguin 1987
Brown, Robert Craig, and Ramsay Cook. *Canada 1876–1921: A Nation Transformed*. Toronto: McClelland and Stewart 1974
Buitenhuis, Elspeth. *Robertson Davies*. Toronto: Forum House 1972
Cixous, Hélène, and Catherine Clément. *La Jeune Née*. Paris: UGE 1975
Cluett, Robert. *Canadian Literary Prose: A Preliminary Stylistic Atlas*. Toronto: ECW 1990
Copithorne, Judith. 'Wild Inlet – a Community.' *Georgia Straight*, 9–16 Sept. 1970, 5–6
Culler, Jonathan. *The Pursuit of Signs*. Ithaca: Cornell UP 1981
Curtis, Bo, and J.A. Kraulis. *Canada from the Air*. Edmonton: Hurtig 1981

Daly, Mary. *Gyn/Ecology*. Boston: Beacon 1978

Dancocks, Daniel. *Legacy of Valour: The Canadians at Passchendaele.* Edmonton: Hurtig 1986

– *Spearhead to Victory: Canada and the Great War*. Edmonton: Hurtig 1987

Davey, Frank. *Reading Canadian Reading*. Winnipeg: Turnstone 1988

Davies, Robertson. *Fifth Business*. Toronto: Macmillan 1970

Derrida, Jacques. *Of Grammatology*. Trans. Gayatri Chakravorti Spivak. Baltimore: Johns Hopkins UP 1976 [1967]

Eagleton, Terry. *Criticism and Ideology*. London: NLB 1976

Farrar, Janet, and Stewart Farrar. *The Witches' Goddess*. London: Robert Hale 1987

Findley, Timothy. *The Wars*. Toronto: Clarke Irwin 1977

Finlay, John L., and D.N. Sprague. *The Structure of Canadian History*. Scarborough, Ont.: Prentice-Hall 1979

Fletcher, John. 'Freud and His Uses: Psychoanalysis and Gay Theory.' In *Coming on Strong*. Ed. Simon Shepherd and Mich Wallos. London: Unwin Hyman 1989, 90–118

Foucault, Michel. *Les Mots et les choses*. Paris: Gallimard 1966.

Frye, Northrop. *Anatomy of Criticism*. Princeton: Princeton UP 1957

– 'Conclusion.' In *The Literary History of Canada*. Ed. Carl F. Klinck. Vol. 2. Toronto: U of Toronto P 1976, 333–61

Godard, Barbara. 'The *Diviners* as Supplement: (M)othering the Text.' *Open Letter* 7, no. 7 (Spring 1990), 26–73

– 'The Politics of Representation: Some Native Canadian Women Writers.' *Canadian Literature* 124–25 (Spring-Summer 1990), 183–228

Grace, Sherrill. ' "Listen to the Voice": Dialogism and the Canadian Novel.' In *Future Indicative: Literary Theory and Canadian Literature*. Ed. John Moss. Ottawa: U of Ottawa P, 1987, 117–36

Gray, John. *Billy Bishop Goes to War*. Vancouver: Talonbooks 1981

Hirst, Paul Q. *On Law and Ideology*. Atlantic Highlands, NJ: Humanities P, 1979

Howells, Coral Ann. *Private and Fictional Worlds*. London: Methuen 1987

Hutcheon, Linda. 'History and/as Intertext.' In *Future Indicative: Literary Theory and Canadian Literature*. Ed. John Moss. Ottawa: U of Ottawa P 1987, 169–84

Irigaray, Luce. *Speculum of the Other Woman*. Trans. Gillian G. Gill. Ithaca: Cornell UP 1985 [1974]

– *This Sex Which Is Not One*. Trans. Catherine Porter. Ithaca: Cornell UP 1985 [1977]

Jameson, Laura E. 'Where White and Brown Men Meet.' *Canadian Forum* 21, no. 247 (1941), 146

Jones, D.G. *Butterfly on Rock*. Toronto: U of Toronto P 1970

Keith, W.J. *Canadian Literature in English*. New York: Longman 1985

Kilbourn, William. 'Introduction.' In *Canada: a Guide to the Peaceable Kingdom*. Toronto: Macmillan 1970, xi–xviii

Kobayashi, Cassandra, and Roy Miki, eds. *Spirit of Redress*. Vancouver: J.C. Publications 1989

Kogawa, Joy. *Obasan*. Toronto: Lester and Orpen Dennys 1981

Kopay, David, and Perry Deane Young. *The David Kopay Story*. New York: Arbor House 1977

Kostash, Myrna. 'A White Man's View of Big Bear.' *Saturday Night*, Feb. 1974, 32

Kristeva, Julia. *Desire in Language*. Ed. Leon S. Roudiez. Trans. Thomas Gora, Alice Jardine, and Leon S. Roudiez. New York: Columbia UP, 1980 [1977]

Kroetsch, Robert. *But We Are Exiles*. Toronto: Macmillan 1965

– *The Words of My Roaring*. Toronto: Macmillan 1966

– *The Studhorse Man*. Toronto: Macmillan 1969

– *Badlands*. Toronto: New Press 1975

– *Alibi*. Toronto: Stoddart 1983

Lacan, Jacques. *Écrits*. Paris: Seuil 1966

– *Encore: Le séminaire XX, 1972–73*. Paris: Seuil 1975

–, and the *école freudienne*. *Feminine Sexuality*. Ed. Juliet Mitchell and Jacqueline Rose. Trans. Jacqueline Rose. New York: Norton 1985

Laurence, Margaret. *The Diviners*. Toronto: McClelland and Stewart 1974

Lecker, Robert. 'The Canonization of Canadian Literature: An Inquiry into Value.' *Critical Inquiry* 16, no. 3 (Spring 1990), 656–71

Lower, Arthur. *From Colony to Nation*. Toronto: Longmans Green 1946

McGregor, Gaile. *The Wacousta Syndrome*. Toronto: U of Toronto P 1985

Macherey, Pierre. *A Theory of Literary Production*. Trans. Geoffrey Wall. London: Routledge 1978 [1966]

McLuhan, Marshall. *The Mechanical Bride*. New York: Vanguard 1951

Macrea, Mary. *Montreal Magic*. Montreal: Optimum 1982

Mandel, Eli. *The Family Romance*. Winnipeg: Turnstone 1985

Marin, Louis. *La Critique du discours*. Paris: Minuit 1975

Marlatt, Daphne. *Ana Historic*. Toronto: Coach House Press 1988

Michel, Andrée. *Le Féminisme*. Paris: Presses Universitaires de France 1980

Moi, Toril. *Sexual/Textual Politics*. London: Routledge 1988 [1985]

Moir, Alfred. *Caravaggio*. New York: Abrams 1982

Morton, W.L. *The Kingdom of Canada*. Toronto: McClelland and Stewart 1963

Moss, John. *Patterns of Isolation*. Toronto: McClelland and Stewart 1974

Neff, Stephen C. *Friends but No Allies*. New York: Columbia UP, 1990

Newlove, John. 'The Pride.' *Weekend Magazine*, 28 Dec. 1974, 14–15. First published in *Tamarack Review* 36 (1965)

Newton, Stan. *Paul Bunyan of the Great Lakes*. Chicago: Packard 1946

Nowlan, Alden. 'Sable Island: Symbol of Enduring Life.' *Atlantic Advocate* 71, no. 10 (June 1981), 86

Ondaatje, Michael. *In the Skin of a Lion*. Toronto: McClelland and Stewart 1987

'One Canada or Two.' *National Geographic*, April 1977, 436–65

Ong, Walter J. *Orality and Literacy*. London: Methuen 1982

Parker, Charles. *The Oilman*. New York: Rinehart 1952

Pearse, Peter H. 'Building on Our Strengths.' *Globe and Mail*, 10 Jan. 1992, A13

Pêcheux, Michel. *Language, Semantics and Ideology: Stating the Obvious*. Trans. Harbans Nagpal. London: Macmillan 1982 [1975]

Reiss, Timothy. *The Discourse of Modernism*. Ithaca: Cornell UP 1982

Richards, David Adams. *Nights below Station Street*. Toronto: McClelland and Stewart 1988

Richler, Mordecai. *Joshua Then and Now*. Toronto: McClelland and Stewart 1980

Roudiez, Leon S. 'Introduction.' In *Desire in Language*. By Julia Kristeva. Ithaca: Cornell UP 1980, 1–20

'Satisfaction Guaranteed.' *Ontario Indian* 5, no. 1 (1982), 24–7

Scott, Gail. *Heroine*. Toronto: Coach House Press 1987

Shaw, Flora L. 'Klondike.' *Proceedings of the Royal Canadian Institute* 30 (1898–9), 104–17

Smith, A.J.M. *Towards a View of Canadian Letters: Selected Critical Essays, 1928–1971*. Vancouver: U of British Columbia P 1973

Sternberg, C.H. *Hunting Dinosaurs in the Bad Lands of the Red Deer River, Alberta, Canada*. Laurence, Kan.: C.H. Sternberg 1917

Sutherland, Ronald. *Second Image: Comparative Studies in Quebec/Canadian Literature*. Toronto: New Press 1971

Swan, Susan. *The Biggest Modern Woman of the World*. Toronto: Lester and Orpen Dennys 1983

Takata, Toyo. *Nikkei Legacy*. Toronto: NC Press 1983

Thompson, Eric. 'Of Wars and Men.' *Canadian Literature* 78 (Autumn 1978), 99–101

Thorsell, William. 'In Our Brave New World the Old Ideas of Independence Are on the Run.' Editorial. *Globe and Mail*, 7 Sept. 1991, D6

Todorov, Tzvetan. *Les Genres du discours*. Paris: Seuil 1978

Van Herk, Aritha. *The Tent Peg*. Toronto: McClelland and Stewart 1981

Vauthier, Simone. 'The Dubious Battle of Story-Telling: Narrative Strategies in Timothy Findley's *The Wars.'* In *Gaining Ground: European Critics on Canadian Writing.* Ed. Robert Kroetsch and Reingard Nischik. Edmonton: NeWest Press 1985, 11–39

Wiebe, Rudy. *The Temptations of Big Bear.* Toronto: McClelland and Stewart 1973

Woodcock, George. *Odysseus Ever Returning.* Toronto: McClelland and Stewart 1970

– 'Gabriel Dumont: The Forgotten Hero.' *Saturday Night,* July 1973, 19–20

– 'The Mirror of Narcissus.' *Saturday Night,* Sept. 1978, 29–30

– *Northern Spring: The Flowering of Canadian Literature.* Vancouver: Douglas and McIntyre 1987

Index

— genre / rhetoric / social & political positions
          & how they impact on texts.